IN BEAR COUNTRY

BY THE SAME AUTHOR

Hail Mary Corner

IN BEAR COUNTRY
A Global Journey in
Vanishing Wilderness

Brian Payton

Published 2007 by Old Street Publishing Ltd,
14 Bowling Green Lane, London EC1R 0BD

Originally published by Bloomsbury USA as *Shadow of the Bear: Travels in Vanishing Wilderness*

ISBN: 1-905847- ISBN-13: 978-1-905847

A CIP catalogue record for this book is available from the British Library.

Printed in Great Britain by Creative Print and Design

for Lily

CONTENTS

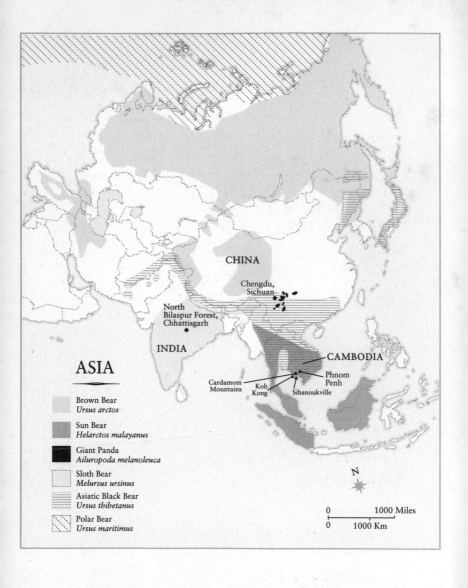

ASIA

Brown Bear
Ursus arctos

Sun Bear
Helarctos malayanus

Giant Panda
Ailuropoda melanoleuca

Sloth Bear
Melursus ursinus

Asiatic Black Bear
Ursus thibetanus

Polar Bear
Ursus maritimus

CHINA

Chengdu,
Sichuan

North
Bilaspur Forest,
Chhattisgarh

INDIA

CAMBODIA

Phnom
Penh

Cardamom
Mountains   Koh
             Kong   Sihanoukville

N

0   1000 Miles
0   1000 Km

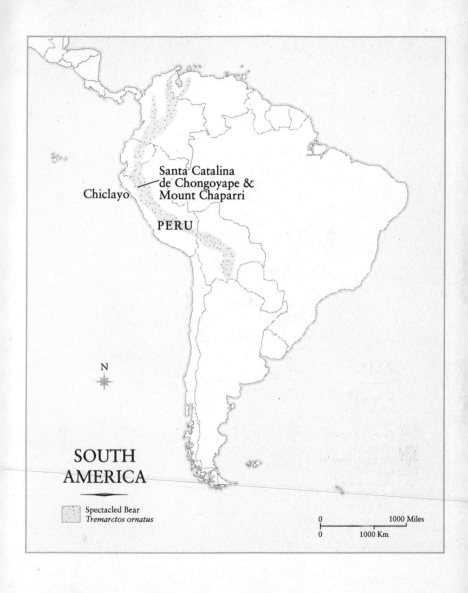

Santa Catalina
de Chongoyape &
Mount Chaparri

Chiclayo

PERU

N

SOUTH
AMERICA

Spectacled Bear
Tremarctos ornatus

0   1000 Miles
0   1000 Km

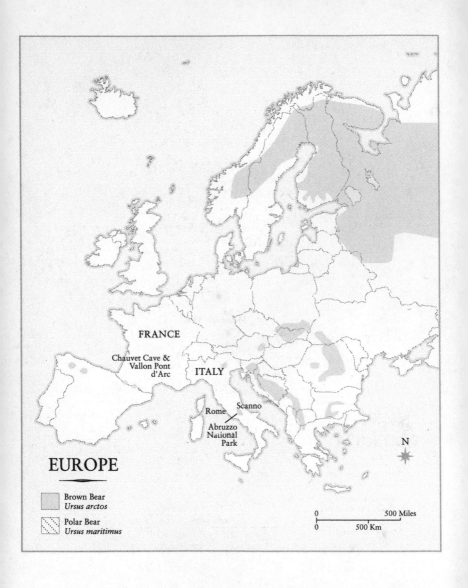

FRANCE

Chauvet Cave &
Vallon Pont
d'Arc

ITALY

Rome   Scanno

Abruzzo
National
Park

N

EUROPE

Brown Bear
Ursus arctos

Polar Bear
Ursus maritimus

0   500 Miles
0   500 Km

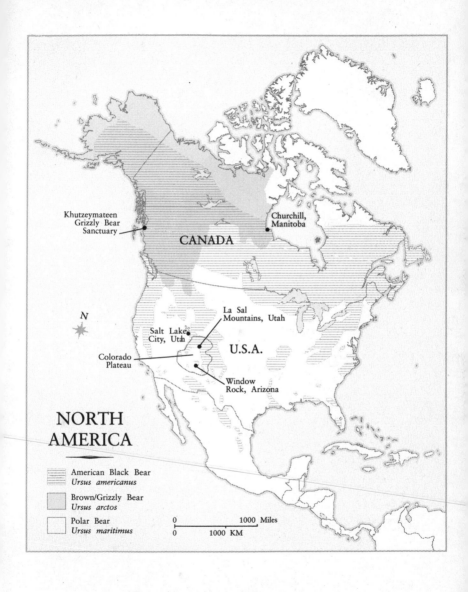

Khutzeymateen
Grizzly Bear
Sanctuary

Churchill,
Manitoba

CANADA

N

La Sal
Mountains, Utah

Salt Lake
City, Utah

Colorado
Plateau

U.S.A.

Window
Rock, Arizona

NORTH
AMERICA

American Black Bear
Ursus americanus

Brown/Grizzly Bear
Ursus arctos

Polar Bear
Ursus maritimus

0   1000 Miles
0   1000 KM

INTRODUCTION
A Sleuth of Bears

THERE ARE MOMENTS of clarity in life, instances that so completely focus the senses, there is no yesterday or tomorrow—only the absolute here and now. Such a moment came for me in the spring of 2000, on the coast of British Columbia, when my guide reached for the oar in the bottom of our boat and accidentally spooked a grizzly cub on shore.

The overgrown three-year-old bawled and temporarily lost his footing. His mother, grazing sedge nearby, spun around and stopped mid-chew. We were so close, I could see the foamy, green saliva at the corners of her mouth—so close I could see her eyes focus on me. Several heart-pounding seconds passed as we stared at one another, reading body language, plotting possible outcomes. Then all at once she turned and sat down. Seemingly unconcerned with our presence, she kept her back to us and her cub as she continued munching on stems and blades.

From what I'd gathered about meeting bears in the wilderness, coming upon a mother and cub seemed like the worst-case scenario. And yet somehow these bears put me at ease. Convinced he'd established who was in charge, the cub scrambled up a large rock for a better view. He yawned, licked his paws, and even dozed off for a while. He resembled a young royal, aware of the flashing cameras but intent on maintaining the pretense of normalcy.

A few minutes later, the pair slowly ambled away from the water's edge and disappeared into the forest.

WE'VE BEEN MEETING them in the wilderness, and in our dreams, since the dawn of human history. Bears have been celebrated in art and myth since we began drawing on the walls of caves. No beast casts a longer shadow over our collective subconscious. Perhaps more than any other animal, the bear remains at the very heart of our concept of wilderness.

The hope of seeing grizzlies in their natural habitat brought me and six companions to the mouth of the Khutzeymateen (KOOT-suh-mah-teen) River in Canada's only grizzly bear sanctuary. The inlet reaches twelve miles in from Chatham Sound, forming an arm of the Pacific Ocean that ends in fingers full of rich green sedge. After emerging from hibernation, grizzlies make their way down to the marsh to feast on the bounty of new shoots that offer up to 28 percent protein. A place of plenty, the marsh attracts dozens of bears each spring. After establishing a pecking order, these ordinarily solitary creatures graze in close proximity. This gathering, known as a sleuth of bears, is something that rarely happens in the wild.

I was determined to get up close and experience being in a place where humans are not the masters of all we see—a place where we are at least one link down the food chain. For four days, guide Tom Ellison's seventy-two-foot ketch served as our mother ship for exploration. Anchored in a sheltered cove, we were surrounded by slopes of old-growth cedar and snowy peaks soaring nearly seven thousand feet above the tide. Himself an imposing figure, Ellison's weathered features betrayed a long association with the wilderness and the sea. He knew these bears better than anyone.

We wandered the rainforest in heavy downpours and soft, persistent mist. More than nine feet of precipitation soaks this part of the coast each year and the resulting jungle is dark and primeval. Grizzly bears play an integral role in this environment, consuming huge quantities of salmon and conveying valuable nitrogen fertilizer deep into the forest. They are the unwitting gardeners of some of the world's oldest, biggest trees. In North America, before the advent of industrial logging, temperate rainforests once stretched along the West Coast from California's giant sequoias to Alaska's majestic Sitka spruce. Among the world's rarest ecosystems, temperate rainforests never covered more than one-fifth of 1 percent of the planet's land surface. Today, less than one-half of that small amount remains.

On one of our forest walks, we found a bear trail below an old hemlock tree. Unlike other animal or human paths, where an unbroken line is traced on the earth, here each bear carefully placed its paws in exactly the same spot as the bears that passed before it. The result was a series of round, measured paw pads in the bright green moss. Some speculate that these trails are ancient pathways, trod by untold generations. Passing bears have also left their marks on nearby scratch trees, which provide temporary relief from an itchy back and serve as a kind of social register with scent, bits of fur, and claw marks that let other bears know who's in the neighborhood.

I was fully aware that these bears could tear me apart. Although the vast majority of encounters between people and bears are peaceful in this part of the world, every couple of years someone gets killed. However, within this protected, pristine environment, bears have not learned to fear humans or associate us with handouts or garbage. Here, it is possible to meet them on unencumbered terms.

I discovered that the same government that protects the sixty grizzlies in this estuary sanctions the killing of approximately three hundred others in British Columbia's annual grizzly bear hunt. It is estimated that another three hundred are victims of poaching. A considerable number of these are killed only for their gallbladders, which end up as medicine in Asian apothecaries, or for their paws, which are served as exotic delicacies in restaurants around the world. Despite the numbers directly killed by humans, it is believed that habitat destruction remains the most serious threat to the survival of these and most other bears.

"We're losing this coast," Ellison said one night over dinner. "If people can't be bothered to save the salmon or trees, maybe they'll be motivated to save these magnificent creatures. And the only way they're going to want to save the bears is if they get to know them."

Ellison spent a long time becoming acquainted with the female bear we met a few days before. Her story began in the early 1990s, when a dominant male encountered her family when she was just a yearling. Male grizzlies are known to attack and kill cubs. This tactic is used to bring females into estrus so they will be receptive to mating, according to some researchers; others are not so sure. Whatever the motivation, the family was attacked. The mother was killed along with one of her cubs. The surviving cub wasn't expected to make it through the season.

"When winter came, we were sure we'd never see her again," Ellison said. "But in the spring, there she was—alive and kicking. She had survived the winter alone in the den. Sometimes she'd see us coming and swim to the boat. I'd have to gently push her paw away with the oar so she wouldn't climb aboard.

"As she matured, she would lure the big males out of the forest to dance with them and tease them on shore. When she was in estrus, she would chase them if they wandered off. She wanted to be mated. One time, we saw her lure a big male into a secluded spot in the bush and make quite a lot of noise. She reemerged with fur rubbed off her shoulders. Then we realized who she was mating with—the same bear who killed her mother and sibling. The result was the cub you've been watching the past two days.

"When the fight was really heating up to save this place, we were able to bring influential people to see the bears," Ellison explained. "She gave many of them an opportunity to get up close and have a personal experience. That bear let us into her life and helped save this valley. This is a special place where these kinds of meetings can happen."

OVER A STRETCH of four unforgettable days, I saw grizzlies crash through the brush, dig up clams, and paddle along the shore. I saw male and female grizzlies, cubs, and numerous shy black bears. On the final day, we set a course for a waist-high field of sedge.

The light and weather were changing, casting the mountains in shadow and bathing the shore in amber hues. At the far end of the estuary, shafts of light beamed down from the heavens as in a Renaissance painting. We landed near a patch of purple lupine and proceeded unarmed (save for a large can of bear spray) in the general direction of an adult male grizzly. Ellison didn't recognize this bear but guessed it was a fifteen-year-old male, perhaps 550 pounds. Once we were within a hundred yards, we quietly sat down.

Despite his powerful build, this bear was the picture of laziness. He ate the sedge within easy reach, then sprawled on his stomach to reach some more. When those blades were finally clipped, he got up, took a deep breath, and moved in our direction. He sauntered for thirty yards or so, stopped, and stuck his nose in the air. He took a long, ponderous whiff. Satisfied with our nonthreatening odor, he resumed his grazing.

Then the bear moved closer still. All was silent, save the click and whirr of our cameras. I stopped staring through the viewfinder and slowly rested the camera in my lap. As we sat frozen, mouths agape, it dawned on me that we were in a rare place in our modern world—at the mercy of a large, wild animal.

As it closed the gap between us, I had another of those moments of clarity. My heart was not racing, I felt no panic welling up inside. But I did feel as if the tables had turned, as if I had become the object of curiosity. Ellison spoke in a soothing voice, informing the bear of our intentions, then quietly suggested that we take a few steps back—which I was happy to do. Choosing to leave us unchallenged and undisturbed, the bear continued past and up an embankment. I inhaled deeply through my nose in a vain attempt to pick up his scent. At the top of the rise, he stopped, took a final look over his shoulder, then lumbered into the woods.

———

MY JOURNEY BEGAN with a dream. Before I left for the Khutzeymateen, I dreamt that I was walking in the woods and saw something, or someone, sitting on a log in the distance. It had its back to me, but I knew it was a bear. It was wearing tattered overalls and mumbling unintelligible words. It turned and acknowledged me with a grunt. As I approached, I saw that it held something in its paws. A book? It was trying to sound out words as it squinted through old, broken spectacles. I sat down next to the bear and began to teach it how to read.

A product of North American culture, I've had two distinct and competing images of the bear imprinted in my subconscious: the clown of enchanted forests and the relentless killing machine that stalks the night. As infants, teddy bears are among the first items placed inside our cribs. As we grow, we are fed a steady diet of children's stories and cartoons about lovable, huggable bears. Eventually, we are exposed to society's enduring and macabre fascination with bear attacks. The result is that many of us tend to either anthropomorphize or demonize bears out of ignorance or expediency. I was determined to move beyond all that and hopefully get a glimpse of what these creatures really are.

The connection between bears and humans is primal—it reaches back into the shadows beyond both myth and memory. We have always recognized bears as extraordinary, intelligent, and powerful beasts that share our preferred environments. More than that, they can stand on their hind legs like us. This ability inspires awe in modern viewers, just as it did our ancestors. Archeologists report that bears have been feared, revered, and even worshiped since the earliest times.

Now they fill a new and emerging role. Where bears still roam, biologists say they act as an indicator of the general health of the ecosystem that supports them. Bears are considered an "umbrella" species. If they are protected and thriving, so the theory goes, then so too will a whole range of animals and plants on the food chain below them. Inspired by this idea, conservationists launched an international campaign to rechristen a five-million-acre chunk of Canada's West Coast "the Great Bear Rainforest." The area is home to thousands of bears: grizzlies, black bears, and even a rare, all-white subspecies of black bear known as the Kermode, or Spirit Bear. If people wouldn't save the wilderness for its own sake, perhaps they would save it for the bears. Following a ten-year struggle, a historic agreement was reached among Native groups, government, and industry to protect the world's largest remaining intact coastal rainforest. Proof of the power of metaphor.

When I returned from the Khutzeymateen, I continued my research. Aside from North America's three bear species— grizzly/brown bear, black bear, and polar bear—I was aware only of China's giant panda and Russia's brown bear. To my surprise, I discovered there are bears in Southeast Asia, Western Europe, India, and South America—eight surviving species in all. Termite-eating bears, feisty little jungle bears, and even bears with pale rings around their eyes that make them appear as if they're wearing spectacles. I found numerous books about bears, including many natural histories of bears living in or near U.S. national parks. Information about bears beyond North America was scarce in the extreme.

It seemed to me that one could probably tell a lot about a society by the way it treats its bears. Outside rare environments like the Khutzeymateen Grizzly Bear Sanctuary, people and bears compete for shrinking space and resources. From the beginning, bears and other large predators have shaped our development by forcing us to cooperate for the protection of each other's lives and, eventually, livestock. Now we shape their destiny.

Scientists tell us that we are in the midst of the Sixth Extinction, a time when species are disappearing at a rate one hundred times faster than normal. All bear species have declined in number and range due to human activities. The IUCN, the World Conservation Union, publishes a Red List of Threatened Species to call attention to those animals facing a high risk of global extinction. Six out of the eight bear species are on that list: the Asiatic black bear, the spectacled bear, the sun bear, the sloth bear, the giant panda, and the polar bear. Saving them will require an enormous test of our ability to cooperate; failing—at the very least—will mean the irretrievable loss of a way to understand ourselves.

Too many fundamental questions about bears remain unanswered, questions only disciplined scientific study can address. But beyond biology and ecology, what kind of political, economic, and cultural environments do bears inhabit? I felt compelled to go and find out. As I embarked on this series of journeys, I was unsure what I hoped to gain, other than some understanding of our relationship to these remarkable beasts and why they continue to inspire fear, fascination, and reverence.

It has been said that there are two concentric circles of knowledge. The inner circle holds everything you know, while the outer circle contains those things you know you don't know (like how to speak Phoenician). Beyond is that universe of things of which you are completely unaware. In my limited experience, I had already moved one small but unassailable fact into my inner circle—spend time in bear country and something interesting is bound to happen. Armed with little more knowledge than this, I set out to wander beyond the outer ring.

1

UNDER THE MAHUA TREE
Chhattisgarh, India

ON A COOL, still morning in 2003, village elder Ranasha Ram arose from bed at 5 A.M. When he stepped out of his mud-brick house, the approaching day was little more than a warm glow in the trees beyond his field. Ram walked barefoot through the furrowed rows, carrying a metal jug of water. He chose a spot near a tree, unwrapped his *dhoti*, and squatted down. Then he pulled out his *Janaio*, a traditional cotton necklace, and wound it around his left ear. It is widely believed that this form of acupressure aids in the movement of the bowels.

His attacker came silently, out of the shadows. It grabbed him by the shoulder and pulled him to the ground. It jumped on his back, pinned him down, and bit through his forearm. Then it tore into his calf. Ram was able to turn himself over, but then it went for his belly. He protected himself with his hands as best he could, but these were savaged as well. Somehow, he managed to push the beast off his body, then it finally ran way.

Ram has short gray hair, dark skin, and eyes clouded with age. He is unsure how old he is, but guesses he is somewhere between seventy and seventy-five. The attack left plenty of scars on his

abdomen and back, plus four puncture wounds in his bony leg.
Nerve damage in his right hand robbed him of strength in his
thumb and fingers—along with his ability to work. He counts
himself fortunate to have a son and daughters to care for him.
These days, he spends much of his time puttering around the
house. Remarkably, Ram holds no grudge against his attacker.
Sloth bears have every right to live in the jungle as they always
have, he says. They are only doing their job, living according to
their nature.

Ram makes his home in the village of Padkhuri, among the
most aggressive and dangerous bears in the world. This fragment
of degraded sal forest has been home to sloth bears since before
recorded time. But as the human population expands, the pressure on the forest intensifies. A fight for survival ensues. Throughout the world where bears still exist, this scenario leads to their
speedy demise. But India is a world unto itself, a place where extraordinary accommodations are made—a place where outcomes
are rarely certain.

THE RAMAYANA, the classical epic of India, was written around
300 BC. It tells the story of the god Ram and his battle against the
evil Ravana. Ram, who happens to be blue, embodies all that is
righteous and good. The tale recounts how the forces of evil conspired against the young god and resulted in all-out war with the
army of Ravana. In this supernatural struggle, Ram was aided by
many allies, including Lord Hanuman, the Monkey God, and
Jambavan, King of the Bears. Jambavan and his legions of sloth
bears fought bravely at Ram's side. They helped defeat the forces
of darkness.

Jambavan was a sloth bear, *Melursus ursinus*; a species endemic
to the Indian subcontinent. Today, sloth bears can be found in
India, Sri Lanka, Nepal, Bhutan, and Bangladesh. Adult Sloth
bears weigh between 175 and 320 pounds and have a body length
of sixty to seventy-five inches. They have shaggy black coats—

especially long around the head and ears—and a cream-colored chest patch in the shape of a V. Sloth bears have physical adaptations to support their appetite for termites and ants, including a long snout, a concave palate, absent upper-middle incisors, and protrusible lips, which work together to form a powerful sucking appendage. They have long claws for digging and slashing, and large canines in proportion to their body size. These weapons come in handy when they are attacked by leopards or tigers.

In the eighteenth century, a specimen of the animal known as *bhalu* in northern India, and *reech* in the south, eventually found its way to Europe. There, museum curators dubbed it the "sloth-like bear" for a perceived resemblance to the well-clawed, tree-dwelling South American sloth. By the time later taxonomists realized there was no relation to the New World animal, it was too late. The misnomer stuck. In fact, *sloth* is a sin these bears avoid. Sloth bears are capable of impressive bursts of speed and have a low tolerance for humans and other large mammals. Due to the high frequency of sloth bear attacks, they are among the most dangerous and feared animals in India.

Sloth bears are found in a wide variety of habitats, from grasslands to sal and evergreen forests. Although they favor ants and termites, sloth bears eat all kinds of fruit, flowers, nuts, and, of course, honey. Sloth bears do not hibernate and can be active day or night. Although they are by nature solitary creatures (outside breeding season), they have also been observed in groups of between five and seven individuals. Female sloth bears usually give birth to two cubs between November and January. The cubs are invariably carried on the mother's back wherever she goes. Beyond these simple facts, precious little is known about sloth bear behavior or distribution. Although population estimates range from 10,000 to 23,000, scientists caution that these numbers are essentially meaningless because the data used to extrapolate is highly suspect. Anecdotal evidence suggests that—other than in a few places of relative stability—sloth bears are in general and widespread decline. The IUCN Bear Specialist Group has identified sloth bears as vulnerable to extinction. Under CITES (the Convention on International Trade in Endangered Species of Wild Fauna and Flora), sloth bears are designated as an Appendix I endangered species to afford them maximum protection.

Historically, sloth bears ranged throughout the Indian subcontinent. Overhunting and habitat destruction led to a rapid reduction in their numbers during the nineteenth century, and by the 1950s, sloth bear sightings had become increasingly rare. This dramatic decline was slowed, somewhat, by the Indian Wildlife Protection Act of 1972, which made both the hunting of sloth bears and the trade in their parts a criminal offense. Enforcement is, at best, patchy. Sloth bears can only be killed in cases of self-defense, although this is rare. When physical confrontations occur between sloth bears and humans, the bears usually win.

I first learned of Chhattisgarh's sloth bears from Dr. Harendra Singh Bargali, a remarkably focused and driven thirty-year-old Indian zoologist. He presented an abstract of his PhD thesis at the 2004 International Conference on Bear Research and Management in San Diego. His report seemed beyond belief. The 540-square-mile study area, the North Bilaspur Forest Division, was home to 180,000 people, 129,000 cattle, and 250 bears. Of the 178 villages in the area, 122 were plagued by bear attacks. With financial support from the Wildlife Institute of India, he conducted an in-depth investigation of 137 incidences of "maulings and killings" that occurred between April 1998 and December 2000. Bargali personally interviewed each survivor, or witnesses to the fatal attacks.

I caught up with Bargali a year later at Keoladeo Ghana National Park in Rajasthan, one of the most important bird sanctuaries in India. There, he confirmed that the North Bilaspur Forest Division has recorded more bear attacks than anywhere else on earth. Although he is currently assigned to wetland and bird conservation, he confesses that he can't wait to get back to working for the protection of sloth bears and their habitat.

"We must save the sloth bear," he says, "because by saving the sloth bear we save more than the sloth bear. We save their habitat and all the other species below them."

India is home to four bear species. In addition to the sloth bear, there is the rare Himalayan brown bear (*Ursus arctos linnacus*) and the Asiatic black bear (*Ursus thibetanus*), whose status in India is unknown but thought to be decreasing. Sun bears (*Helarctos malayanus*) were thought to be extinct in India, but a few have recently been found hanging on in the northeastern states of Arunachal Pradesh and Manipur. Bargali is fighting an uphill battle to raise awareness and money for conservation and research to help the sloth bear avoid a similar fate. Despite the fame of Rudyard Kipling's classic *Jungle Book*, which features Baloo the Bear, sloth bears are almost completely unknown outside the Indian subcontinent. The more glamorous species get all the resources and attention, both at home and abroad. Nothing illustrates this fact better than the Indian ten-rupee note, probably the most commonly used denomination in the country. It features Mahatma Gandhi on one side and an unlikely grouping of an Indian tiger, elephant, and rhino on the other. The international funds that come pouring in for these high-profile endangered species don't trickle down to sloth bears.

In North America, the smallest details of bear biology and behavior are funded for study while India's sloth bears remain largely unknown. Even among the international bear science community, there is relatively little knowledge of *Melursus ursinus*. Bargali remembers going to a bear conference in Norway where a researcher stood up and spoke at length about a project studying the "problem" of attacks in that country. What to do? There had been a single attack in the region. Bargali was reluctant to deliver his findings on India's numerous sloth bear attacks for fear of embarrassing his hosts.

As for the jungle in Chhattisgarh, he says, there are too many stories to tell. Stories of bad luck, courage, and terror—stories I will have to discover on my own. Through all the harrowing tales of violence and loss, the lasting impression he took from the jungle was that of the generosity, gentleness, and patience of the people—these "tribal" people, he says. Even after all they have endured, they still don't want any harm to come to the bears. This sentiment touched him deeply.

While Bargali was conducting his research in the region, villagers discovered an abandoned sloth bear cub and brought it to him. *Bhaluwa wale*, they called the young scientist, "he who belongs to the bear." Bargali named the cub Monica and raised her by hand. She would sit on a chair beside him each night as he typed up his attack reports. Bargali acted as surrogate mother, feeding and playing with the cub as often as he could. Even though he was in "the prime time to be looking for a wife," he was feeling the growing bonds of affection for a bear. This experience helped him understand his subject with an intimacy he never thought possible. Although his work has taken him six hundred miles away, it is his dream to see Monica, her jungle, and its people once again.

Sadly, he is unable to accompany me. Instead, he arranges for my train ticket and local guide—then wishes me the best of luck.

———

THE MORNING I arrive in Padkhuri, the mahua flowers are falling from branches sixty feet above. With the size and density of a large table grape, these fleshy flowers bounce when they hit the ground. Two women in gold and tangerine saris are doubled over, collecting them in baskets. I pick up a flower that has just come to rest at my boots. Its soft, pearly flesh is opaque and resembles lychee in both taste and texture. Most of the flowers gathered by these women will be dried and sold in local markets, fed to cows to sweeten their milk, or fermented to produce wine.

In recognition of the importance of the mahua tree (*Madhuca latifolia*) in this society, the annual Harchhat festival includes a feast in which every dish is made from its flowers, including *chapatis, roti, dal,* and *chai.* One of the most important crops of the year, mahua flowers are also highly prized by bears.

Although I am the subject of intense curiosity, these women try hard not to stare. I gather that foreigners are not in the habit of showing up in these parts, so far from any city or tourist destination. Padkhuri is one of many villages scattered throughout the jungle, where the local tribal people, or Adavasis, continue their traditional way of life. They have lived in and around this jungle forever, they say. But as their families and herds continue to grow, the jungle slowly withers away.

In addition to mahua, the forest consists of large sal trees that are also in full bloom. Their small white flowers give off a scent reminiscent of jasmine. The other tree in conspicuous bloom is the palash, which is aflame with red-orange flowers the color of midcentury lipstick. While beautiful, these flowers are not edible. For the fortnight mahua is falling, it is the most important tree in the forest. The flowers drop throughout the evening and early morning. Men, women, and children begin collecting them before dawn.

I wander through this clean and orderly village with Avneesh Pandey, whose given name means "god of the earth." A slight, twenty-eight-year-old man of the Brahmin caste, he has a shiny black moustache, a receding hairline, and an exceedingly gracious manner. He has agreed to act as my interpreter and guide among these tribal people and has fast become a friend. In his other life, Pandey is an instructor at his family-owned computer training school in Pendra (pop. 25,000), a town seventy-five miles away. There are no computers in these tribal villages—electricity has only just arrived.

We stroll among insouciant cows and pampered Brahma bulls. The tall piles of golden hay, rough-hewn oxcarts, and wooden plows bring to mind a medieval pastoral scene. The modest homes of the village are mud brick with two or three rooms (including an indoor stable) built around an *angan*, a small open courtyard. The floors are finished with what appears to be concrete, but is actually a mixture of cow dung and water, troweled hard and smooth. Each home has at least one wall painted sky blue, which reminds the people of Ram, Krishna, and heaven. On the sunny side of some houses, cow patties (used for fuel) have been slapped up on the wall to dry—each with a feminine handprint still clearly defined. Above or near many front doors are two common symbols: one is *om*, a venerated Hindu sign and an important mantra, the other is the swastika. An ancient and nearly universal creation symbol, the swastika has been found in Celtic, Byzantine, Greek, Buddhist, and Mesoamerican cultures. Although it has been ruined for the rest of the world since the rise of Germany's National Socialists (who used an inverted version as their symbol), the swastika is still highly popular in India.

At the edge of the village are rocky hillocks consisting of granite boulders the size of minivans. They rise some 150 feet above the otherwise flat terrain and are where sloth bears make their dens. Villagers know where each animal lives, the trail it takes to and from the den, and its usual pattern of movement. Now, in the late morning heat, the chances of attack are low. Having filled their baskets in the forest, the women hoist loads of mahua flowers up onto their heads and return to the village.

Although their traditions predate the Vedic Aryans and Dravidians, tribal people have been marginalized by the dominant culture. There are an estimated sixty million Adavasis in India. The government refers to them as Other Backward Tribes. Here in the North Bilaspur Forest, the people consider themselves Hindu (like over 80 percent of all other Indians), but are especially dedicated to local gods and adhere to local customs. In the past, relations between the tribal communities and the larger Indian society were largely peaceful and cooperative until many

Adavasis were forced off their land following Indian independence. A sizable percentage are now impoverished laborers. They are largely uneducated and their more savvy neighbors have been known to take advantage. To help redress the situation, the central government has created special programs to ensure that Adavasis have access to higher education. A quota system guarantees them parliamentary representation—a right unavailable to aboriginal peoples in Australia or North America.

Here, the tribal economy is based entirely on agriculture. They have few possessions, and earn about twenty to fifty rupees ($0.45–$1.14) a day. Despite their low net worth in the eyes of the global economy, they live relatively healthy and peaceful lives. After crop failure, their biggest fear is sloth bear attack.

When I arrive at the place called Chuwabahara, I find a giant mahua tree less than a hundred yards from a well-known bear denning site. In the parched field across the road, villagers are busy digging out a large reservoir to capture and keep more of the monsoon rains due to arrive in June. About sixty people are at work—half of them women. Men in loose *dhotis* and flip-flops wield pickaxes and shovels while the women do the heavy lifting, carrying baskets of rocks and soil on their heads. From my perspective above the pit, the drift of violet, green, and golden saris below makes it appear as a roost of tropical butterflies.

It is announced that a foreigner is in their midst and a crowd quickly gathers. The men leave the worksite en masse, happily tossing aside their tools. I am soon surrounded by men in the shade of the mahua tree. The women—including a pregnant girl who appears eight months along—continue hauling and dumping soil.

Although I've been hearing stories of bear attacks since my arrival in India, one particular event is repeated time and again by scientists, forest officials, and villagers. There are slight variations in the accounts, but the salient facts are remarkably consistent.

It is possibly the most horrific account of a bear attack ever recorded in India—or anywhere else for that matter. I have come to visit the site and try to piece together the story that, despite hundreds of subsequent attacks, people still recount with dread.

But the men have more recent stories to tell. Out of the thirty men surrounding me, all have family members who have been attacked. One young man is too shy to speak, but quickly hikes up his *dhoti* to show me the scars, which I am encouraged to touch. Once he sees that I am suitably impressed with the puncture wounds and the eighteen-inch scar running down his thigh, he is ready to tell his tale.

I squat down along with these tribal men, but it is clear that I am not built for such a pose. This is their preferred posture for conversing in the field. It reminds me of the way my own grandfather would squat and talk to me in his garden. Squatting was the mark of field hands and sharecroppers, people of the soil. My grandfather married into a large family of immigrants who brought the squat with them from Italy. It is the same squat found in the fields of Arkansas, China, Cambodia, and now here in central India. It is the way of poor people the world over. My father later pointed out that this tradition was fading away. He was sad to see it go, but recognized it for the "progress" that it was. And so I balance on the balls of my feet, listening, never quite at ease.

Kanshlal is twenty-three years old. He is powerfully built with full cheeks and cinnamon-colored skin. One evening two months ago, he was walking in the village. He came upon a bear that had been eating fruit from a neighbor's kitchen garden. He never approached the bear or made any aggressive movements. The bear looked up, dropped the fruit, and burst into a full gallop toward him. It bit his leg and then ran away. The leg became infected. Under a recent government compensation program, he received six thousand rupees (about $137), which almost covered the doctor's bill. The pain lasted two months, during which he could not work or provide for his wife and two small children. If he had died, there would have been no one left to feed them.

Fifty-year-old Mangalu is eager to show me the gray scars on his black cheeks, chin, and hands. His associates hold his head and direct the chin toward me, pointing at the marks, ostensibly for a better view. There are also bite marks on his thigh, shoulder, and on the top of his head. Mangalu was tending his cattle in a field just below a known den site. After the attack, he passed out. Someone found him bleeding in the field and took him back to the village. Although this attack happened in 1998, it is still fresh in his mind. His injuries required seventy-five stitches. Before the attack, he was forever having nightmares involving bears. Once a bear mauled him in his waking life, the dreams went away. He fears bears and is "very much disappointed" in their behavior, but doesn't want any harm to come to them. He wouldn't mind if the government decided to round them up and move them someplace else, but he doesn't want to see them killed.

I gesture to the hillock and den sites. Everyone knows the bears live there and depend on this forest for their food. So why come here? Why build houses and fields right next to the bears' home, especially when the danger is well-known? They have no choice, he says. They are poor and must build their homes and fields where they can. They need the food and fuel of the forest.

A third man shows the scars on his thigh and knees. He too was tending cattle when a bear came out of nowhere and attacked. He always carries a stick for just such an occasion, but for some reason forgot to bring it that day. He fought the bear with his bare hands and shouted for help until it ran way. Leopards never attack people this way, he says. No other animal is as dangerous as the bear.

I ask if they have heard of Jambavan. Of course they know Jambavan and his role in helping Ram triumph over evil. They know *The Ramayana* and believe it to be true. But when a bear attacks people they wonder if it has forgotten its allegiance to Ram and defected to the army of the wicked Ravana.

Although their injuries were painful, these men say that they are nothing compared to what women suffer when attacked. Everyone knows that bears prefer women because they like to rape them. In one famous case, a woman was kidnapped by a bear and held in a cave for a week. The bear had an ingenious plan; it licked the soles of her feet until all the callous had worn away and she was unable to walk, let alone escape. The bear raped her repeatedly for seven days until she was rescued. This happened four years ago. Sloth bears also prefer women, they say, because they like to eat their breasts.

I glance around at the men's faces—everyone heartily agrees. Then I look down at the women in the pit. I watch a woman balance fifty pounds of soil on her head while retaining the poise and grace to straighten her scarf.

Although none of the men know the rape victim's name, or where she was from, they are convinced of the story's authenticity. In fact, they cannot name a single woman who has been raped by a bear. However, they all believe it happens because their elders tell them so. Besides, they know bears prefer women because they saw what happened on this very spot ten years ago.

My thighs are on fire. I give up squatting and sit in the dirt, Indian-style, and let the story unfold.

AT HALF-PAST NINE on the morning of January 12, 1995, two women passed this tree on their way to the jungle where they planned to collect sal leaves. These thick, broad leaves are pressed into paper bowls for serving food on the street in Pendra, and to hungry travelers passing through Chhattisgarh by train. The women never reached the jungle. They were set upon by a large male bear.

During this initial attack, the women shouted and screamed for their lives. Three men working in a nearby field heard the cries and rushed to the scene. By the time they arrived, they found one woman dead—the other had run away. The bear ignored the men, and continued eating the woman. They shouted in an attempt to frighten the bear away, but it attacked them instead. It succeeded in killing two of the men, while the third managed to escape. The surviving man ran all the way to the village. A messenger was sent to forestry officials in nearby Marwahi to see if they could help. By the time the forest guards (rangers) finally arrived, villagers were reporting more shouts and cries from this same location. They found two women up the tree, weeping hysterically. The forest guards told the women to calm themselves, all was well in hand. But all was not well; the bear was still at the base of the tree feasting on the woman it had slain.

Meanwhile, most of the men and boys from the village had arrived, some brandishing sticks and axes. The guards ordered them to hold their attack. They had sent to Marwahi for a gun. The bear continued to eat as the villagers looked on in horror. The men decided they could no longer wait and moved together toward the bear. Instead of running away, the bear turned and attacked the mob—the people fled in panic. The bear caught the slowest member of the group, which it killed and began to consume. Finding this flesh not to its liking, it returned to the carcass of the woman.

The gun arrived at 1 P.M. The crowd held its breath as the guard took aim, but the single bullet proved to be a dud. It was thirty years old. Everyone watched in disbelief as the bear continued to eat. Eventually, more forest guards arrived with more bullets. This time the bullets worked but the men were terrible shots, having never had a chance to practice. (A vegetarian population, a law prohibiting the private ownership of firearms, and the resulting lack of gun-related crime means that even the police almost never have need of guns.)

Finally, one of the bullets hit the bear in the foreleg, which only served to enrage it. Although by this time the crowd had grown to over four hundred people, the bear launched another attack. In the ensuing panic, the slowest and unluckiest man was again culled from the mob, pulled to the ground, and mauled to death. Now five bodies lie in the shade of the mahua tree.

By this time, the superintendent of police had arrived from Pendra. He was not impressed with the locals. He said, "Give me the gun," and then shot the bear in the stomach and shoulder. The bear fell, but the superintendent continued firing just the same. Although it was clear the bear was dead, the people were too frightened to approach. Two or three of the bravest men— those with the "biggest hearts"—went to what was left of the woman. Her entrails were strewn about and much of her flesh had been consumed. The skull had been opened and the brains removed. In the words of one eyewitness, it looked "just like an empty pot."

In the branches above, the two women continued to weep. A strong young man tried to climb up to help them, but the trunk was too slippery. It seemed a miracle that the women were able to climb it. The men had to lean against the tree and stand on each other's shoulders to form a human ladder.

The bear was taken to Pendra for an autopsy to find out why it had gone berserk. It had killed five people, consuming one almost entirely, and had charged a crowd of over four hundred people. This kind of behavior had never been seen before. The bear's stomach was bloated. When the dissection began, they tried using surgical scalpels intended for humans, but these were unable to pierce the bear's thick skin. Someone offered an ax. When they hacked a hole in the abdominal cavity, the escaping gas was so noxious that everyone was forced to flee. People reported an over- powering stench up to a kilometer away. Two hours later, when the air had begun to clear, they returned and continued the work.

The bear had not had time to digest. When the bloated stom- ach was opened, parts of the woman came spilling out, including hair, clothes, muscles, and skin. While there had been countless attacks in the region, no one could remember a case of a bear consuming human flesh. The people wondered: What had turned this termite- and fruit-loving bear into a man-eating monster? The autopsy turned up neither rabies nor any other disease. The bear was a large male and it was mating season, but that was no answer. They reasoned that the bears could not find enough to eat. The people had taken too much from the jungle. That's why this bear had attacked and sloth bear attacks in general were on the rise. Three years later, Drs. Harendra Singh Bargali and Naim Akhtar arrived to study the problem.

THE TEMPERATURE CONTINUES to rise until it reaches the upper eighties. In summer, it can top 105. Even though it is only the mild days of March, I notice cattle and their people are most active in the morning and late afternoon, taking shady midday breaks that often include a nap.

After collecting a series of horrific tales, we break for lunch at a villager's home. The gracious owner invites us to recline on the low bench in the shade of his porch where we spread out the vegetarian lunch Pandey's sisters have prepared in advance, which includes butter *roti*, pickled mangoes, *cholay* (curried chickpeas), and *aloo gobi* (cauliflower and potatoes).

I have been keeping an eye on my left hand. Like all truly great men, I am left-handed and this talent causes me only small inconvenience in my life back home. While traveling in Latin America, however, I was called *siniestro* (sinister) when I scribbled in my notebook. Now I try to be discreet. Here, as in much of the world, personal ablutions are performed with the left hand—all higher tasks are reserved for the right. This is especially important to remember at mealtime. Food, plates, and serving spoons may be touched with the right hand only. This custom—and the fact that food is scooped, daubed, and gathered with *rotis* and *chipatis*—has me on edge. It requires fine motor skills. I have been vigilant against mistakes. Pandey is a patient teacher and any slip-ups are forgiven because I show such a genuine passion for Indian cuisine. After lunch, we laze in the shade.

When we finally step back onto the road, a barefoot man appears from out of nowhere. He presses his palms together, symbolizing the meeting of two souls, and bends down before me in *pranam*. He touches his forehead to my feet, then with his right hand, he touches the middle of his chest and then the middle of mine. He bows with deep respect to the all-knowing, all-loving god he believes dwells inside me and every other human being.

"He is respecting you," Pandey explains. "He welcomes you to this village. For us you are a respectable person. Here we say *Atithi Devo Bhavah*: Guest is God."

TWO BRAVE BOYS have volunteered to lead the way to the dens. They are in their mid-teens, have fuzz on their upper lips, and walk the trail in front of us holding hands. They know where the bears live and say they are unafraid.

The hillock rises from the surrounding fields and trees like the ruins of an ancient civilization. The hike up along the bear trail—through parched trees, thorns, and scrub—comes to an abrupt end at the mound of boulders that tops this and all the other hillocks in the region. The absence of such boulders in the rest of the plain reinforces the impression that they have been gathered here for a purpose lost near the beginning of time. Perhaps it was the fortress of giants or gods, a place from which to repulse determined enemies.

According to Dr. Harendra Singh Bargali, the denning behavior of the sloth bears in this region is unique in the bear world—even among sloth bears. Solitary creatures who usually prefer to avoid their own kind, no fewer than ten sloth bears make their home on this small hillock, both males and females with cubs. Whereas bears in northern lands use dens for maternity or hibernation, sloth bears do not hibernate and occupy their dens year-round. They follow semiregular patterns of sleeping, and then come down into the jungle to forage. They are most active at dawn and dusk. We pass a shallow cave where large bats stare back with accusing eyes. They stay put; a flight of butterflies comes spilling out instead.

Our guides confidently predict that the bears will be out at work this afternoon. They hop between boulders in plastic flip-flops without the slightest hesitation. Eventually, they stop in front of a small cave, scratch themselves, then point with satisfaction. They climb the last few steps up to the entrance and disappear inside.

Several piles of scat are in evidence. While I wait to see if the boys survive, I bend down and pick up a piece with my right hand. Pandey doesn't notice so I quickly switch to the left. It is surprisingly light and has an almost brasslike sheen. It has baked solid in the sun. I break it in half and a confetti of exoskeletons comes tumbling out. Some of the termites are still intact, although they are hollowed out by powerful bile and stomach acid. Other than a few strands of what appear to be splinters, the pile seems almost entirely composed of termites.

I haven't decided whether or not to be afraid. So far, I've taken my cues from the locals, who by now should have a healthy respect for the dangers posed by their resident bears. But then I remember what it was like to be sixteen and suddenly I don't feel so secure. In his dress shoes, pressed slacks, and long-sleeved shirt, Pandey carefully peeks over the entrance of the den and then waves down to me. I decide to place my faith in my ability to outrun the competition.

It is clear we are not the first people to visit. Inside the den, there is writing on the boulder above the pit. The Hindi words are in white chalk and I imagine it is some kind of warning, or prayer to the beast that sleeps in the hollow below. Pandey explains that it is only graffiti declaring some village boy's love for some village girl.

The top of the hill affords a commanding view over the forest and plain below. The terms *forest* and *jungle* have been bandied about to describe what I would call patchy clumps of trees; now these words earn their keep. From here, the forest cover is revealed as a canopy extending for miles around. Some of the mud-brick homes on the periphery of the village can be seen, as well as the fields and walled kitchen gardens. Other hillocks rise just above the trees. They contain boulders and bear dens of their own.

A hot breeze blows over the boulders where a few bamboo poles have been planted at the summit. Near the poles are collections of small earthenware saucers known as *deepaks*. These palm-sized vessels are used in prayer. A candle is lit inside the bowl, then held in the right hand and moved in a clockwise motion in front of the chest as an offering to the gods.

We take a look at another fortunately vacant den and still more stool samples. Then all at once I've had enough. The heat is making me dizzy and I can feel our luck pressing back. On our way down, we follow the same trail. Only this time I notice a spindly hut near the base of the hillock. Inside sits a *baba*, a holy man from the village. He is about a hundred yards from the nearest bear den, lost in meditation, with only a few withered leaves and twigs to protect him.

Back in the village, we pass women carrying all manner of items on their heads: rocks, cow dung, soil, mahua flowers, bundles of wood. The men never seem to be carrying anything. They have, however, volunteered to help me find a bear.

The elders of the community, strong young men, and yet more cocky boys have assembled with sticks and clubs. They all know where to find a bear and argue among themselves about who should lead the expedition. Another barefoot *baba* arrives with his painted forehead, walking staff, and minimal clothes. He will lend his spiritual intuition to the search. While they debate about which way to go, I pull out my notebook. A hush falls over the two dozen men who now huddle in close to watch. Curious, smiling faces press in front, from the sides, and over my shoulder to see what it is that I am doing with my nasty left hand. Suddenly seized with a case of stage fright, I scribble the words *They're all watching me!* Having long since given up on privacy—or the writer's privilege to shield unfinished work—I hold up the book and show the scribbles to anyone who wants to see. Nods all around.

Other than bicycles, there are no vehicles in this village—save the jeep that brought me here. We squeeze in and speed away while the rest hoof it or pedal bikes over shortcuts through the fields of green wheat and *chana* (chickpeas). Five minutes later, we arrive at the other side of the same hillock where we inspected the dens. I see a few men are armed with their tiny tribal axes which, with their three-inch blades, seem custom-made for children. One man has a bottle of kerosene. Thus prepared to face whatever danger awaits, we all march off into the trees with much fanfare and the continuing debate over who will get to lead. The village men crunch loudly over leaves, break branches to make yet more clubs, and generally talk up a storm. Any creature, wild or tame, has long since fled the region. What was I thinking? Vegetarians since the time before time, they long ago lost any instinct for the hunt.

We march along a bear trail for the better part of an hour. Eventually, the futility of continued pursuit dawns on even the most persistent. Amid the shrugging of shoulders and the shaking of heads, the *baba* wanders off and the parade shuffles back to the village.

THE OFFICE OF A. S. Patel appears as a minor colonial outpost from the height of the British Raj. The walls are painted the same faded blue so popular in the villages—and in Greek restaurants around the world. Shelves sag under moldering books and oversized ledgers. The three hardwood desks that fill the room are piled shoulder high with yet more dossiers and files. A ceiling fan lazily stirs the air overhead, offering the only proof that we are in the Electrical Age. Needless to say, there is not a computer or calculator in sight. I can hear the wheels of opportunity spinning inside Avneesh Pandey's head.

Forest Manager Patel is dressed in a version of the khaki uniform worn by forest guards and rangers in other jurisdictions. I suppose the enforcement nature of the job makes them a certain class of soldier, but these guys look kitted-out for the Battle of Verdun. This is the office that dispatched the gun and the vintage bullet during the Massacre of '95, the one that failed to pop.

Patel is a middle-aged man who orders his staff about with a formality that also seems antique. Still, he has graciously set aside some time to meet me and answer my questions about bear attacks and government compensation. He marvels at the fact that someone from so far away could be interested in Marwahi.

From the shelf he pulls out one of hundreds of giant ledgers and lands it on the desk between us. He opens it to January 2004, and runs his finger down the page. He reads aloud a catalog of bites, slashes, cuts, bruises, broken bones, and disemboweling. Eight pages in, he finally comes to the end of the casualties. In the North Bilaspur Forest Division, the jungle under his watch, there were twenty-four sloth bear attacks reported last year—a slow year, but an average of one every other week.

Patel also lists amounts of compensation paid to the victims, money made available by the central government and distributed by this office. Bites and slashing that do not result in lasting disability net between 200 and 7,000 rupees ($4.58–$160.20). The rate climbs in relation to the severity of the injury. He realizes that this may seem somewhat insignificant, but one has to remember that this money is intended to cover hospital expenses only, plus a little extra for the crippled. In cases of death, the family of the deceased gets a hundred thousand rupees (just shy of $2,300). I am reminded that India is a developing country, and that until the 1990s, there was no compensation of any kind.

Victims tell me that the government's compensation money often does not cover their doctor's bills. As I listen to the roll call of the wounded, I can't help but think of the ubiquitous multimillion-dollar personal injury lawsuits in the United States— which can compensate victims for wounds, pain and suffering, mental anguish, loss of future income, and diminished quality of life. There, a strategically spilled cup of drive-thru coffee can net a fortune.

In these jungles, jackals and hyenas also attack, Patel explains. But they mostly target sheep. In the few instances when humans are attacked, the injuries are rarely severe. Bears are the most dangerous animal in the jungle, he says. And because bears and people depend on some of the same sources of food, there is conflict. Although there are no tigers in this forest, where they exist in nearby jurisdictions there are few attacks on humans because Hindus don't compete with tigers for game meat. However, if a tiger messes with a villager's cattle, there will be hell to pay. The villager will locate the carcass of his cow in a tree (where tigers like to stash their kill), inject it with poison, and thereby extract vengeance for the "murder."

It boils down to this, Patel explains. People cut the trees and the forest is being nibbled away. People encroach on the forest and this leads to attacks. And then there is the problem of politics in this, the world's largest democracy. "Politicians choose people over forest animals," he says, "because animals do not vote."

Although the human population continues to increase as the forest steadily contracts, he believes the numbers of bears is on the rise. Sloth bears are found in other areas, including national parks and sanctuaries, but there they do not have much of a problem because the interaction between people and bears is limited. There is currently no plan to declare a national park or sanctuary in this region. Sadly, Patel predicts that they won't be able to stop further encroachment in the forest and that the number and severity of attacks will increase.

As an aside, he says there was another attack that involved the death and consumption of a villager a few years ago. Again, two women were in a field. A bear appeared from out of nowhere and killed one of them. The second woman escaped, then returned to the scene with some villagers. They came to kill this bear. When they arrived, they saw the bear consuming the woman's flesh. Before they could act, the bear left the corpse and ran straight toward the villagers. But this time the son of the slain woman stood and fought. The bear easily gained the upper hand. When the boy's father arrived and saw the body of his wife, and his son under attack, he threw himself at the bear. Although the men fought bravely, both were badly mauled. The villagers were sure this would be the end of the family. It is accepted local wisdom that a sloth bear possesses ten men's strength and twelve men's cunning. Somehow, the father grabbed the bear by the ears and wrestled it to the ground. The son picked up a large rock and brought it down on the bear's skull. To the best of Patel's knowledge, this is only the second case of a sloth bear eating human flesh—and of people killing bears in self-defense. Most bears get away with murder.

Sloth bears are fascinating creatures, Patel says by way of summation. He has personally watched sloth bears engage in intercourse "nonstop" for half an hour. "And they were having sex like us," he says, "face to face."

BACK IN PADKHURI, the people are turning out in droves to hear the Muslim *baba*. Men wear their cleanest Western shirts and pants. Women in resplendent saris clutch scrubbed and obedient children. Many are wearing shoes. With few exceptions, these tribal people are self-described Hindus but they see no conflict in hearing what the Muslim has to say. Any *baba*—Hindu, Muslim, or Jain—is welcome to come and the people will show up to listen. If they like what they hear, they may add a new god to the mix. Although there are no Christians in these villages, in Pendra some Hindus visit the Christian church and develop an interest in Jesus, praying to him along with Ram, Ganesh, and Hanuman.

We take tea with the faithful in a restaurant beside the *baba's* white and green *Dera* (meeting place). Chai is an important daily ritual, usually taken together by men two or three times a day. Dark and strong, it is served in four-ounce glasses with rich, fresh milk. It is a habit I quickly adopt.

A crowd soon gathers around me. People look me up and down and then ask for my story. While it is true that I haven't seen a single foreigner since stepping on the train in Rajasthan ten days ago, I still can't get over the reaction. They must have seen Westerners before.

"No," Pandey says. "You are the first one they have seen. You are the first to visit their villages."

Surely he is mistaken. I turn to the oldest man at an adjacent table. He looks to be about seventy. "Ask him," I say. "Ask him if he has ever seen a Westerner before."

The man looks up and thinks for a moment. "Two Westerners came to this place four years ago," he says at last. "They came to pay their respects to a white crow that had been born here and lived in the trees of this village. The men were from Pakistan."

"You are the first real foreigner they have seen," Pandey says. "I tell them where you are from and they don't understand. *Canada* is a new word for them."

They are curious about this distant country and its inhabitants. I explain that there are European, Asian, and African people— even people from India. There are also indigenous "tribal" people like themselves, also known as Indians.

Eyes blink at the conundrum.

"But we are Indians," they say.

"Yes, but Christopher Columbus . . . You know, when he reached the New World and thought he was in India?"

Blank stares.

I can't tell whether being the one to tell them this is a kind of privilege or curse. When I explain the planet's most fantastical case of mistaken identity, and the fact that an entire race of people—spanning two continents—still bear the wrong name, they shake their heads in dismay. Truly, I come from a strange land.

ANY LINGERING DOUBT about the danger posed by sloth bears is forever stripped away inside the humble mud-brick home of Prem Singh. He wanted to come and meet me, but is unable to travel. He sent a boy to fetch me.

We are welcomed into his *angan* where I am offered a low stool under a poster of elephant-faced Ganesh. Although he is fifty years old, Singh looks closer to eighty. He wears a sagging *dhoti* above knotted knees and walks with a pronounced limp. His face, the upper half of it anyway, has been ripped away. The bridge of his nose is gone and his left eye is missing. The one that remains is opaque. The brow ridge over both eye sockets, the bridge of his nose, and the front of his skull are gone. What remains is bubbly skin that has been stretched and sewn back in place over the brain, which—like the soft spot of a newborn baby's head— pulses with the beat of his heart. His hearing is wrecked, he has puncture wounds on his legs, shoulders, chest, and stomach. There is nerve damage in his right hand and leg. Unable to work, and with no children to care for him, his wife must go out and earn their living. Afraid to leave the safety of his home, he is a prisoner of his fears.

Singh has been attacked twice by sloth bears. The first incident, which claimed his face and eye, took place in 2002.

"I was going out to defecate in the field," he says. "I was carrying a jug of water, which I set on the ground. I was untying my underwear when a bear attacked from behind and bit my foot. It never made a sound. Then another bear attacked my leg. I fell down and one of the bears came and sat on my stomach. I was shouting for help and then the bear bit my mouth and began ripping the skin on my face. I fought with that bear. When the second bear attacked my head, I lost all sense. People heard my shouts and came running. They chased the bears away."

As he tells this story in Hindi, I recognize only the word *bhalu*, but I understand the distorted, muffled voice. While his nostrils remain, his nose is gone and what comes out of his mouth is muted. His tone is anxious, confused.

The second attack happened a year later. He remembers three bears in the field where he was going to work. One of them ran straight for him, biting and slashing his back and shoulders before finally running away. The government gave him seven thousand rupees ($160.20) for the first attack, five thousand ($114.50) for the second. Neither covered his medical bills. His life is over, he says.

"What should be done about the bears?" I ask.

"I have no right to give you an opinion."

"Some people think they should be captured and moved some-place else."

"I don't want the bears to be killed but . . . I have no power," he says. "My opinion doesn't matter. Of that I am certain."

As I gaze at his mangled face, I realize that this is more than I had hoped for, more than I had imagined this story could be. And now I feel ashamed that I have come all this way to get it. I feel like a tourist in other people's misfortune. I ask him why he agreed to see me and he says he wants this story told. He does not hate bears, or call for vengeance, but this thing has happened to him and people should know. If I want, he says, I can take his picture.

And so I arrange him and his wife up against the cool blue wall inside their safe little courtyard, then snap a single frame. I thank him, bow with respect, and—before he can refuse—press money into his hand. I tell him *Jay Ram Ji Ki*, the local salutation that means both "Good-bye" and "Win with Ram."

MARKET DAY IN the jungle has the feel of a summer carnival. In a parched clearing the size of two cricket pitches, men and

women from the surrounding villages unfurl blankets and set up
shop at the edge of the forest. Metal pots, mini-axes, and posters
of the gods are for sale. There are piles of powdered cumin, pepper, and coriander, plus waxy green and red chilies ablaze in the
setting sun. At the edge of the market is the *paan wallah*—the
man who freshens breath.

Paan is an explosive bundle of sweet, spicy, and aromatic flavors
packed in a green banana leaf. Betel nut, lime paste, caraway
seeds, plus half a dozen other condiments and spices are smeared
on a cool patch of leaf before being folded into a tight packet and
impaled with a toothpick. I am told it is for cleansing the palate
after meals, but it is much more than that. It is a habit-forming
stimulant akin to a double espresso or a wad of chewing tobacco.
The teeth of those who consistently indulge rot into points and
are stained the color of blood. I had my first *paan* experience the
day I arrived in Chhattisgarh—and promptly spat it out. Now I'm
a connoisseur.

There are hundreds of people in the field today. Middle-aged
men shoot the breeze while young men wander the market in
pairs with arms intertwined, draped around each other's hips, or
simply holding hands. While public displays of affection between
the sexes are taboo, these youth seem to make up for the lack
with each other. I am assured it is simply a sign of platonic affection that does not ordinarily lead to "wrong actions." But the
intimacy—the familiar way they handle each other's bodies—
makes it clear that there is, at least, infatuation. The girls and
young women feign disinterest in the doings of boys and young
men. They are too busy weighing spices, minding siblings, closing
deals.

Beyond the market, we pass grown women washing clothes and
bathing fully dressed in the river, then stop at a small mud-brick
house on a rise above the bank.

Phool Mati is not happy to see us. The thirty-five-year-old has
her hands full with a pair of demanding kids, bawling goats, and a

million more important things to do. She covers her neck with
her purple scarf. By the set of her jaw and the roll of her eyes, it
is clear she does not welcome the intrusion of strange men while
her husband is out. Still, she offers me a seat on a newish-looking
burlap sack on the dung patio.

In addition to Pandey and our driver, my entourage now consists of a local guide, a forest guard, and numerous neighborhood men and boys who unfortunately saw us arrive. Everyone
crowds around to help me conduct the interview. I take deep
breaths, cross my arms, and even shake my head in disbelief, but
no one seems to decipher my nonverbal cues. I explain that I
prefer conducting interviews alone, without the help of villagers or officials, but no one understands how this could be. It
is getting late so I relent and ask Phool Mati about the attack.
The men shout back answers and descriptions before she has a
chance to open her mouth. According to them, she was attacked while tending sheep. I ask for details, and if she has received compensation. This is the first she has heard of such a
thing. The forest guard vigorously disagrees, but she refuses to
change her tune.

Then, I lose my patience. In what instantly feels like classic
colonial style, I wave my hand and tell the men to be quiet and
go stand by the jeep. It mostly works. Better still, her husband arrives and puts her at ease. He is a silver-haired gentleman with
tattered clothes and a noble bearing. He seems pleased with all
the attention and urges his wife to continue.

She was grazing her sheep in the jungle at ten in the morning.
By the time she saw the mother bear on one side of her flock, and
two cubs on the other, it was too late. The bear charged straight
at her, slashing and biting her legs and breasts. In the shock and
adrenalin of the moment, she thought only of her sheep and
didn't realize the extent of her injuries. The attack was over as
swiftly as it had begun and the bear ran away. Despite it all, Phool
Mati had the presence of mind to round up her flock and bring it

safely home. Her husband took her to the hospital where they treated her injuries. No one said a word about compensation.

The breeze blows the scarf from her neck and she pulls it back in place again.

Does she believe bears attack women more than men? What if this bear had been a male? Did she fear being raped? She's heard these stories before but does not believe them. While the bear did bite her breasts, she points out that it bit her legs and arms as well. Despite the attack, she does not think anyone should harm the bears. She inadvertently came between a mother and her cubs, she says. As a mother herself, she understands what this means.

A FEW MILES down the road, we leave the last human habitation and enter the "core" forest area. As twilight approaches, the trees and bush close in. We park the jeep and follow a road to the base of yet another rocky hillock and well-known bear denning site. A troop of black-faced Hanuman langurs study our every move. The sweet, heavy perfume of sal blossoms hangs in the air, along with the lonesome howl of a jackal.

Our party consists of nine members, including a forest guard and three local guides—tall boys in their late teens with wide shoulders and intelligent eyes. They are the picture of health, save their prematurely graying hair. They have no doubt that we will encounter a bear. When I ask why they aren't afraid, they reply that we are well-prepared and that there are enough of us to discourage an attack. I can feel my eyebrows rise. I wonder if they were old enough to join the crowd at the Massacre of '95.

In the heart of this remnant forest, we pick a spot atop a rocky ravine on the far side of the road. It offers a view toward the darkening hillock and a well-defined bear trail. The men divvy up axes and sticks; I am handed a club as long as my leg. One of the boys makes a Molotov cocktail with a bottle of kerosene. Arif Tenvir, a friend of Avneesh Pandey's, is along for the ride. He has brought an old bicycle tire, which he hacks in two. He ties the halves to separate sticks, creating a pair of crude shepherd's staffs.

As we prepare for the bear's arrival, I learn that this hillock (like all hillocks) is inhabited by a local god. The one that lives here, *Bhuthi*, is known as the Vampire goddess. Like the bear dens, her temple is somewhere in the boulders. Although she is depicted with a menacing face and fangs, she is actually a good goddess and likes having the bears around. "We don't pray to any bad gods," the villagers say.

Our deliberations are interrupted by distant screams. We freeze and listen to a woman's desperate cry for help somewhere in the jungle. The forest guard grabs a stick and one of the boys, then jogs off into the trees.

While we wait and wait for news of this disturbing development, the remains of the day slip beyond the horizon as the stars multiply. We sit on sun-warmed stones with our weapons at the ready, divining shadows in the half-moonlight. Soon, a swarm of fireflies flashes before our eyes.

Because market day has come to an end, people begin filing past on the road. Mostly single men pedaling bikes, they whisk by without noticing us, singing to calm themselves through what must be unnerving territory. An adolescent boy appears with a couple of cows, tapping them on the rump with a stick to urge them on a little faster.

The forest guard returns and tells us not to worry. The woman's sheep were attacked by jackals, nothing more. I don't feel relieved. In this meager light, I can barely see the road in front of me. If a jackal, hyena, or bear shows up, how will we see it? And now more people are passing by. One man has an enormous metal speaker bolted to his bike, blaring loud music. Even the guard is forced to concede that perhaps we have picked the wrong day.

Still, we stare into the night. Several times I think I see something moving in the shadows—and then it is gone. Two of the boys climb the nearest tree for a better view. The rest of us squeeze in close on the rock, axes and clubs in hand.

What I am doing here? To be sure, lying in wait for a sloth bear with half a dozen men has not the slightest whiff of bravery. Bravery would be what the locals do each morning, stumbling outside at dawn to relieve themselves, working alone in the fields, letting their children out to play. Or, in the case of twice-mauled Prem Singh, facing the mirror each day. Suddenly, my presence here seems foolish. All introspection comes to an end when we hear a snuffling noise nearby. The men point into a clearing and everyone strains to see. I see nothing other than some possible shadows within shadows. When the snuffling stops, the forest guard hustles into the dark. With his departure, and the boys up the tree, I am feeling a little exposed.

The forest guard returns and we hear the sound again. Now it seems everyone else can actually see it. One of the boys dashes behind me, takes my head in his hands, and points me in the right direction. I think I can see something, but I am unsure. The guard clucks and tells us to follow him. We race off into the dark-ness and then all at once I see it: a waist-high mass of shadow gal-loping toward us. We let out a collective roar and instinctively circle in tight—backs together, weapons pointed out. On the first strike, Tenvir miraculously manages to light a match, then the Molotov cocktail, and finally those ingenious tire torches. In the sudden flash, I clearly see the bear halt its advance about twenty yards away. Then—in almost cartoonlike fashion—it spins on its heels and bounds off the way it came.

Wild-eyed and shaking, we turn to one another and let out a profound and primeval cheer. We hug and slap each other on the back, congratulating ourselves for having narrowly escaped death or mauling. In that moment, we are united in an ancient, funda-mental way that speaks of cooperation, fire . . . humanity. We swagger back to the jeep with our torches held high, dripping molten rubber—a blazing trail of warning in our evolutionary path.

DRUMS CAN BE HEARD as soon as we enter the village. We have arrived to a celebration. As we stop to listen, one of the boys asks if we would like to see some traditional dancing. A wedding is taking place for one of his friends, and as guests in this village we are welcome to attend. Keenly aware of the popularity of wedding crashers back home, I send him ahead to make doubly sure.

Past the door and into the *angan*, a crowd of smiling faces turns toward me and my companions. A dim, naked bulb is the only light inside. Near the door, two men sit on the dung floor pounding large *nandara* drums in a complicated, hypnotic beat. I am offered a seat of honor, a mat next to a newborn calf. The calf seems unfazed by the activity and noise, so I sit with my elbow resting on its haunch. My new circle of friends crowd in close, leaning on my shoulder, back, and knee.

A lanky boy, about sixteen, and a fifteen-year-old girl in a magnificent sari, are carried out and set in the center of the courtyard. They are carried by their mothers. The stiff, barefoot couple sit side by side as the drummers pick up the beat. The mothers are both in their early thirties. They reach into bowls of *haldi* (turmeric) and *ata* (flour), then dust the heads of their children yellow and white, ensuring their fertility and abundance.

The boy has long, storklike legs and big, bony feet. His mother reaches down and scoops him up in her arms. He wraps his legs around her waist and his arms around her neck, and then she dances across the room. She dances with her arms floating at her sides as the boy hangs on like an enormous toddler. She moves across the room with poise and grace, defying the weight, dancing with her grown son. His feet never touch the ground. Two other women dance onto the floor. As soon as the mother sets him down, the aunts each take a turn with the groom. This dance speaks with an eloquence beyond words. More than a celebration of maternal love, it is a moving tribute to the feminine strength that builds and sustains this community.

The boys pass me a kind of cigarette wrapped in a tendu leaf. Smiling faces press in to watch. I am no smoker, but I recognize this as an appropriate time to start. I pull the tangy smoke into my lungs and let it out again in a controlled, steady stream. I cough only twice.

The music changes as the bride is danced around the floor by her female relatives in similar fashion. She is a fragile beauty. Her dark, wide eyes concerned but resolute.

The local vintner has learned of my interest in mahua. When the dancers take a break, he lures me away from the celebration to show me how tribal wine is made. I purchase a liter, which he pours fresh from a large clay pot into a grimy plastic bottle. Pandey and Tenvir politely decline but are eager to see me try. I drink a toast to them and the boys, the bear—and, of course, the happy couple. The sour-sweet potion warms all the way down.

WHEN I FIRST arrived in India, Dr. Harendra Singh Bargali explained that there is another Indian tribal group that is famous for traditional dance—only this dance is not performed by people. The Kalandars, a nomadic tribe descended from Muslim gypsies, have long relied on "dancing" bears as a way to make a living.

For untold generations, Kalandars have traveled into the jungle to capture sloth bear cubs, which often involves killing the mother. It is estimated that a hundred cubs are captured each year but only half survive the ordeal. Once brought into a Kalandar community, cubs are subjected to a series of cruel "dance" lessons. First, a hot poker is used to pierce the cub's sensitive snout clear through the skin, cartilage, nasal passage, and the roof of its mouth. A rope is then inserted through the wound. A loop is formed and tied to a leash, which the master tugs to encourage the cub to stand on its hind legs. The cub sways and lifts its limbs in a further attempt to alleviate the pain and this produces the "dance" that tourists pay to see. Locals are fond of the Kalandar's dancing bears for their entertainment value, and for their purported healing properties. Sick children are placed on a sloth bear's back for a short ride in the hope this will cure them. To protect against the Evil Eye, amulets are made from the bear's claws and fur.

Estimates of India's dancing bear population run as high as twelve hundred. Many dancing bears live with endless infection; more are malnourished. Although the practice has been illegal since 1992, Kalandars are still seen with sloth bears along the road between Jaipur and Agra—home of the Taj Mahal. They favor this road for the steady stream of tourists willing to pay to see the bears raise their paws and sway back and forth in a "dance." Dancing bears are, of course, not unique to India. In Western Europe, dancing bears were popular for centuries until the practice came to an end (in the case of Greece) only a few years ago. Dancing bears can still be found in Central and Eastern Europe, Turkey, and Russia—although in steadily falling numbers.

In India, the problem seemed worst in Agra. With the support of numerous animal welfare organizations (Wildlife S.O.S., World Society for the Protection of Animals, International Animal Rescue, and Free the Bears Fund), police have recently begun targeted raids in Kalandar communities and are in the midst of a general crackdown on the dancing bear trade. This has resulted in the confiscation of numerous dancing bears—which end up at the Agra Bear Rescue Centre, a sanctuary designed to rehabilitate and house former dancing bears in a seminatural state. People convicted of possessing or trafficking in sloth bears face as much as five years in prison. To help the Kalandars find other ways of making money, and to ensure they do not reoffend, animal welfare organizations offer them the opportunity to surrender their bears in exchange for a transition grant. So far, over fifty have accepted the offer, resulting in new lives for them, their families, and the bears.

Through the media, these animal welfare organizations have been highly successful at raising awareness of the dancing bear problem in India. Due to the power of public opinion, this has had a direct and measurable impact on ending the exploitation of many sloth bears. While the practice won't completely disappear for some time to come, Bargali is confident its days are numbered. My time would be better spent in remnant forests where sloth bear habitat still exists, he said. Only by seeing the way humans and wildlife compete for space and resources could I hope to understand the greatest threat to the sloth bear's survival.

OBSERVING SLOTH BEARS in their natural habitat, however, is proving a difficult task. Having only seen a charging sloth bear in a kerosene flash, I am eager for a closer look at a less agitated specimen. The best place to do that is at a tiny zoo in Pendra where it is possible to get remarkably close to the star attraction— Monica, the orphaned cub that was hand-raised by Bargali.

When I arrive, Monica is fast asleep in her cell. She is an undefined mound of fur. When I call her name, she looks up with drowsy, searching eyes. For my benefit, the staff decide to let her out to play. They say she is allowed outside to exercise "now and then," but I have my doubts. Letting her out is a bit of an ordeal. A man enters her small exercise yard and locks the gate behind him. He then approaches the cell where Monica rests and carefully unlocks the door. She barely seems to notice. Slowly, he pulls open the heavy iron door about a third of the way—then turns and sprints through the yard and scrambles up the ten-foot fence. I think to myself, *There must be a better way.*

Monica is soon up and moving. Just as the man finally climbs over the top to safety, the suddenly energized bear is bounding out into the center of the yard. No one knows how much danger he was in. Although Monica was hand-raised by Bargali, she has not been allowed direct human contact for some years now. Despite this slapstick routine, her keepers say they err on the side of caution.

Slight by sloth bear standards, Monica still seems rather fit. She bounds toward the fence, then jumps up on hind legs—raising her claws as if playing up some tired bear cliché. She roams in circles like a prize-fighter, throwing taunts, spoiling for a bout. The langurs chained to the fence do not take this display lightly; they scream in real terror. Pulling at their chains and collars, they frantically try to escape. For her part, Monica seemingly enjoys the spectacle and does the pose again. Finally, the keepers unchain the terrified monkeys and evacuate them to a distant tree.

Monica is distracted by ants near her wading pool and begins snuffling around. Her shaggy black coat is offset by the ivory of her chest patch and her formidable claws. She flings dirt and grass behind her, then inhales the tiny prey. Suddenly losing interest, she picks up a wicker basket and begins tossing it in the air like a cat toying with an expired rodent.

A small group of local kids and families have gathered to watch. Despite the pain and suffering these bears have caused in local villages, the people's faces are fixed with wonder. Try as we might to deny the fact—or rise above it with reason and sophistication—it seems our fate as human beings to thrill in the close proximity of dangerous, unpredictable beasts. It is an existential paradox that the fear of violent death makes us feel more alive.

THIS NIGHT I am surprised by many things, the first of which is the fact that Arif Tenvir is a Muslim. Because I am so new to this country, I suppose it is really no surprise at all. Friend of Avneesh Pandey and fire master from the night of the sloth bear charge, Tenvir is committed to classical Indian culture and is the director of Pendra's Traditional Music Research Center. He knows only a smattering of English but has decided to befriend me anyway.

I have been raving about India's vegetarian cuisine but Tenvir insists I try chicken biriani. We walk to a small outdoor grill in a dark corner of town. There, I am instantly surrounded by local men who regard me as an interplanetary alien. When they learn where I'm from—the world's second-largest country that sprawls across the top of North America—their eyes grow large and their mouths gape. Their first and only question is, "Who is the god of Canada?" I try to explain that—coming from Vancouver, a city where half the people are of Asian descent—the question is not so easy to answer. As Indians, they understand religious diversity. Equivocations aside, one man is willing to bet on the prophet Jesus.

After the meal of savory chicken and rice, Tenvir invites me back to his home for music and dessert, where Avneesh Pandey and his sister Chaia are already waiting inside. Like Tenvir, Pandey is turned out in a crisp white *kurta*, the traditional Indian long shirt. His sister is in a lime-green sari.

The small brick-and-stucco room is remarkably spare. There is no furniture, so we sit on the floor among a collection of traditional musical instruments. With Pandey on the *tabla* and Tenvir on the harmonium, they launch into an old love song. As Tenvir sings the warbling melody, the pride and determination is written on his face—his red, *paan*-stained teeth flash in the dim light. Pandey and his sister sing the refrain. It is the song of a man who must leave his family to make money elsewhere, and the wife who begs him to stay.

A crack appears in the curtain over the back room and the hand of a young woman sends out four small bowls of *kheer*, a sweet rice pudding. Although I am not introduced, and her existence is never mentioned, it is clear that this is Tenvir's wife. In the shadows I can see that she is holding a baby but clearly doesn't want to be seen. I praise the *kheer* to the heavens and still she will not show her face. Later I can see one eye peering from behind a scarf as she stares back from the darkened room.

I have asked a million questions, I say. Is there anything they want to know about me or life on the other side of the world? Chaia asks if it is true that there are no more families in North America, if we all lead more or less separate lives. I survey their faces—all three genuinely wonder if this is true.

After dessert, and another traditional Indian song, they want a song from me. I surprise myself by asking if they've ever heard "Amazing Grace." My religious years ended half a lifetime ago, but this is the song that elbows its way to the front of my mind. They've never heard it before. After a minute or two a cappella, I find myself accompanied on tabla and harmonium. On the second refrain, Tenvir even sings along phonetically. By the time the song comes to rest it feels as if we have created something new.

THERE ARE MANY more villagers to meet; a seemingly inexhaustible supply of scars and stories. Many people are attacked by sloth bears in the early morning, either on the way to, during, or returning from relieving themselves. Others get into trouble while collecting flowers or fruit, or tending livestock. In one story, a bear knocked a man to the ground and proceeded to maul him. Then his cattle came to the rescue. They charged and chased the bear away, saving their master's life. Over and over again I hear that, despite the danger, villagers do not want any harm to come to the bears. They want them to stay because they believe bears guard the jungle. If the bears disappear, then so will the trees and rain.

I meet one boy who probably lives closer to a wild bear than anyone else on earth. Thirteen-year-old Vishnu Prashad is about five feet tall and has intense, sober eyes. He takes me through his father's house to the dung patio out back where there is a well, a place to bathe, a hay pile, a small garden with fruit trees, and—about fifty yards from the door—a mound of boulders two stories high. Here lives the bear that slashed his back, stomach, and side.

The attack happened when he was "just a child" (two years before). He was going out to pick fruit from his father's trees between the house and the den. It was late in the morning and he didn't see the bear; it simply appeared and attacked. The boy pulls off his shirt to show the damage. The bear lashed out with its claw and caught him just above the navel. It tore the skin over his belly, up toward his rib cage, and around to his left side. A second swipe caught him on the back, leaving a scar that required many stitches. In addition to the long scars are numerous puncture wounds. All this damage was done by the bear's claws, he says. Strangely, it never bit him.

The neighbors heard his cries and came running. They were able to chase the bear away. His father carried him to Marwahi, but they were unable to deal with such an injury. They stopped the flow of blood and sent the boy on a seventy-mile journey to the city of Bilaspur (pop. 265,000), where he remained hospitalized for a month. It was his first trip beyond the local villages. Was he afraid to stay in a big city so far from home?

"No," he says, pulling on his shirt. "I am only afraid of the bear."

The same bear that continues to sleep in the den behind his house.

"I still go back there to collect fruit and other things. I have to go there. Sometimes I am afraid; other times I am not."

Does he want to kill the bear to prevent another attack on himself or members of his family?

"No," he says, with only the slightest hesitation. "Other people might like to kill bears, but they fear punishment from the government more than they fear the bears . . . I don't want to kill them. You can take them to another part of the jungle, where there is more room, but do not kill them."

Why? Because this is the bear's home. They have always lived in the jungle. They are only trying to survive, just like him and his family. Because people and bears like the same food, he says, problems are bound to occur.

LATE THAT AFTERNOON, we set off for Ghusariya, another core forest area of towering sal, mahua, and palash trees. We pass a pair of women walking out with bundles of leaves balanced on their heads. In every direction the jungle appears healthy and whole. A closer look, however, reveals that the cutting of branches and trees is well under way. Little by little, year by year, the villagers gnaw away at what remains. After half an hour, we arrive at one of the largest hills in the region, a place of numerous sloth bear dens.

Because there are only four of us, our guide is uneasy. Phool Singh is a wiry man with ebony skin and narrow, attentive eyes. He wants to fetch a few more men to bolster our meager group. This means he and the driver will leave Pandey and me atop the granite boulders and bear dens to watch for signs of movement. For protection, he leaves two axes.

An hour later, he returns with a pair of village men and three boys in their mid-to-late teens. We are now eight in number and have three axes, a couple of sticks, and a torch between us. We sit on the highest point of rock as the parakeets, Long-tailed Night-jar, and Black Drongo call and respond through the valley below. The avian commotion increases in advance of the setting sun.

We hear the rustle of dry leaves on the opposite hill. Eventually, we spot a black form grazing under a mahua tree. We watch as the bear consumes the fallen flowers, then continues on its way. Eventually, we lose sight of the bear but can hear it—plus the crunch and crash of a second bear foraging the forest floor. When their paths intersect, there is a low growl.

A boy slips away from the safety of our group, scrambles down the boulders and out into the open. Phool Singh and the boy's father snap their fingers and signal him to return, but he ignores them. By now it is clear that one of the bears is approaching. Although it remains unseen, its advance can be clearly heard. As it nears the boy, I feel a tightening inside. His hands are empty; he carries no ax or club. How effective will his flip-flops be if he is forced to run for his life?

This is my fault. These people are here to impress me with their knowledge and bravery. They are taking unusual risks and now this boy is in danger. No one asked him to act as bait, but I have set this drama in motion.

Phool Singh now seems frantic but the boy's father appears only mildly concerned. A decision is made and we proceed down from the rocks in a tight group to surround the boy—who is waving excitedly because he wants us to come and see.

When we meet him at the base of the hill, he is beaming. He points his long brown arm at a sloth bear, foraging in the leaves about fifty yards away. It is twice the size of Monica. We squat down together, in tight formation.

Although I know the light is weak, I set my ax down and raise my camera. The automatic flash agrees with me, blasting between us and the bear—which suddenly stops moving. The bear lifts its head, revealing its long snout and the white chest patch. I fire again and this time the flash reflects off its retinas: a pair of rubies in the dusk. The bear is sizing us up, deciphering what we are and if we pose any kind of threat. Then, without breaking its gaze, it assumes an aggressive, head-down stance. Again I trigger the shutter release and the flash lights up its eyes. After a half-second deliberation, the bear turns and bounds off the way it came.

The boys and men stand with weapons raised in triumph. Emboldened, they want to pursue and confront the bear yet again. But before they do, I call off the chase. I am content to leave the bear as it has left us—in a stunned but respectful peace.

THE DRIVE BACK from the jungle is fragrant with flowering trees and the smoke of cow dung fires. Darkness is now complete, save for the light emanating from open doors of village homes and the curious village shops. These little wooden boxes are elevated on stilts, about four feet off the ground. They are large enough only for a man, seated Indian-style, and his meager stock of *gutkha*—a stimulating mixture of tobacco, betel nut, and spices. We travel past wide open fields and along narrow lanes where the houses are packed so tight I'm forced to pull my elbow in. Eventually, we arrive at the Marwahi–Pendra road, which has recently been paved. It serves as the region's highway.

Cows wander in and out of traffic with practiced nonchalance. Seemingly aware that they have the absolute and sacred right of way, they appear unconcerned by trucks and motorcycles speeding past. Our headlights show up a young bull lying with his rump in the road, tail swishing the flies away. Like everyone else, we gear down and adjust our plans accordingly.

Just when I think that no other animal could afford to be quite so brazen, I see a dog sleeping in the middle of the road. I watch as a truck comes barreling down the line. *Surely he's going to . . .* But the driver makes not the slightest deviation. He speeds directly over the sleeping dog, its fur and ears flapping in the onrush of wind. The dog raises its head ever so slightly, as if trying to recall some long-forgotten fact, then lies back down again. We too pass directly over the dog. I turn to see how it fared between the tires. Again, the dog raises its head, then lies back down to sleep.

As we travel from the jungle to Pendra, I am struck by competing visions of where we've come from and where we seemed destined to go. I have stolen a glimpse of our ancient relationship to bears, from a time when the balance of power was not tilted so completely in our favor. It's also as if I have seen the future: a time when our needs will crowd out all other considerations, a place where "wilderness" will be tattered islands—souvenirs of a world we used to know. Here at least, the jungle still has defenders.

Midway through our journey, Avneesh Pandey turns to me and

asks if I would like to see the two-headed calf. This is that rare kind of question that gets asked, perhaps, once every couple of lifetimes. A question to which there could be only one answer.

Ten minutes later, we pull off a side road at a small house surrounded by night. We remove our shoes on the cow dung terrace and enter the home of a tribal family clearly in mourning. Unfortunately, we are too late.

Bathed in candlelight, the family is gathered in the main room. I count ten people in all. Although they look up at me in wonder, it is as if they have been expecting my arrival. This calf's birth is thought to have presaged the arrival of the god Brahma in their midst, who is usually depicted with multiple heads. They are proud their family was chosen, but sad that the calf stayed such a short time. However, the miracle visited on this family continues to astound. The man of the house, a farmer in his forties, welcomes me as a respected mourner from a strange and distant land.

I am directed to the small shrine in the corner. It consists of a plate of rice, an Indian sweet, incense, a candle, and a portrait of the deceased. The photo features the entire family in happier times, with the calf resting in the lap of the farmer. Everyone has big, radiant smiles. The newborn calf is ghost white. It has a normal calf's head on top, and then—where the jaw is supposed to be—a second set of eyes and nose. The two "heads" share a mouth. It is a beloved, four-eyed little monster. I am truly sorry for their loss. When these words are translated, the man nods and gently replaces the photo on the shrine.

Outside, with the help of Ursa Major and Ursa Minor, I seek and find the pole star. The lowing of the cattle and the miraculous birth put me in mind of the manger in Bethlehem. But this is India and I am no wise man—just a traveler caught up in curiosity, coincidence, and wonder.

2

NATIONAL TREASURES
Sichuan, People's Republic of China

A FOREST of black mold has colonized the water-stained ceiling. The wallpaper is peeling, but not to worry—it is being held in place with white masking tape that dates from the dawn of Deng Xiaoping. Luckily, the heater is way up on the top corner of the wall so the tepid air can rise the short distance to the mold, which probably appreciates this for the help it affords in incubating the next generation of spores. In the cold, cut-rate room below, the jaundiced pillows have no cases. Continuous conversation is broadcast from the large Chinese family sitting in the hotel's tea garden, which is located directly outside my wafer-thin window. One guy is even leaning his chair against the glass. I consider stripping down to nothing, throwing open the curtains, and making lots of direct eye contact. But I don't. It's too cold to contemplate anything other than hiding beneath the covers with the remote control.

This year marks the fiftieth anniversary of the National People's Congress. I have tuned in just in time to catch the hard-hitting "coverage" of the historic session on CCTV 9, the English-language mouthpiece of the Chinese central government.

There is a large congregation of faded old men with unnaturally black hair, long shots of appreciative applause, and lots of pretty flowers under the blaze of red flags. There is no debate, criticism, or controversy; everything is reported as simple fact. In a post-modern moment, it is announced from the dais that the People's Congress has voted unanimously to recognize private property. Half a century later, it seems the Running Dog capitalists have been welcomed in from the cold. I wonder what this will mean for the bears.

It is late afternoon and the guidebook says it's unsafe to go out alone at night in Chengdu, a city of over ten million people. But it has missed the mark before. It also promised "clean and comfortable" budget accommodations.

I walk for hours through the crush of people filing home from work on foot, by bike, and in wave after wave of traffic. People over forty avoid catching my eye out of, I suspect, a reflexive response to years of being told to avoid foreigners for the trouble we can bring. Young people, however, stare unabashedly as if I were wearing a fruit turban, à la Carmen Miranda. Mothers point and hold up their babies for a better view of the *gui lao*, the foreign devil—the white ghost in their midst.

At last I arrive at a little dive called the Global Station, which advertises its name in English. Inside are the flags of various European nations, Canada, and the USA. Scrawled across the walls in black felt marker are the graffiti greetings of travelers from around the world. The menu is in Mandarin and English. It is a place for young, beer-swilling backpackers intent on partying their way across the Orient, and lonely writers in search of a little conversation. The place is completely deserted.

Frank, the proprietor, pokes his head out of the kitchen. He's friendly, chain smokes, and speaks near-perfect English. Frank isn't his real name; he's chosen an English name, as do many Chinese people who have contact with foreigners, because we have such a hard time pronouncing anything in Mandarin.

Frank wants to know where I'm from and what I'm doing in Chengdu. I tell him I've come to learn about the plight of the Asiatic black bears, or moon bears as they're commonly known. While I'm in the neighborhood, I figure I'll stop in for a peek at the giant panda breeding center to get the lowdown on the world's most famous endangered species. For some reason, I've developed an irrational prejudice against giant pandas. Perhaps it's because their plight is so well-known around the world while moon bears languish in obscurity. Although Frank knows little about moon bears, he's visited the pandas "hundreds" of times. However, he won't discuss the subject until I've had a chance to see for myself. Come back after I've had a look, he says. Then he'll share his opinion.

We drink and discuss the People's Congress, the Cultural Revolution, and Socialism with Chinese Characteristics. We marvel at how, despite having been born in the same year (1966), our lives have been so utterly different. Frank says he was brought up to believe that workers in Western countries would welcome an invasion from their Chinese socialist brothers. They would rise up, he was taught, if only China could lend a hand. It was China's patriotic duty to help the proletariat in the United States and Western Europe. He was convinced it would someday fall to his generation to act. Imagine that, he says—one nation believing it had the responsibility to liberate the other. "It seems ridiculous now, doesn't it?"

ADULT CONTENT. Sexually suggestive scenes. Graphic imagery. These would be the warnings applied to the museum at the Chengdu Research Base of Giant Panda Breeding in nearby Fu Tou Shan, if one could imagine the existence of such a place in North America, which I cannot.

In stark contrast to the official One Child policy that rules most of China's human population, this institution is completely concerned with sex, fertility, and the making of babies—panda babies, and plenty of them. Its approach to presenting the sex lives of giant pandas (*Ailuropoda melanoleuca*) in a graphic, voyeuristic style would be unimaginable back home, where the topic of sex—even animal sex—in a venue where children are permitted is either infantilized or sanitized to the point of obscurity. Here, I'm sure much of the local innuendo fails to make the leap across the linguistic and cultural divide. The result is an unintentionally humorous attempt to make the science of breeding a critically endangered species accessible to a general audience.

The museum has several sections to explore, including "Joy of Drinking," "Bamboo Recluses," and "Marriage." This three-part act, it seems to me, might sum up a pretty good life. Although the first two sections hold out the promise of colorful anecdotes, they are composed mostly of dry didactic panels, where we learn that giant pandas—honored as the "national treasure"—are now found only in a tiny fraction of their historic range, which once included much of eastern and southern China and as far north as Beijing. Giant panda bones have even been found in Vietnam and Myanmar. Today, a few wild pandas hang on in Shanxi and Gansu provinces, but 85 percent live here in Sichuan. Their remaining habitat covers an area of about 5,800 square miles, roughly the size of Connecticut. Despite the government's efforts, the rate of habitat loss is accelerating.

Giant pandas have many handicaps, chief among them being their preference for bamboo, which makes up 99 percent of their diet. Their physiology is not really suited to their vegetarian inclinations. Adult male pandas weigh between 185 and 275 pounds; females are about 20 percent smaller. In order to survive, they must eat at least a third of their body weight in bamboo leaves each day. And then there is the problem of the mass die-off of bamboo, which happens at regular intervals, leaving giant pandas vulnerable to starvation. The exhibits include skulls, skins, and specimens of panda scat displayed in little glass boxes. The fecal collection is presented as precious fossils or porcelain from the Ming Dynasty. However, it is the Marriage section that captivates this visitor's attention. One panel declares:

> When flowers burst into bloom, male and female pandas break the habit of being solitary to run to each other, fall in love, and mate. Wedding ceremony is often in the field, sometimes in the trees. After mating, male and female pandas depart. Before the baby panda is coming, mother panda selects old tree hole or cave as her maternity den. In late August or early September, the lovely little baby is born, 1–2 cubs in a litter.

Next to this wholesome birds-and-bees treatment of panda courtship rituals is a complete set of one panda's internal organs, preserved in an enormous jar of formaldehyde. Adjacent to this grisly display are similar jars containing complete sets of male and female sex organs. The genitals have turned white and waxy in their embalming bath. The little disembodied strings of fallopian tubes and egglike testes are decidedly unsexy, despite all the talk of romance. Above the jar containing the male's equipment is a sign that would surely result in the entire gender dying of shame if only it could read the Mandarin and English inscriptions below.

> Male panda's penis is so short and female's vagina is so long relatively, that the insemination rate is low . . . This is one of the main causes which make the giant panda become scarce.

Where to begin in assessing the self-esteem and performance-anxiety issues? I take a second look at the diminutive organ in question. Apparently, it grows to only about 2½ inches fully erect. The other problem is that the giant panda's baculum— the stiffening bone found in the penis of most mammals and all primates (except humans)—is decidedly different than that of other members of the bear family. Where in other bears it is straight and directed forward, in the panda it is S shaped and directed backward. Somehow, it still works (after a fashion). There are three photos of pandas caught in flagrante delicto. These are found under the caption "Natural Copulation." The photos show typical sexual positions—rear entry being the favorite. One randy young male has a very expressive face that shows he's giving it his all, despite his limited endowment.

The most disturbing images, by far, are found under the banner "Get Semen By Electric Stimulation." The main photo shows five men in white medical smocks and a cameraman eagerly recording the action. They are all assembled at the pelvis of an anesthetized panda lying spread-eagle on an operating table. The victim seems, at least in this picture, unresponsive. The next photo, however, is titled, "Collecte Semen." The image shows a medicinal-type brown glass bottle covering the panda's electrified penis. Three pairs of gloved human hands reach for—and in one case grips—the penis-shrouding bottle. In addition to the photographer who captured this image, another grinning photographer is shown snapping yet another photo of the violation. After an hour in the museum, I can confidently predict that I will never think of pandas the same way again.

Outside, I take a deep breath of the cool March air. En route to the panda enclosures I encounter the first of many plaques spaced out like mileposts along the meandering, bamboo-lined path. The inscription reads:

TO BE FRIENDS WITH THE ENVIRONMENT,
TREAT IT AS YOUR FRIENDS

IT ISN'T LONG until I happen upon Ms. Luo Lan. We've been corresponding for several months now and she is a little taken aback when I call out her name. She is a slight, cordial woman in her forties with braces on her teeth that she habitually covers with her hand when she smiles, which is often. She has been working at the breeding center since 1994 as a translator and more recently as vice-curator of the Education Department. Judging by her expression as she gazes at the panda cubs in the adjacent enclosure, she still hasn't lost her enchantment.

The cubs play with brightly colored plastic toys, somersault down the knoll, and cling to the leg of the female handler. They huff with delight and swing their heads from side to side, vying for more attention from their surrogate mother. With their clean black-and-white coats and indigo eyes, they evoke protective feelings in all who gaze upon them. The German and North American tourists snap endless pictures, and each new gesture— a raised paw, yawn, or scramble up the jungle gym—elicits a collective intake of breath.

We visit male and female, adult and sub-adult pandas that are surprisingly easy to see. It is nine o'clock in the morning, feeding time, and they sit enthroned on their bamboo couches grazing on the bamboo leaves that are served by an accommodating staff. My favorite pair is a couple of adolescents who lounge side by side, rhythmically pulling the leaves into a paw with their nearly opposable "thumb" (actually an elongated wrist bone) and then lazily chewing a fistful at a time.

By now, giant pandas have become arguably the most widely recognized species of bear on the planet. That is, if you consider them "bears." The controversy over the panda's taxonomy has mostly died down, but dissenters remain. Most scientists now consider the giant panda a member of the bear family (*Ursidae*) instead of the raccoon family (*Procyonidae*), which includes the red panda, or even a separate family of its own (*Ailuropodidae*). Fossils of ancestral giant pandas date back eighteen million years, only about two million years after the emergence of the first creatures recognizable as bears. DNA genotyping makes the case for bearness more solid. Bears, belonging to the order Carnivora, evolved from predators called Miacids some fifty-seven million years ago. Bears are closely related to raccoons, dogs, and weasels. Today, the bear family comprises three genera (*Ailuropoda*, *Ursus*, and *Tremarctos*) and eight living species. The bamboo-loving giant panda is the oldest living bear.

Unlike tigers or monkeys, giant pandas are not deeply woven into the fabric of Chinese culture, history, art, literature, or legend. While Chinese art is awash in images of mountains and bamboo— and even the odd moon bear—there are few depictions of giant pandas before the twentieth century. Perhaps this is because giant pandas were rarely seen by people and lived in such remote regions, high in the mountains, whereas moon bears prefer middle and lower elevations that bring them into more frequent contact with humans. The giant panda's appellation as China's "national treasure" goes back only as far as the 1960s. Scholars have searched Chinese texts to find some ancient relationship between pandas and people. Their work has yielded only a few dozen mentions, many of which may or may not actually refer to giant pandas. There are a few early references to pandas being held in the garden of an emperor of the Western Han Dynasty (206 BC–AD 24), and a Tang Dynasty (AD 589–960) emperor sending a pair of pandas to Japan as a gesture of goodwill. A more modern and famous example of what would become known as "panda diplomacy" took place in 1972 when a pair of pandas (Ling-Ling and Hsing-Hsing) was presented as a gift to U.S. President Richard Nixon on his groundbreaking summit with Chairman Mao Zedong.

Since China began its preservation efforts in the 1960s, the giant panda has rapidly been adopted as the planet's poster child of endangered wildlife. Giant pandas have been the subject of a great many documentaries, books, magazine articles, and children's cartoons. They are the mascot of countless products, organizations, and services—everything from the WWF (World Wildlife Fund) to Pride, one of the most popular cigarette brands in China. There are an estimated one thousand pandas left in the wild, and their numbers, while still at a critical level, have stabilized in recent years. If anything, their predicament may perhaps be a little overexposed. And yet they will melt even the most jaded heart.

I hadn't planned to fall in love, but there is little I could have done to stop it. There is an aesthetic perfection that culminates in the panda: the distinctive black-on-white color pattern, pleasing round proportions, short snout, black eye patches encircling large almond eyes, the graceful way it gathers and consumes its bamboo salad. It seems I too am a sucker for the appeal of neoteny, the retention of juvenile characteristics in adult members of a species. Some scientists argue that we breed our domesticated animals for this nonthreatening trait (witness pugs and Jersey cows) and it affects us on some deep level. It seems to stimulate the secretion of "cute and cuddly" sensations that give us all pause. But why deconstruct love at first sight? Pandas are dolls animated, mythical creatures come to life. The urge to reach out and touch them overwhelms. Realizing this, someone has placed another plaque nearby. It features a quote by naturalist Edwin Way Teale:

THOSE WHO WISH TO PET WILDLIFE LOVE THEM,
BUT THOSE WHO RESPECT THEIR NATURES
AND WISH THEM TO LIVE NATURAL LIVES
LOVE THEM MORE

Despite the moats separating the pandas from the people, some visitors feel the need to be even closer. Luo says that on several occasions, visitors have disregarded the multilingual warning signs and hopped into the panda enclosures to join them. She says those who land in the adult males' enclosure are in for a rude awakening because the animals are, in fact, very territorial and will furiously defend themselves because there is nowhere to run and hide.

The yearling cubs we're watching seem rather less threatening. The handler encourages them to wrestle and play—particularly the somersaults that the audience clearly favors.

"We give them many things to do, like climbing and exercises," Luo explains. "We give them an opportunity to develop relationships with their peers. We learned from the mistakes of the past."

Little was known of the panda's natural behavior before the 1940s when scientists first began to observe them in the wild. Since the breeding program began, scientists have learned that it was a mistake to wean cubs from their mothers too early. In their desperation to increase the population as rapidly as possible, they broke the mother-cub bond early, so females would go into estrus again. The unforeseen result was young male pandas with little interest in sex and less understanding of what to do if they were interested. This troublingly low libido resulted in researchers at other panda facilities showing "panda porn" on large-screen TVs to arouse some interest. Luo reports that the results of the pilot project were disappointing. However, researchers have made some headway in the race to understand and unlock the erogenous nature of the beast. For example, they have recently discovered that panda mothers play a pivotal role in the sexual maturity of male offspring in the wild. This has resulted in a change of approach at the breeding center.

"Mothers will introduce the young boys to the meeting area to watch the other pandas mating," Luo explains. "If the mother has a girl, she doesn't do that. Only with boys. We've learned that the mother is extremely important. We've also learned that the hand-raised cubs must stay longer with their mother. Although a baby panda will only nurse with its own mother, female pandas will happily take care of and play with any panda baby.

"We have several males entering the age group [six to seven] where they are ready to mate," she says. "We're looking forward to seeing if these males succeed. They spent much more time with their mothers . . . We keep them in good health at all times and give them access to watching other pandas mate. This is more successful."

Oh, and they've also recently determined that the male panda's equipment is not to blame. It turns out that penis size doesn't matter after all. Someday, they'll get around to updating the information in the museum, she says.

Luo and I wander over to a grassy enclosure and watch a lone female pacing back and forth near the wall. This is not the repetitive behavior of an overstressed animal; it is the healthy behavior of a female panda in estrus, Luo explains. In an adjacent enclosure, a lone male ignores us, sniffs the air, and turns his head from side to side to inhale even more of the pheromones emitted by the unseen female. This male is clearly captivated by the scent. Luo points out the jungle gyms that are designed to help the males build their thigh muscles "for good mating."

"We are confident that two of our boys will be successful," she says, pointing at the panda. "See, he will smell her and pace the ground nearby. She will engage in a lot of courtship behavior in the neutral cell they both use at different times. This room is used to introduce the pair so they familiarize themselves with each other. At other [nonestrus] times, they would fight with and sometimes injure each other. But now the males will be very interested in the smell of the female markings.

"We're involved in both artificial insemination and natural mating at this facility," Luo explains, in case I've missed the Marriage display. Sometimes females will mate naturally and also receive artificial insemination. After the cub is born, a test is done to determine if the natural or artificial method was successful.

From an original group of six pandas captured from the wild, ninety-seven have been born at this facility. Through trades to zoos and other breeding centers throughout China and around the world, the population here at the Chengdu facility is down to forty-three individuals. It is both a moral and financial burden to care for them, Luo says.

"We dare not release them until the environment is safe. For pandas, the wilderness is their idea of heaven. Releasing these pandas is a big hope . . . [but] that's not likely to happen." She catches herself, then offers a more optimistic assessment. "We don't have a date set for any release of pandas back into the wild. This is our last goal. This possibility depends on the success of habitat protection. I'm a little worried about the panda's habitat . . . Deforestation is banned in the panda's home but some people still do it. The government is trying to encourage tourism but the people end up scaring all the animals away. I don't think the government understands."

One bright spot is the increasing number of panda reserves. In 1963, there were only three reserves; as of 2004 there were thirty-two areas dedicated to the preservation of the panda in Sichuan, forty nationwide. However, two-thirds of the remaining wild population still lives outside protected areas. The central government is now talking about wildlife corridors between reserves to promote genetic diversity, she says. Still, it's tough when local people demand more and more resources. And then there is the exploding urban population.

"People don't even think about wildlife because we are so far away from it," Luo explains. "The younger people have more interest, but in general people don't have enough information about wildlife."

I tell her of my upcoming visit to the China Bear Rescue Center. If China has this much trouble protecting the panda, the national treasure, how much energy and resources will be left for the protection of the less glamorous moon bear?

"It's sad for the moon bear," Luo says. "Chinese culture with the moon bear is good and bad. In China, people dream of eating the bear's paw because this is an exotic food that the poor cannot afford. Sick people will do anything to make their family healthy, even though they may feel guilty about killing the bear for its gallbladder. I think it is cruel. I hate it. I think if people knew how they got bear bile, they wouldn't do it. But you have to give people an alternative. People here will use Western medicine, but if it doesn't work they will use Chinese medicine—which they think is really better because it's more natural."

Why is moon bear bile used in traditional Chinese medicine while panda bile is not?

"In the Chinese medicine book, pandas were one of the few plants or animals that weren't recorded," she says. "So we are lucky with the panda."

Back in Luo's office, the phone keeps ringing and colleagues hover at the door. I say good-bye and thank her for her time. I wander back out for a final look at the pandas but they have finished eating and have moved inside their warm enclosures. Most of the visitors have long since departed. While I wait for my bus back to Chengdu, I am left to ponder a final plaque bearing a poorly translated quote from Indira Gandhi:

THE GREATNESS OF A NATION AND MORAL
PROGRESS CAN BE JUDGED BY THE [WAY]
ANIMALS ARE TREATED

In Chengdu, Frank sits with his back to the window, silhouetted by the gray light of late afternoon and the muted blur of bicycles flashing past the Global Station. The smoke from his cigarette is a blue haze between us.

Frank is very interested in the story of my visit with the pandas but first wants me to taste his inaugural attempt at brownies. He has never had a brownie himself and wouldn't know if he had succeeded or failed. He had to go to an obscure store in order to procure the chocolate, which he claims is a "crap" domestic variety, the only one available. Chinese people aren't much good at chocolate things like brownies and cookies, he says. But he's willing to try for the sake of his international clientele. He found the recipe on the Internet. I take a bite of the bitter, gelatinous goo and try to swallow, but I'm forced to eject it into a napkin. Frank laughs and leans back in his chair.

Before settling down to manage the Global Station, Frank spent many years as a tour guide. This career took him all over China and, miraculously, to Europe. As a guide and translator, he took "countless" tourists to the panda breeding center over the years. He has serious reservations about the facility.

"How can it be good for the baby pandas to get touched by fifteen or thirty tourists per day? You can see they don't like being held." He refers to the practice of letting tourists touch the pandas—for a price. Although I did not see this myself, it has been mentioned in guidebooks. "They strain and try to get away," he explains. "Sometimes they scratch at the face of the tourist holding them. They don't want to be held by people. All of this for one hundred Yuan ($12) for the sub-adults and three hundred Yuan ($36) for the babies. This is nothing to be able to touch China's national treasure."

Frank says it was common to have half of his large tour groups pay to have their picture taken with the cubs. The workers at the breeding center see this as a way of earning extra cash. Frank wonders aloud if the death of a cub last year was the result of a tourist taking flash photography of infant pandas in the incubators. The other major problem he sees is the fact that few Chinese people have a chance to visit the facility. Only foreigners can visit the panda center now because most Chinese people cannot afford it. If the government really cared about pandas, they wouldn't allow this to happen. He believes the place for pandas is their native bamboo forest. Unfortunately, the forest isn't safe.

"The poor people in the woods are illiterate," he explains. "They can only read one word at a time . . . Chinese people don't care about wildlife. They can't see a difference between a rat and a panda. People are too busy making a living, and people in the country don't know about laws protecting animals. Some of them don't even know about laws to protect the panda. The land where they live is no good for farming so they do what they have to in order to feed their wife and kid. Many of them have never been out of their area . . . My uncle lives out there. I go to his house and there is not one newspaper or book in the whole place. They don't care. They have no time for anything other than making enough money to eat."

Frank says the constant push for numbers of captive-born baby pandas, never to return to the wild, is the result of a long-standing mania in his country. It shows a disconnect between "numbers" and any practical goal.

"Back in the 1950s, we had to measure our success by how much agricultural production we gained out of one hectare," he explains. "So when it came time to measure the production, the people would get in line with their baskets of rice and measure it once and then walk around to the back of the line and measure it over and over again until they had ten times what a normal hectare could produce. If one farm or one region pointed a finger and said, 'It's impossible to get such a yield out of one hectare,' the government would point a finger back and say, 'You are jealous, envious. You are bad.' Then you go to jail or they will kill you. Same if you say you are a counterrevolutionary. If you say that, you will be killed.

"Then the people would be asked to measure our success as a nation by how much steel we produced. We were in competition with Russia and the U.S. So, in order to raise our steel production, we had to give the government our pans, stoves—our front gate if was made out of steel. All of this was melted down so China could say to all the world, 'Look at this: We have a very high steel production.' But the next year everything went back to normal, and many people went hungry. People knew these things were big lies, but there was nothing you could say about it. You were too busy working and trying to make a living.

"But people did believe Chairman Mao. He would say, 'If you

can dream it, if you can think it, then you can do it.' When we were trying to develop a petroleum region, he said that if the people want it bad enough, and cry out for it, the earth will open up and petroleum will spill out. People believed him."

Real customers have arrived. Frank greets them warmly without breaking his train of thought.

"If you tell a lie a thousand times, it becomes the truth . . . People are too busy making money to worry about wildlife. People will still hunt a panda in the woods if they see one because they could make money from the skin. If they know they could go to jail or be killed, they don't care. They have to make the money for their family. They have no choice."

Frank discards the stillborn brownies and delivers menus to his customers. He has been extraordinarily generous with his time and opinions and I have kept him from his duties for far too long. I wave good-bye and slip into the night. On the long walk back to the hotel, I collect suspicious stares as I plot my escape from the city.

IN A SECLUDED yard bordered by farmers' fields and the shallow Pi River, a lone moon bear reclines on the grass near the village of Qingqiao, twenty miles north of Chengdu. It is a cool, clear morning and the promise of spring is in the air. Rupert, as this bear is known, closes his eyes and enjoys a nap in the sun. At long last, he has found himself in a permanent home where he can live out his remaining days in peace.

In one of the stucco walls surrounding his domain is a window into an apartment where Jill Robinson gazes out on the fruit of her labor. Over a cup of tea, she explains that before Rupert's arrival at this rescue center, he endured a life of agony. After years imprisoned in a restrictive cage, he sustained permanent physical and mental damage. As a result, his movements are slow, his reactions are clumsy, and his face is strangely lopsided. He doesn't understand electric fences and cannot tolerate the presence of other members of his species, so he is kept in this special pen next to Robinson's quarters, which she calls the Secret Garden.

In the spring of 1993, when Robinson was working for the International Fund for Animal Welfare in Hong Kong, she received a call from a journalist at the *South China Morning Post*. He tipped her off to the location of a bear "farm" on mainland China where bears, kept in abominable conditions, were systematically drained of their bile (the alkaline fluid that aids in digestion). Bear bile is used to treat a variety of ailments in traditional Chinese medicine. Robinson immediately made plans to go. An Englishwoman with long blond hair, she posed as a tourist and attempted to "blend in" with a group of Japanese and Taiwanese businessmen who were taking a guided tour of the facility. During a lecture on the medicinal benefits of bear bile, she slipped away from the group and descended into a dark basement where she discovered thirty-two bears locked in tiny metal cages.

"I just walked around in shock," Robinson says, reliving the event. "I couldn't believe what I was seeing. I mean the cages are bad enough. But just knowing that this is a wild species that roams over many kilometers throughout its natural life . . . There was this one animal. I backed into her cage and felt something touch my shoulder, so I cried out. I looked around and there was this bear with her paw through the bars of the cage." Unaware of how unpredictable bears can be, Robinson tentatively reached out her hand and the bear gently squeezed her fingers. "At the time, I didn't know how special that was," she says. "Our eyes connected for a bit. What happened then was very special and there was a message there. I felt a connection . . . I knew then that bear farming was inherently wrong."

In the early 1980s, the demand for bear bile as a traditional Chinese medicine had grown so strong that the central government sanctioned the capture and breeding of wild bears to be kept alive on bear farms so they could be "milked" of their bile on an ongoing basis. The traditional method of collecting bile—killing wild bears—results in only a single gallbladder per animal, a one-time economic opportunity. Keeping a bear alive indefinitely and draining its gallbladder on a daily basis can produce 5½ pounds of precious bile a year over the productive life of a bear, which averages about ten years. It is a practice that originated in Korea and has spread throughout China and Southeast Asia. Robinson has committed herself to stopping it.

It didn't take long for the enormity of the task to sink in. Although she has no formal training in biology, pharmacology, or zoology, Robinson knew she was going to have to become an expert in the very thing that repelled her: the collection and use of bear bile. She left her job to concentrate her efforts on rescuing China's farmed bears. "One of the first things I learned was that bear bile can be replaced," she says, referring to synthetic and herbal alternatives. "No one is going to die for the lack of bear bile. And as soon as I knew that, I knew we had a chance."

FOR OVER A DECADE, Robinson has been working to convince the government that bear farming is not only inhumane, but is also a stain on China's international reputation. Incredibly, they agreed, and now work in partnership with Robinson's Animal Asia Foundation to begin closing China's bear farms.

In 1999, the last year official figures were available, the government counted 247 farms containing seven thousand bears. Half of these animals are kept for bile; half are used for breeding. Although the numbers of bears in need is staggering, Robinson works methodically, persistently, toward her goal. When I remark on her apparent determination, she smiles and looks at her shoes. Originally from Nottingham, she's lived in Hong Kong since 1985. She spends two weeks a month here in Sichuan, and the rest of her time at Animal Asia's Hong Kong headquarters or traveling the world to raise money and awareness. She is eager to give me the tour.

The China Bear Rescue Center covers twenty-two acres and contains a small animal hospital and recovery wards, kitchen facilities, an educational display, offices, staff accommodations, plus a series of bear pens, yards, and thick stands of bamboo. In addition to a veterinary staff of five, over fifty local people have been hired to help care for the bears. Currently, 116 Asiatic black bears live on-site, and there are plans to bring many, many more. They are segregated according to size and physical ability. The recently arrived bears reside in a series of roomy cages where they begin the process of rehabilitation and socialization. Twice a day, they have access to a large open yard, where they can run, stretch, and play. Inside their cages are ergonomically designed metal beds, elevated and curved to mimic the feeding platforms wild Asiatic black bears are known to make in trees. Some of the newer cages have lengths of bamboo instead of metal bars, and beds resembling stylish, oversized patio furniture. The center's bamboo forest, where the rehabilitated bears are at liberty to roam, offers something akin to a free-range existence. They never had it so good.

We pass a pair of bears sitting on a bed together, gently pawing one another's muzzles. We see bears chase each other between one cage and the next and then lounge together on the floor. Occasionally, there is huffing and jaw "popping" to communicate irritation or frustration. Now and then, a roar. Most bears are interested in us. They approach the bars, stand on hind legs, and reach out for whatever we may be offering. Many of the bears at this facility are missing parts; paws lost in snares, claws ripped out by farmers, and canines either forcibly extracted or broken from repeatedly biting the bars of their cage. Given what they've been through, it's remarkable that they don't cower in our presence.

Asiatic black bears (*Ursus thibetanus*), or moon bears, range in weight from as little as 110 pounds for adult females to 485 pounds for males. They have large Mickey Mouse ears, black shaggy coats,

and a cream- or rust-colored chest patch that can resemble a crescent moon. They are closely related to American black bears. Females often have pronounced manes around their necks. They
prefer living in the woods—from deciduous oak forests to tropical
rainforests—and, like most bears, are omnivorous opportunists.
Beyond that, little else is known about them. Moon bears remain
something of a mystery because there is virtually no funding for
scientific research on the species. In Asia, their value rests almost solely on their ability to produce bile.

The central government claims there are 45,530 wild moon
bears in the People's Republic of China. Others come up with a
different figure. TRAFFIC, the wildlife-trade monitoring network, works to stop trade in wild plants and animals. A joint project of WWF and the IUCN, TRAFFIC has offices around the
world and collaborates with the Convention on International
Trade in Endangered Species of Wild Fauna and Flora (CITES).
TRAFFIC estimates the worldwide population of the species is a
mere 25,000. The IUCN includes them in its Red List of Threatened Species and reports that there are no real conservation efforts to protect them. Moon bears still range into Southeast
Asia, in fragmented groups as far west as Afghanistan, and in isolated groups in the Russian Far East and Japan. Most, however

(16,000–20,000) are found in China—particularly Sichuan. As with giant pandas and brown bears, China's other surviving bear species, moon bears suffer from overhunting and a recent, dramatic loss of habitat. Unfortunately, they are also the preferred species of the bile trade.

Part of the official rationale for allowing bear farming was the hope that it would help slow the rate of poaching, but according to Robinson, this has not been the case. Instead, the increased amount of bear bile on the market has only stoked demand. Before bear farms began producing bile in large quantities, domestic demand was approximately five hundred kilos a year. As of 2004, the annual consumption had risen to four thousand kilos, with a wholesale value of $250 per gram. Meanwhile, the number of wild bears continues to decline.

We stop at a heap of rusting metal, a collection of two dozen cages confiscated from bear farmers—the very cages that once imprisoned some of the bears I've met today. The largest are barely big enough to enclose an adult bear, and leave virtually no room to maneuver. Some are as small as 18"x18"x45" and are reminiscent of medieval iron maidens. Robinson points out a special "crush" cage that has a second, internal set of bars in the top that can be pushed down to further immobilize the bear within. This is an especially cruel and convenient way to ensure an easy "milking" session free of snapping teeth or slashing claws. Bears are often kept this way for months, forcing them to eat, defecate, and sleep in the same position. For nearly half of the moon bears in China, this is the only life they will ever know.

"It seems impossible that you could fit a fully grown bear in there," Robinson says, "but believe me, they do. You get a small female in there, say fifty or sixty kilos. They keep growing until they can't grow anymore. That's why they have scars the same size and shape as the bars. When we got one bear out of his cage, he really wanted to eat but after several mouthfuls, he stopped. We had to euthanize him. In the postmortem, we found that his chest cavity had constricted all his internal organs. He just couldn't get food down." Robinson has interviewed farmers who've admitted to keeping bears in the crush position for months at a time. They've also kept bears confined in these tiny cages and milked their bile for up to twenty-two years.

"I think in fifty or a hundred years' time people will look back and wonder how, how could human beings be so barbaric to animals? We're living in an age now where we think we're sophisticated. We think we're living in a more conscionable and respectable society, but we're not . . . It just riles you. You just get blown away and overwhelmed with madness, anger, and sadness."

She points to the tiny feeding slot beneath the floor of a cage.

"You see?" she says. "It's all done for a reason. It's disgusting. They have to lie facedown. They have to flatten their bodies down to the bottom of the cage to feed. This is when they are held down so the farmer can remove the bile from the catheter, or in the new method, stick in a rod so the bile drips out."

I try and force open the small door of a cage, but it's rusted in place.

"It just reminds me of when we sleep at night," Robinson says. "You know that feeling when you have to turn over? Why would a bear be any different? You can see them now in their recovery cages, turning over, making themselves a little more comfortable, doing everything we take for granted . . . They are not even allowed to have that simple comfort on a bear farm." She folds her arms tight across her chest. The emotions no longer simmer just under the surface; they are warming up to a boil.

Traditionally, she says, Chinese people have believed that animals don't feel pain the way humans do. In fact, she conducted a survey in Hong Kong some years back and found that 7 percent of people there believe animals are *incapable* of feeling pain—and this was cosmopolitan Hong Kong. The proportion of people who hold that belief here in rural Sichuan, she says, is much, much higher. "When we began, there wasn't a term in Mandarin for 'animal welfare.' People have said that it's because of the work we've done that the term is now known."

But what of the mistreatment of animals in the West? We've exterminated brown bears from most of their range. Where do we get off telling the Chinese how to treat their animals when we've given the world the gift of factory-farmed chicken and pigs? She heartily agrees that we in the West, with our concept of "dominion" over other beings, have plenty of work to do. Many Chinese people also have a hard time understanding why her organization spends so much money helping animals. Shouldn't people come first? She's heard this argument time and time again.

"With so many other groups out there addressing human issues, I think it's about time the animals had their day in China and Asia," she says. "It's time we developed a more conscious attitude. Wasn't it Gandhi who said that the consciousness of a nation is how you are treating your animal species? I think a lot of people in China are beginning to recognize that. They do understand that animals feel pain and mental trauma as much as any human being. And if we can evolve to understand that, we can be a more conscious and forgiving species toward each other."

Robinson checks her watch. "There's something I want you to see."

In the "rehab" yard adjacent to the cages, staff members retrieve buckets and head for the exit. They lock the gate and switch on the electric fence behind them. When they signal the all's clear, a bell rings, gates slide open, and a flood of black fur comes streaming onto the grass. Depending on their physical ability, bears hobble or gallop into the yard as fast as they can and head straight for the jungle gym, logs, and hay piles that have been placed there by the staff. Hidden in the nooks and crannies throughout the yard are chunks of watermelon, banana, cabbage, and apple. The bears seek out and find these treats with remarkable speed—getting the food out of its hiding place is another matter. This often requires work and ingenuity. This "enrichment" is designed to aid in their recovery and keep them sharp, healthy, and happy in the long term.

Bears lick honey off rocks, pick apple slices out of bamboo tubes, and knock down bamboo stalks. Even the bears with missing limbs get in on the action. When the treats are gone, they play together or alone as their temperament dictates. They swat each other, somersault, and wrestle while standing on hind legs. They gnaw on one another's necks trying to pull each other down. Others amuse themselves by wallowing in the hay, tossing it up in the air and letting it rain down on their heads. It doesn't take a specialist in animal behavior to detect the joy. In their previous lives, many of them were unable to stretch their limbs or even touch the ground. Witnessing this scene instills a deep respect for their astonishing will to live.

THE SURGICAL TEAM stands silently in the on-site operating room. The monitors have been calibrated; the clamps, swabs, and scalpels are all assembled and accounted for. There's nothing left to do. Assistant surgeon Dr. Lim Kwok Zu from Hong Kong, two English veterinary nurses, Jill Robinson, and I watch the clock on the tiled wall; 8:35 A.M. Eventually, Dr. Gail Cochrane enters the room and nods—the anesthetic has taken effect. She had just returned from the pre-op ward, where she gave the patient a poke with a loaded jab stick. On her orders, we file out of the OR and down the hall.

In the foyer, six men wait beside a gurney. The anesthetized bear is rolled out in its cage; the men open the door and duck in. After gently shifting the bear onto a litter, they all take hold and hoist it out and onto the floor. The center of all this attention is a 490-pound brown bear lying flat on its back. Her name is Caesar. She, along with a male named Emma (a rare moon bear/brown bear hybrid), was recently rescued from an elderly farmer who decided to get out of the bile trade. Robinson named the bears at the request of donors before anyone knew their sex. She sees no need to switch them now.

Caesar and Emma have come a long way. Robinson and a team of eight people undertook a three-day, two-thousand-mile round-trip to Tianjin in northeast China to rescue them. Animal Asia works with the Chinese government to compensate bear farmers who are willing to shut down their operations. The amount of compensation, which is kept secret, is negotiated by the government and paid almost entirely by Animal Asia.

After checking the pulse, the first order of business is the removal of the permanent metal girdle that was affixed to Caesar some nine years ago. The contraption is made of steel rods, bolts, and plates and is held in place by thick canvas straps. It weighs twenty-two pounds and is designed to hold a latex catheter in the gallbladder and to keep the bear from licking or otherwise touching the permanently open sore. It has worn off much of the fur around Caesar's back and shoulders. The veterinarian team refers to it as the Full Metal Jacket.

"This is the catheter method," Robinson says, pointing out the latex tube inserted in Caesar's abdomen. "It's been overtaken by something called the free drip method."

This new method is held up as an example of "humane" bile farming techniques. Compared to the Full Metal Jacket, the drip method employs a less restrictive device for collecting the bile and the bears are given more room to move. Calling this method *humane* is nonsense, Robinson says. The animals still suffer from the open wound in their bodies where an unsanitary catheter is shoved up into their gallbladder. In this method, the gallbladder is surgically moved to the front of the abdomen where a permanent hole, or fistula, is created. From here the bile is meant to leak out conveniently into a bowl.

"Of course it doesn't," Dr. Gail Cochrane adds. "Apart from leaking out, it also leaks back into the abdomen and that's how you get peritonitis." Peritonitis is acute or chronic inflammation of the peritoneum, the membrane that lines the abdominal cavity. Symptoms include severe abdominal pain, vomiting, massive inflammation, and high fever. This results from the introduction of bacteria, either by the initial surgery or through the catheter. Cochrane says she's forced to euthanize bears who have it.

A local TV crew is covering part of the event and Cochrane looks up from her work now and then to allow for the best possible shots. A wired and engaging Glaswegian, she has short, bleached hair and a mischievous smile. She's done this routine many times before. In addition to running an animal clinic in Hong Kong, Cochrane has performed over three hundred anesthetic surgeries on moon bears for Animal Asia—to the best of her knowledge, more than anyone else on the planet. Caesar will be her first brown bear. Once the jacket is photographed and disposed of, Caesar is lifted onto the gurney and wheeled to the operating room.

CAESAR'S SUFFERING is a modern, industrial twist on a Chinese practice that dates back over three thousand years. Various parts of the bear are used in traditional Chinese medicine—from brain and spinal tissue to fat—but the animal's bile is by far the most valuable. It is used as a medicine to treat everything from cancer, burns, and redness of the eyes, to asthma, sinusitis, liver disorders, and pain in general. The active ingredient in the bile is ursodeoxycholic acid (UDCA), and bears are the only mammals that produce significant amounts. Giant pandas, however, do not. This may explain their omission from the traditional Chinese pharmacopoeia. UDCA is used in the West for dissolving gallstones and has shown promise as a treatment for a fatal form of cirrhosis.

It is estimated that Chinese bear farms produce over fifteen thousand pounds of bear bile annually, primarily from moon bears. There are effective synthetic and plant-based alternatives to bear bile—at least fifty-four herbal alternatives are known. Together, China, Japan, and South Korea consume approximately one hundred tons of synthetic UDCA annually. Despite the availability of alternative versions of the substance, poaching and bear farming persists.

Animal Asia works with well-respected traditional Chinese medicine practitioners to bring its message to the medical community. Its chief ally, Professor Liu Zheng Cai, national director of Traditional Chinese Medicine Academic Inheritors, has over forty years' experience and has even served the military in Beijing. Hailed as one of China's top five hundred doctors, he calls for an end to the use of bear bile and is an active promoter of herbal alternatives, which he believes are superior.

"I think once they recognize that the reputation of Chinese medicine could be affected—that it is associated with animal cruelty—it starts to register," Dr. Cochrane says, taking a long look inside Caesar's mouth. "And a lot of Chinese doctors don't know how bear bile is extracted. They just hear from the farmers that they have new, humane techniques, and the doctors believe it."

Caesar is stabilized on the respirator, shaved, and cleaned of years' worth of accumulated filth. The cleaning alone takes forty minutes. An IV is inserted and blood is taken for analysis. As Dr. Lim preps her for the incision, the nurses perform what they call the ten-thousand-mile checkup, which includes a thorough ear cleaning and ultrasonic teeth scaling. Caesar's paw pads are overgrown and cracked from never having the chance to stand on solid ground. Robinson clips claws that have grown far too long. With farmed bears, she explains, the claws sometimes grow right back into the pads, causing huge abscesses. Throughout the operation, the veterinary team monitors the limbs closely. In a recent operation, a bear began to rouse and wave its paw in the air. They had to hold the bear down while Cochrane administered another injection.

The respirator clicks and wheezes; the pulse oximeter glows

and beeps. Cochrane reckons that this is the best-equipped animal hospital in all of Asia. Considering the electronic equipment and the medical hardware, drugs, gas, sutures, gloves, and swabs—not to mention the hours of expertise assembled in this room—one wonders if the Chinese wouldn't appreciate this sort of free medical care being lavished on the human population.

Robinson says they spend $57,000 a month on these bears. This includes staffing, bear food, enrichment, communication, land lease, supplies, transport, utilities, and office costs. The budget for an expansion project is about $3 million, and will allow the facility to accommodate up to eight hundred bears. Sound expensive? Robinson offers a comparison with the new rainforest exhibit at the Bronx Zoo, which she claims cost $43 million, or the new exhibit housing two jaguars in the Hong Kong Zoo, which cost about $1 million. Because operating costs are relatively low here in Sichuan, money can go a long way. Most of the funding comes from individuals in the UK, Germany, Australia, and Hong Kong.

I place a stethoscope on Caesar's chest and catch the sound of rushing wind. I run my hand down her broad snout, stroke her massive paw, and look into her unconscious eyes. The pupils are dilated so Cochrane can peer inside before gently pulling the lids closed. It is noted that all four canines have been broken—in this case as a result of biting the bars of her cage—and will have to come out during a future operation. Once the bear is prepped, the team dons surgical smocks and gloves, and the first incision is made.

I've heard it said that when a bear's body is skinned it looks remarkably human, although on a larger scale. Flat on her back and with her torso shaved, Caesar's belly button doesn't look much different from mine. The sight of this powerful animal, helpless on its back, paws spread out in total surrender, provokes an overwhelming feeling of responsibility.

"Bears are very different from people and other animals,"

Cochrane explains. "If you put any other animal through this you'd have skin and bones. If a person is in bed for five months, they lose something like seventy percent of their muscle mass . . . You take a bear and it goes into its den. It does bugger all for five months and when it comes out it [has] only lost about twenty percent [of its body mass]. So that's how they can survive. NASA is really interested in how bears do it."

Cochrane clamps off arteries, swabs up blood, and slices through fibrous flesh without breaking the conversation. She pauses only occasionally to ask for assistance.

"Even though they came out of these disgusting cages, they can recover—no problem," she says. "It's amazing. They get up and walk. Some of them have stiff joints because they've been in the cages for so long, but with the physiotherapy we get them to stand up. I can't imagine any other animal being able to survive what they've been through and end up like that. It only takes about six months from the time they get out of the bear cage. That's one of the things that makes them so interesting from a veterinarian's point of view. I'm constantly amazed at what they can survive and how they can adapt and recover."

She straightens and stretches for a moment, giving her back a rest.

"Nobody is researching Asiatic black bears," she says. "And so many other countries have had their populations decimated because of the gallbladder trade. That's what happened in South Korea. That's what happened in Taiwan . . . The bear farms grew so quickly in Vietnam. Now they're getting their bears from Cambodia, Laos, and Burma because Vietnam is running out of bears in the wild. They look at bears as a 'resource.' I hate that word."

At long last, with the help of Dr. Lim, Cochrane lifts the gallbladder from the abdominal cavity. They work in a blur of hands and clamps to cut all around the fist-sized organ until it is free. I lean in for a closer look. I'm told that Caesar's abused gallbladder is only half the size it should be. Cochrane shows me where the catheter pokes through one side of the gallbladder and nearly out the other. Had it managed to poke all the way through, it would have spilled the bile into the body cavity and it would have been lights out for Caesar. Cochrane says neither bears nor humans really need gallbladders, which store and concentrate bile. When humans have their gallbladders removed, doctors simply tell them not to eat too much rich food and they live perfectly normal lives. Here, she says, rich food isn't a problem.

After laying it out on the metal tray, Cochrane dissects, measures, and photographs the organ, then records the information. Next, she reaches inside the open cavity all the way up to her elbow. She roots around, feeling for whatever she can find— tumors, cysts, pregnancy, or cotton swabs left inside from the two previous operations this bear has endured. Happily, nothing is out of place. Lim sutures up the abdominal wall first, then the outside skin. Three hours and five minutes after the first incision, Caesar is wheeled out and placed in a recovery cage.

Before securing the cage door, Robinson climbs in to perform a ritual she observes with all the bears. She places a few drops of homeopathic Bach Rescue Remedy on Caesar's tongue. Aromatherapy, she explains. Robinson wants the first conscious breath this bear takes in her new life to be a sweet one.

THE FOLLOWING DAY, I notice that the staff is acting strangely. They've turned out in their best clothes, continually preen their hair, and exchange excited whispers everywhere I turn. It isn't until I'm well into the morning that I discover the cause of all the excitement: Karen Mok is about to arrive.

You'll be forgiven if you do not recognize the name Karen Mok. The only reason it sounded familiar to me is that I'd watched a half-hour television special about her when I collapsed in front of the tube on my first night in Hong Kong. Karen Mok is the reigning pop princess of the Chinese universe, the top recording artist in Asia. She's also an actress. The only Western analogy to draw, Jill Robinson claims, is that it's like having a visitation from the likes of Madonna. Turns out that Karen Mok has taken an interest in Animal Asia's China Bear Rescue and, out of the blue, called to find out how she can help.

The sun breaks through the dull haze and the temperature begins to rise. It's going to be a beautiful day. As the staff sweeps the sand paths and otherwise cleans up the compound, Robinson takes a break from the preparations to walk with me. I ask if it is difficult for her, as a woman, to confront both government and business in China. The Chinese men haven't been the problem, she says. As a woman, she is seen as less of a threat.

"But you have to be very strong to counter some of the scientific objections to what we're doing," she says. "There are a lot of people who talk about 'sustainable use' and say there are enough bears in the world. [They say] why shouldn't we be doing this bile extraction? And you have to be a very strong person to come up against that."

She says the sexism she's encountered along the way has mostly come from Western scientists. All that began to change when she was made a Member of the British Empire (MBE). "When I got the letters behind my name, there was a change," she explains. "It's a horrible thing to say, but it's true. It helped. People will look at it and say, 'She has achieved something because she has an award from the queen.' And perhaps they will listen a little bit more. You have these people who are scientifically qualified and they're almost talking down at me. Then they will ask for my business card and say, 'Ah, you've got an MBE.' Straight away you see their whole image of me change. In some ways it makes me sick, but in other ways it's okay. Whatever gets the job done. I will prostitute it. I don't care. You can quote that."

The bears watch closely as the workers smear peanut butter on the jungle gym in preparation for the twice-daily exercise and enrichment session. The staff members seem to enjoy hiding the stuff almost as much as the bears do finding it.

"My mum developed peritonitis when I was six months of age," Robinson says. "She died of septicemia [blood poisoning]. My dad said she died very quickly but it was a very painful death. He always said she died screaming in agony. I never knew her." Many of the farmed bears that arrive at the rescue center are dying of the same thing due to the catheter implants. When postmortems are performed, lumps filled with puss are found all over their bodies. The bears suffer in this condition for months. "And that just completely broke me up. For a long time it affected me very badly. To see them dying with the same thing that killed my mum . . . It's just a deep connection.

"I don't have kids of my own, but I have a five-year-old niece, and I just wonder what the hell she's going to inherit sometimes . . . The way we're corrupting and destroying this planet is really unconscionable. And everyone thinks you are a screaming radical because you're talking about compassion. Why shouldn't you be understanding? You know bears feel pain the same way we do. Why shouldn't you be saying this is wrong? This is utterly wrong to be causing this amount of harm. How dare we just abuse a species we share the planet with?"

Then she poses the ultimate hypothetical question, a question I didn't ask, the question that must trouble her the most: If she had to kill a bear in order to save her niece, would she do it? Robinson says she doesn't think she could. I think of my own nieces and nephews and realize instantly that it is no choice for me. I would kill a bear.

Robinson shades her eyes from the sun and we both turn to watch the expectant moon bears watch us from their cages.

Defending hypothetical positions has a way of diverting energy from the cause of dealing with actual issues. Robinson must feel pressured to do it. It is in fact unnecessary to make these kinds of choices in relation to bears. Not with effective replacements for bear bile. Over the past fifty years, the decline of moon bears has been precipitous. If all concerned parties don't work together to face reality soon, moon bears will continue to disappear from the wild and die in inhumane conditions. And when they're gone, a way of understanding the natural world will perish with them.

The place vibrates with anticipation of the imminent arrival of Ms. Mok. Staff members jostle for positions and the best sight lines. I bow out of the scene and visit Caesar in the isolation ward of the hospital.

I peek through the half-open door and watch as she lies on her back, stretching her arm, considering the back of her paw. I make no sound, but it isn't long until she catches my scent and slowly rolls her head in my direction. I push open the door and offer a gentle greeting. I wonder how she'll make out as the lone brown bear surrounded by over a hundred moon bears. Given her size, fairly well, I imagine. Caesar considers me for a time, then her head becomes heavy. She lies back down and covers her eyes with her paw.

KAREN MOK arrives in a caravan of vehicles stuffed with over three dozen members of the media, fans, and assorted hangers-on. When she steps out of the car and gives a wave, the ordinarily staid Chinese staff let out a cheer. Mok approaches the bear cages to the flash of digital cameras. She is tall, confident, and unconventionally beautiful. Several video crews record her every move as she feeds the caged bears watermelon and lets them lick honey from her fingers. The crowd gasps in wonder.

Mok is positioned for a second photo op in front of the rehab yard as the moon bears stream from open cages, as they do each afternoon in their manic treasure hunt. This time, however, the cameras are rolling. After ten minutes of delighting in the scene, the celebrity and her retinue retire to Robinson's apartment for a meeting.

Toby Zhang, Animal Asia's education officer, taps me on the shoulder. He is a big, confident man who seems pleased with the unfolding of the day's events. I've been waiting for him to fill me in on the Chinese folk perspective on moon bears. Unfortunately, he says, they receive none of the reverence shown to pandas. Moon bears are thought to be stupid. Not "ugly" stupid, but "lovely" stupid. Chinese people also believe that moon bears have very poor eyesight, and use the expression "bear blind" for a dim-witted person who hangs around aimlessly and can't see the opportunities in front of him.

"Bears are always stealing corn from the field," he says, relaying a common folktale. "But they are too stupid to make much of the opportunity. They put an ear of corn under each armpit, then go to the next corn plant and drop the previous ears replacing them with new ones. And then they go to the next one, drop the old corn and put the new ears under their armpits and so on. At last, the bear will have only two ears of corn for all his work."

As a publicist for the cause of moon bears, Zhang clearly has his work cut out for him.

"Local people have a long way to go to understand what we're doing," he says. "Especially the villagers. Some of them might think we are making money from the bile or conducting some kind of research. We are planning a kind of open day for the local people. I believe that if they see what's happening here, they will understand."

When Robinson, Mok, and company finally resurface, it is announced that the superstar wants to make the China Bear Rescue her personal cause. She will help in any way she can and wants to donate the proceeds of an upcoming concert. Robinson is beaming. It couldn't have gone better.

In the scrum of Chinese journalists and pop music fans, a tall redhead catches my eye. Originally from the UK, she is here as a "foreign expert" teaching English to journalists in Chengdu. She wants to know what paper I work for and if she can be of assistance. When she discovers that this is my first trip to China, she smiles and says she can save me some time. She has discovered the perfect shorthand explanation for the difference between Chinese and Western cultures. Western society is built on guilt, she says. Eastern society is built on shame.

"Plus we're afraid of physical contact," she says. "British people are so reserved. We don't touch each other. I know people who grew up in England and their parents never touched or kissed them. We're starved for physical contact. Maybe that's why we're mad on cats and dogs. We're allowed to touch *them*. We should touch each other more, as the Chinese do. It's more natural, don't you think?"

THE FOLLOWING AFTERNOON, I unfold a sticky menu in a small working-class restaurant near the heart of Chengdu. All eight pages are in Mandarin so I smile, point at the first item on page three, and hope there are some vegetables involved. They've put me at a table with an ashen young man hunched over a book. He does little more than glance up to acknowledge my presence. When my meal arrives—pig intestine, chilies, and noodles—I smile to myself, grab the chopsticks, and dig in.

"You are very skilled with chopsticks," he observes in measured English. He is in his mid-twenties and I take him for a student.

I quickly learn that Jerry is an investment advisor, a man who counts Warren Buffett among his heroes. A nascent capitalist, he has all his money in futures (soybeans, copper, and rubber). He chose his English name after seeing a movie that featured a very clever character named Jerry. He tells me that he respects George Washington because he seized power for the people and then gave it away. He respects Nelson Mandela because he seized power, then gave it away. Mao Zedong? He seized power for the people and held it for himself.

Jerry lives in a town about four hours south of Chengdu by train. He does most of his work on the Internet, but must occasionally come into the city. He's only ever spoken with two other Westerners, for five minutes each. This is the longest conversation he's ever had with a white person. Two hours after I sat down, Jerry invites me back to his hotel for tea.

Although it costs the same ($9), his hotel is in much better shape than mine. Jerry's room is heated and even has a little sitting area. We settle in and continue our discussion of politics, economics, and family over the drone of traffic in the dark.

Jerry is hopeful about the liberalization of Chinese society and the possibility of some kind of democracy, but he's most interested in the possibilities for business. He sees himself as a pragmatist, a man willing to put his efforts behind what is possible while avoiding what is not. "When a man is fifteen," he says, "he wants to change the world. When a man is thirty, he wants to change his country. When a man is forty-five, he wants to change his family. When a man is sixty, he wants to change himself."

While I admit to clinging to more adolescent aspirations, Jerry says he already feels like an old man.

Then, after a rare break in the conversation, he tells me his body is weak. He is dying of blood cancer. He made the journey to Chengdu to see a specialist and received the results only yesterday. The news is not good. There are almost no white blood cells left in his body and he doesn't know how much longer he will live. Today, he found himself alone in the city, alone with his news, and I was the unlucky stranger who sat down at his table. He offers an apology, which I do not accept. Perhaps, I say, sharing this news with a stranger is the best way to begin. I have been honored to meet him.

It's getting late and Jerry looks exhausted. Before leaving, we arrange to meet tomorrow for lunch. I head back to my cold hotel near the river. On my way through the darkened streets, I walk past idling taxis, old men out for their nightly stroll, and two young soldiers of the People's Army sitting in a truck watching a porno on a portable DVD player. They take no notice of my passing.

JERRY IS WAITING in the lobby of his hotel at noon the following day. He takes me to a restaurant where they serve traditional Sichuan hot pot, which I discover consists of different cuts of meats, tripe, chicken feet, some unidentifiable tadpolelike fish, and an assortment of vegetables on bamboo skewers. These are dipped, fondue-style, into boiling cauldrons of oil and water. I find it spicy, but Jerry sweats profusely. The place is full of families and couples, and even though it is March in a Buddhist country, the stereo plays muzak versions of Christmas tunes, including "The First Noël."

Here, in the light of day, Jerry looks poised but emaciated. He explains a little more about his disease, and laments the emotional and financial burden his illness has placed on his family. During the meal, he receives a text message from his brother who wants to know the test results. His family is worried about him and he's been reluctant to break the news. He will call them this afternoon.

Then I ask about his treatment. He tells me that he takes comfort in Taoism, and spends most of his days reading Chinese philosophy. Naturally, he says, his doctors prescribe traditional Chinese medicine. I feel compelled to ask if bear bile is a part of the regime and suffer both guilt and shame for the impulse. He saves me by rattling off the unpronounceable herbs he takes to ease the pain.

It is then I remember the only time in my life a close friend was seriously ill. In 1987, a classmate was struck by a drunk driver while riding a motorcycle. He spent months in intensive care, and very nearly died. His injuries were numerous and severe. Much later, while convalescing, he was invited to a formal "Game Dinner" being held by his reserve regiment. He could not go unaided, so I tagged along. The elaborate, multicourse menu was filled with wild game, including venison, moose, and even sweet-and-sour cougar. My friend was presented with a large bear steak and was encouraged to clear his plate. The curative properties of bear meat are well-known, the officers said, and would help speed him on the road to recovery. The Chinese are not alone in looking to the bear for strength.

Jerry and I cast off in a pedicab through the growing stream of traffic. The ride gives him a welcome rest. Bikes are used to transport the most amazing array of items in this country, I say. I point out a broom and feather duster salesman, and a bike with baskets of water and live fish. One man rides with a huge, refrigerator-sized bundle of cotton on his back, and then there is a butcher with sides of meat and cleavers swinging on a cart behind. On two wheels, we see every imaginable fruit and vegetable for sale, as well as chickens and ducks. One man rides with a loudspeaker announcing the sale of pots and pans. Finally, we see a bike parked with a rice cooker and propane BBQ attached behind the seat. Its owner sells baked goods and full meals from the back of his bicycle. Jerry asks again about my work and if I might mention him in a book someday. I tell him there's always the chance. On the curb outside his hotel, we shake hands and say good-bye.

That night, I tune into CCTV 9 to find that the People's Congress has now welcomed entrepreneurs into the Communist Party. I want to ask Jerry what he thinks of this. Later, there is a travel show featuring my hometown, Vancouver. It opens on an in-depth profile of our Chinatown and concludes with the "sport-loving" Canadians' infatuation with snowboarding. I feel the sudden, profound need to call my wife.

I rise early to ensure that I catch my flight back to Hong Kong. The cab passes through a city of skyscrapers—some half-built and abandoned, others fully occupied. Bamboo is used as scaffolding and men nimbly scramble between the poles sixty stories up. Everything is covered in gray, chalky dust. As we near the airport, a large billboard comes into view.

I have exercised remarkable restraint when it comes to cataloging the various gems of Chinglish (Chinese-English) I've run across in Sichuan. For someone with only a few words of Mandarin, it would be unseemly. But this sign transcends the ordinary unfortunate spellings and amusing cultural blunders. It feels more like a cosmic riddle, or perhaps a Taoist truism that might take a lifetime to comprehend.

CHENGDU: A CITY YOU WOULD NEVER WANT
TO LEAVE AS YOU COME

3

THE BLESSED CURSE
OF CHAPARRI
Department of Lambayeque, Peru

LONG BEFORE the time of the Inca, when the Moche ruled this land, an entire village disappeared—almost without a trace. Of all the people in Old Ferreñafe, only two young warriors survived, the brothers Chaparri and Yaranwanka. Chaparri was a good man, pure of heart and mind. Yaranwanka, however, had a jealous heart and his thoughts were filled with darkness.

Yaranwanka made his new home on Mount Mulatto, a half-day's walk to the east, while Chaparri remained near his vanished village on a mountain that would later bear his name. Chaparri's mountain was by far the richer of the two. Yaranwanka—who settled in a barren place—wanted all this natural bounty for himself. One day, he gathered a war party and marched toward Chaparri's mountain. Not expecting an attack from his brother, Chaparri was taken by surprise. Yaranwanka slew his brother and kidnapped his sister-in-law. He gathered up the plants and trees and even collected sand from a riverbank on his brother's mountain. He took all these things back to Mount Mulatto.

The people who lived nearby wept for Chaparri. They called out to their gods and asked them to revive the young man so he could walk among them again. The gods granted their wish and Chaparri rose from the dead. He quickly gathered an army and went in search of his wife. When Chaparri arrived at Mount Mulatto, he found Yaranwanka's men celebrating their victory. Chaparri attacked. When the brothers met in combat, Chaparri was forced to kill Yaranwanka—then he turned his brother's army to stone. Finally, Chaparri freed his wife, gathered up the stolen trees and plants, and returned to his mountain.

For Chaparri, there was no celebration. His grief at having killed his brother was so profound that he asked his own soldiers to kill him. He told them to cut out his beating heart, wash it in the Changkai River, and place it on his forehead. They begged him to change his mind, but Chaparri made them promise to fulfill his final command. To this day, it is possible to see the outline of Chaparri's enormous heart on top of his mountain. On Mount Mulatto, the stones still bear the features of Yaranwanka's vanquished army.

WE MARCH AT DAWN up the slopes of a magic mountain. I concentrate on the legs of Javier Vallejos-Guerrero, two pistons pumping relentlessly across rock and scrub. We hike up Chaparri toward the damp and colorless sky in the hope of seeing wildlife. Unfortunately, my interpreter—the third member of our group—is addicted to the sound of his own voice. He shuffles far behind. Still, Vallejos-Guerrero expertly guides us through the cactus and thorns that litter the landscape. Here and there, the blush of bougainvillea.

Vallejos-Guerrero is a warm, able man who possesses considerable knowledge of the land. He is respectful of the spirits that reside here but is no longer afraid of Mount Chaparri, as are most of the men in the nearby community of Santa Catalina de Chongoyape. Vallejos-Guerrero and his family are responsible for the care and feeding of six captive spectacled bears as well as the protection of the wild bears, puma, foxes, deer, and birds that populate this reserve. Vallejos-Guerrero has little time for people who don't work as hard as he does.

We stop and inspect the gnawed trunk of a thin passayo tree, one of the preferred winter foods of the spectacled bears that live in this dry forest. Spectacled bears are named for the distinctive, light-colored circles around their eyes, which someone thought resembled the frames of eyeglasses. They can be found in various habitats throughout Peru—from the dense jungles of the Amazonian basin to the lush cloud forest of the Andes—but Vallejos-Guerrero claims that the ones who live here grow to be the biggest of all. He locates and breaks open some dried bear scat that has baked hard in the sun. The shredded pulp of the passayo tree flakes out and blows away.

Considering this evidence, and surveying the rest of the spare plant life, it seems remarkable that bears can make a go of it here at all. It is important to remember that this is the dry season, Vallejos-Guerrero says. You should see the place green up when the rains start to fall.

After a two-hour hike through arroyos, denuded trees, and parched grass, we rest on a knoll overlooking the face of Mount Chaparri—ablush in the rising sun. Mist blows in from the Pacific, shrouding the peak in a cool fog. As soon as it is completely covered, the winds shift and pull the blanket away. Moments later, the sun reappears, bathing Chaparri's stone heart in a copper glow. Then the wind stalls and damp, gray clouds come racing back again.

Vallejos-Guerrero is from Santa Cruz de Sierra in southern Peru, but he has lived and worked in the shadow of Chaparri for the past six years. He is built solid and low to the ground. At fifty-two, he appears strangely ageless, his jet-black hair shows no signs of retreat. He says that's thanks to his predominantly indigenous blood—the two or three strands of gray on his head are the telltale signs of a Spaniard lurking somewhere near the family tree. He has grown to love this place, is proud of his work, and is only too happy to show it to me.

Vallejos-Guerrero plucks a blade of bromeliad, a plant that can be found growing throughout this forest. Resembling the top of a pineapple, it is a favorite food of spectacled bears. Vallejos-Guerrero explains that the forest depends on two phenomena for its survival. Of primary importance is the mist we've been watching drift in from the sea. The precious moisture is expertly collected by the plants and trees, making life possible during the dry winter months. The other force that sustains this place are the spirits that haunt the mountain.

We trek across boulders and fields, and past waterfalls that have long gone dry. Unsure it wants to reveal itself, the mountain continues its fog striptease. We scramble up a rock perch that, in the wet season, is a small, clear pool. This is where camera traps captured a mother bear and two cubs swimming and playing in the water last summer. Although there may be over a dozen wild bears on the mountain, they are wily. Vallejos-Guerrero finds signs of their presence whenever he ventures into the forest, but has only seen three wild bears in all his time at Chaparri.

Soon, I am told that we've gone far enough. It wouldn't do for a gringo to hike all the way to the top of the 4,265-foot peak. Chaparri is no ordinary mountain. In the Muchik language, *Chaparri* means "the heart that cries." Local people—and shamans throughout Peru—consider it sacred. Out of respect for the community, no one goes up except Vallejos-Guerrero, who must keep watch for poachers. He has spent several nights on the peak and has lived to tell the tale.

TREMARCTOS ORNATUS, the spectacled bear, is the only bear found in South America. It is the sole surviving member of the tremarctine family, which included *Arctodus simus,* or the giant short-faced bear that died out ten thousand years ago. Standing

well over twelve feet tall on its hind legs and weighing up to fifteen hundred pounds, it was the largest land carnivore in North
America during the last Ice Age. A mere shadow of its northern
ancestor, adult male spectacled bears stand between five and
six feet tall and can weight up to three hundred and eighty-five
pounds. Females are about a third smaller. Still, it's enough to
claim the title of South America's largest carnivore.

Spectacled bears can be found throughout the Andes, from the
border of Panama and Columbia, to Venezuela, and down to
Bolivia and Argentina. A close relative of the North American
black bear, spectacled bears occupy a broad range of ecosystems
at elevations between fifteen hundred and twelve thousand
feet. They consume large amounts of bromeliads, herbs, flowering plants, and fruits; their diet is 95 percent vegetarian. They are
the most arboreal of bears, building daybeds in trees by folding
branches into a comfortable and sturdy bunk. They are not known
to hibernate. Although the size and health of the spectacled bear
population is unknown (due to a lack of hard scientific data), estimates range up to eighteen thousand. Peru is believed to have
the largest population. According to the IUCN, spectacled bears
are classed as vulnerable to extinction.

There are significant threats to the spectacled bear's survival.
Hunting continues to be a major concern, as is habitat fragmentation due to agriculture and mining. Unfortunately, bears are
not even safe in national parks, where poaching persists and
farming continues to alter the landscape. In all Andean nations,
it is illegal to hunt spectacled bears but the law is not enforced.
Farmers shoot bears for raiding their crops. The bears themselves
aren't making matters any easier. Spectacled bears usually live in
low densities, reproduce at a slow rate, and, like other bears, have
a relatively long period of parental dependency. At lower elevations, they can fall prey to jaguars. Although there is considerable
anecdotal evidence that wild populations are decreasing, without
proper scientific research, this is impossible to verify.

Created in 2000, the Ecological Reserve of Chaparri is dedicated to the preservation of spectacled bears and their habitat. The bulk of the reserve's land was donated by the community of Santa Catalina de Chongoyape (pop. 18,882), which is located forty-five miles from the mountain. Recognized by the government as the first private ecological reserve in Peru, Chaparri comprises almost 84,000 acres at the southern end of a 125-mile-long stretch of dry forest—one of the largest remaining tracts in the world. The Tumbesian dry forest, as this ecosystem is known, is found only in southwest Ecuador and northwest Peru. It is far more endangered than South America's internationally renowned tropical lowland jungle, more threatened even than the rapidly disappearing Andean cloud forest. Only 5 percent of the continent's original dry forests remain.

The dry forest environment is home to a large number of endemic and threatened species. Nearly 30 percent of the vertebrate species and 20 percent of the estimated 6,300 plant species that live here are found nowhere else. An excellent example of this rare ecosystem, Chaparri is also important for another reason: watershed preservation. Without an intact forest to capture winter rains, Santa Catalina de Chongoyape, an agriculture-based community, would soon wither and die. Believing that the survival of the forest is directly related to their own survival, the community donated the land for conservation. It is the first community in Peru to make such a move. This sentiment is contained in the phrase *el oso es agua* ("the bear is water"), which is emblazoned on Vallejos-Guerrero's T-shirt. Locals believe that preserving the bear means preserving the forest. By preserving the forest, bears preserve the water—and life.

Although spectacled bears have been known to science since the 1800s, research on the species didn't really begin until 1980 with the arrival of American bear researcher Bernard Peyton in Peru. Much of what we know about the spectacled bear today can be attributed directly to him. Peyton spent years in this habitat observing and recording data on these little-known mammals.

Peyton and I (no relation) met six months earlier in San Diego at the International Bear Association Conference, the annual convocation of the world's foremost bear biologists and researchers. A tall, bearded man who appears at once professorial and athletic, Peyton is a past president of the organization and is considered a dean of the international bear science community. Before his work, many South Americans were unaware of the existence of bears on their continent. More than anyone else, Peyton has helped build the scientific case for the protection of the species. His years of dedication—in partnership with Peruvian wildlife photographer Heinz Plenge—led to the creation of the Ecological Reserve of Chaparri.

But science, hard work, and dedication only go so far in Peru. The bears of Chaparri have long relied on something more— something that cannot be quantified, tested, or proven; something beyond the temporal realm.

To THIS DAY, everyone knows that Mount Chaparri swallowed the village of Old Ferreñafe and that the mountain continues to take people now and then. One account involves a shepherd who made the mistake of falling asleep at the base of the mountain. The shepherd worked with experienced dogs and was forever moving his goats from one range to the next. Once, while watching his flock graze near Chaparri, he reclined against the trunk of a tree and fell asleep. The next morning, the man's dogs herded the goats back to the village by themselves. The concerned villagers followed the dogs back to the place the shepherd had fallen asleep. It was clear that the mountain had taken him.

The people returned with a shaman, who proclaimed that the missing man was indeed inside the mountain. He told the family to find three more shamans to help. With their combined power, they would be able to free him. The family came back with four shamans who performed a ceremony in which they saw the mountain open up to reveal the missing shepherd. He was sitting in a park in the village of Old Ferreñafe. Although they were unable to retrieve the man, they could see that he was content.

"Many people have gone missing here," Vallejos-Guerrero explains. These people are presumed dead, consumed by the mountain. "Most people are afraid of dead people, but I am not. I'm afraid of the living. Dead people can't hurt you; live people can."

Because he had only two years of schooling, Vallejos-Guerrero says he never dreamed he could go so far. He essentially runs the reserve on a day-to-day basis; his boss Heinz Plenge spends most of his time traveling on assignment or at home in Lima. He is grateful for the opportunities he's had. "I have even been on *Animal Planet*," he says, in case I didn't know. The pride is evident in the way he carries himself, the determination and purpose with which he moves across the land.

We rest on a large boulder near the source of the spring that feeds the reserve. We have a commanding view out over the valley and arroyo that I'm told can run like a torrent during the rainy season. The boulder, known as Tinajones, has four holes carved out of the stone. Each is perfectly round, about eight inches across and a foot deep. They were left by the Moche. No one knows what they used these holes for, but some speculate they served as a calendar of the seasons or as a way of predicting how much water is available for irrigation and agriculture at certain times of the year. Others think they were used in the ritual human sacrifice the Moche were famous for.

The Moche culture dominated this region one thousand years before the arrival of the Inca Empire. It flourished from AD 100 to 800 and built a highly organized society with advanced art, culture, and elaborate religious beliefs. Directed by an elite class of warrior-priests, the Moche economy was based on agriculture, fishing, and skilled artisans. They traded textiles and other goods with highland peoples. They built huge temples and vast irrigation systems to water their fields. They made fine ceramics and—working with gold, silver, copper, and precious stones—their mastery of metallurgy was unrivaled in the Americas. They are also famous for their sacrificial decapitation and the drinking of human blood. The Museo Tumbas Reales de Sipán, in the city of Lambayeque, holds a resplendent display of the artifacts from the rich burial cache of two Moche warrior-priests, recently unearthed at the royal tombs of Sipán.

Since the time of the Moche, at least, local people have believed that bears are powerful beings. Bears live on the mountains near the gods and therefore must be able to communicate with them. Having the ear of the gods gained bears the respect and reverence of the people, who worshiped them in relation to the passage of the seasons, the transition from adolescence to adulthood, and even the journey from life to death. Some local people still make burnt offerings to the bears with bundles of vicuna meat and coca leaves.

Although Vallejos-Guerrero and his family work here full time, other men have tried and failed. On several occasions he has attempted to hire local men to come up and help with the maintenance, patrolling, and the care and feeding of the bears. Santa Catalina de Chongoyape is a poor community, where a farmer makes only ten soles ($3) a day. Ordinarily, the prospect of such stable employment would draw plenty of eager applicants. After all, providing jobs was part of the objective when the reserve was first established. Unfortunately, it hasn't worked out that way.

One worker came from the neighboring district of Cajamarca. The man was afraid to spend the night, but forced himself to do it. By midnight he was screaming so loudly that Vallejos-Guerrero had to shake him awake. When the man finally calmed down, he claimed that an enormous goat with massive horns had charged down the mountain and attacked him in his bed. The next day, he cleared out and never returned.

Recently, an engineer came up to help build an electric fence and planned to stay a week. He had a nightmare the first night. In his dream, a herd of horses came down from the mountain and destroyed his tent. He was so afraid that, from then on, he came to work during the day but drove back to Santa Catalina de Chongoyape each night—a 2½-hour round-trip over extremely rough roads. Everyone has these dreams, Vallejos-Guerrero says, and they often involve animals. His son had a dream about a giant deer attacking him. In the dream, the deer chased his son over a cliff. He fell from Mount Chaparri into the mouth of an enormous snake that was waiting in the rocks below.

"One night, I forced myself to stay awake to see if there was any-thing to be afraid of," Vallejos-Guerrero says. "That night, I was alone. I told myself, I won't leave no matter what happens. I kept the radio on to keep me awake and I stayed up until five o'clock in the morning. Then I got sleepy and the nightmares returned."

The dreams, he says, often involve an animal attack. The best defense is to sleep with a big dream machete over your bed. That way, when you have a nightmare, you can grab the blade and use it to fight off the attackers.

Because otherwise brave men are afraid of the dark at Chaparri, most people are unwilling to come here even in the full light of day. It is widely believed that if pregnant women or unbaptized children touch the mountain's plants, water, or stones, some terrible fate will befall them. Only yesterday, people from the community were invited—at no charge—to come up, tour the re-serve, and learn about the animals here. There was room for forty people on the chartered bus; fifteen had the guts to come.

We walk back to the reserve center and enjoy an excellent din-ner of barbecue beef, rice, and fried bananas, prepared by Vallejos-Guerrero's wife Pepa. Dinner is served under a palapa be-hind the dark, low-slung building. We dine by candlelight and the dim glow of a solar-powered bulb as semiwild peccaries wan-der in and out of the shadows, sniffing for table scraps.

After dinner, I walk into the night and consider the unfamiliar southern sky. Here, beyond the view of Ursa Major and Ursa Minor, the Milky Way is a luminous cloud running along the entire rift of the valley. In the distance, Vallejos-Guerrero announces the discovery of a treed *oso hormiguero* (anthill bear). We all gather around to see. Also known as a northern tamandua, it is not a bear at all, but a kind of nocturnal anteater. It picks its way through the slender branches, just a few yards above our flashlights. Its long, conical face looks frightened but remains composed as it ponders its next move.

That night, tucked under the wool blanket in my room, I listen to the buzz of the crickets and conjure a long, gleaming broadsword that is as sharp as it is light. In my mind, I slice the air above my head a few times and then, as directed, place it on an imaginary rack above my pillow. I fall into a deep and peaceful sleep.

MORNING LIGHT paints the place in flattering shades of peach. The reserve center itself consists of simple rooms of adobe, stone, and wood, built in homage to the Moche style. The exterior walls are finished in mud plaster with fine renditions of Moche paintings—warrior, animal, and religious images inspired by those found at the archeological site of Sipán. At the peak of the roof is a series of rabbit-ear knobs poking toward the sky. These are designed to disrupt the breeze and encourage it to stick around a little longer on long, hot days. Originally built by Heinz Plenge as a retreat for his family, the place now also serves as a base for invited scientists. Out back, the long palapa offers a view out over the fish-filled pools of a natural spring.

As I snoop around the property, I am stopped in my tracks by the discovery of a sword hanging on the wall outside Plenge's room. No dream sword, this weapon is housed in an intricately designed sheath of leather, shells, snakeskin, and—at the handle—the paw of a spectacled bear. Vallejos-Guerrero explains that this specimen is typical of the swords used by shamans during their ceremonies. Throughout Peru, they believe the "luck" of the bear will be transferred to them as they wield the sword during incantations. I wonder if Plenge has placed it here for luck, magic, or kitsch. I recall my dream sword from the night before. Realizing that I experienced no nightmares or haunting, it seems to have done the trick. I suddenly wish it hadn't.

Plenge greets me as he makes his way out to the field for the day. The descendant of German immigrants, he is a sober, quiet man who—without trying—exudes an air of noble *patróne*. He shakes my hand and says he is looking forward to sitting down with me to answer all my questions. However, he must go. He pulls a sombrero over his graying hair, adjusts the brim, and walks out into the sun.

Beyond the long, shaded palapa, hummingbirds zip between flowers as wary vultures wheel overhead in the pool-blue sky. As I survey the surrounding hills, I am stunned by the number and variety of birds. Before breakfast, I see a flock of scarlet-fronted parakeets and the deeply saturated plumage of the vermillion flycatcher. So far, they've counted over two hundred species of birds on this reserve, including the white-winged guan—which Vallejos-Guerrero is eager to show me.

The white-winged guan seems to have trouble getting off the ground. In Vallejos-Guerrero's estimation, they are "seventy percent turkey, twenty percent vulture, and ten percent dinosaur." I am fortunate enough to see three of them browsing in the bush a short stroll from the reserve center. One awkwardly flaps its way up into the lower branches of a tree. With this relatively easy sighting, I am now the envy of millions of birders the world over. This species, thought to be extinct for over a century, was rediscovered in 1977. There are just three hundred white-winged guans in existence, but thanks in part to the work of the Ecological Reserve of Chaparri, these birds have been reintroduced to the wild.

Birds are quickly putting Chaparri on the map—particularly with Europeans. Although the reserve was originally set up for the protection of spectacled bears and their dry forest habitat, birders have gotten wind of the mountain's astounding variety of avian life and are beginning to make the trek.

Soon, I spot the silhouette of a spectacled bear up a tree and hear the plaintive bleat of another. Vallejos-Guerrero cautions that the bears I'm about to see are much smaller than the ones outside the fence. Former circus performers and orphans, these bears have been in captivity since they were cubs and didn't get their mother's rich milk during their formative years. A little closer and I can see that each has a short, mottled snout and a version of the "spectacle" rings around its eyes. They are pigeon-toed and highly vocal. Elders report that the rings are a recent development and that the faces of the bears (at least in this part of Peru) were once mostly white. These white-faced bears were responsible for eating cows and other livestock. The ones with the circles around their eyes, they say, cause no such trouble. Vallejos-Guerrero confirms that one white-faced specimen lived here for a number of years before dying of old age.

We begin serving breakfast. On the other side of the electric fence, a female spectacled bear—half the size of an adjacent male—keeps her rival at bay by charging and bawling in his face. She stands on hind legs and jumps up and down like a toddler. Determined to be served first, she eventually warns him away. The bears go ape over the long green guava beans, expertly cracking them open to get at the sugary pulp inside. They enjoy everything from cactus to apples, and—as we have seen—the wood of the passayo tree. As with all bears, they are consummate opportunists. Once, Vallejos-Guerrero saw one gnawing on the carcass of a deer that had been killed by a puma.

Handing them guava is far too easy, Vallejos-Guerrero claims. He wants to make them work. These bears live in an enclosure large enough that they can get about half of their food from the wild. The other half comes sailing over the fence. Vallejos-Guerrero picks up a *waraka*, an ancient Incan weapon used for launching stones at the heads of enemies. The sling easily accommodates a full-sized yam that can be thrown more than twice as far as normal with the same effort. After Vallejos-Guerrero demonstrates, I give it a try—sending a few carbohydrate missiles deep into the bush. The bears bound off in hot pursuit.

Although these bears still rely on food provided by humans, Vallejos-Guerrero says, the percentage will decrease over time and eventually they will be set free. One bear, Linda, couldn't wait for this carefully considered program and escaped a few years ago. She had been fed by humans her entire life and had only just begun to forage on her own. Vallejos-Guerrero wondered how she would fare out in the forest where food was often hard to come by during the long dry season. She might not have the knowledge and experience necessary to survive. Linda showed up one year later, traveling near her old enclosure with a healthy new cub. She'd clearly made a successful transition from the life of a captive pet to that of a wild mother.

Across cultures and time, people have always captured and imprisoned bears. The spectacled bear of South America, however, has been known to capture people. The most famous case of this involved Juan Oso (John Bear), an animal whose reputation extends throughout the Andes.

Long ago, a bear called Juan captured a woman, made her pregnant, and kept her as his wife. When the baby was born, it was known as Juan Osito (John Bear Jr.). Being jealous of the people who lived nearby, and suspecting that his wife might try to return to the village, Juan Oso decided to keep his family hidden in a cave—with a giant boulder over the entrance. All day long, he gathered food and water, to bring to his wife and son.

As time passed, little Juan Osito grew big and strong inside the cave. Then one day he had an idea. He asked his mother to tell his father to bring them water—as he had always done—but this time to bring it in a grass basket. The woman spoke to Juan Oso and the next day he complied. He filled the basket with water and brought it to the cave, but by the time he had traveled part way from the spring, all the water had leaked out and the basket was empty. Frustrated, Juan Oso returned to the spring again and again, filling up the basket and traveling to the cave. Each time, the water leaked out and he had to return to start all over again. Knowing that his family needed water, Juan Oso worked faster and faster in order to reach the cave in time. While his father was distracted with this impossible task, Juan Osito pushed the stone from the entrance of the cave and escaped with his mother.

Eventually, a frustrated Juan Oso returned to discover that his family had escaped. He immediately tracked down the pair. Furious that they had deceived him, he beat his wife for what she had done. Wishing to protect his mother, Juan Osito intervened and eventually killed his father.

Some researchers believe this legend appeared after the Conquest, marking a change in the way people related to bears. It is believed that indigenous people shifted their view of bears from being revered intermediaries between the mountain gods and men, to embodying the macho sensibilities of the conquerors. The bear's spiritual association soon gave way to a baser reputation as symbol of brute strength, sexual power, and violence.

In markets throughout Peru, bear fat is sold as an ointment for relieving pain as well as a balm for smearing on the skin of baby boys to ensure their power and potency. Bear baculum is sold in markets and consumed as an aphrodisiac. Bear claws are purchased by young men and used to inflict scratches across their own chests to make them "desirable" to young women.

I saw bear parts for sale in the nearby city of Chiclayo at the Mercado Modelo, which is known as a market for *brujos* (wizards or shamans). It was displayed with heaps of fragrant herbs; snake, skunk, and puma skins; dried birds; stuffed pampas cats and eagles; deer hooves; and, of course, cured bear skull. In fact, one merchant had the entire right arm of a bear, skinned and dried white with the shriveled muscles and tendons still in place. Looking like some prop from a horror movie, the five digits and palm bore a striking resemblance to a flayed human hand.

"People do these things to get the bear's power because they know about the bear's long sexual endurance," Vallejos-Guerrero explains. "I have seen with my own eyes bears mating for an hour and forty-five minutes. And if the female moves, the male bites her. Even if the female is tired and falls, he continues fucking her. When you see the bears having sex, you get tired just watching them."

If only the pandas knew. The spectacled bear, it would seem, is the bear family's Latin Lover.

ON A RISE overlooking the reserve center and valley below, a newly constructed shaman's house faces east to greet the sun. Made from bamboo and constructed in the Moche style, the small dirt-floored hut has an enclosed room with a sleeping bench and an adjacent, open space with a table set for magic. Here, the stone slab covers much of the floor and contains items used in sorcery, including ceramic figurines of animals, men, a vulva, and a Moche couple engaged in sexual congress. Rounding out the collection are numerous spears, a bear paw, a jar of magic herb juice, a bromeliad, and two skulls: one bear, one human.

The house was constructed to honor the fact that Chaparri is a mecca for Peruvian shamans. It also provides a new place for them to come and practice their craft. As I inspect the skulls and fiddle with the amulets and charms, Vallejos-Guerrero tells me that locals believe in the power of shamans; it is ingrained in the culture. People regularly consult them for all kinds of needs, including medical, spiritual, and revenge. They believe what their shaman tells them because this is a land where stories come alive.

Old people from Santa Catalina de Chongoyape tell of an immense bull with solid gold horns that lives on Mount Chaparri. This is not a story, they say; it is real and they have seen it. Occasionally, it comes down from Chaparri while a similar colossal bull with silver horns comes down from Mount Mulatto.

The bulls, they say, come together to fight in the center of the road connecting the two rival mountains. And when they meet, there is always a mighty battle. They tear up the road with their enormous hooves and the soil turns to mud from their saliva. No matter how long the battle rages, one bull always wins. If the winning bull is from Chaparri, the region will have a good year with lots of rain to help with agriculture. If the bull from Mount Mulatto triumphs, the rains will fall over there, near the people of Cutervo. The old men who last saw these bulls say that when the beasts clashed with their horns of silver and gold, chips of fire flew in all directions.

I decide to confirm all these things with a trip to Santa Catalina de Chongoyape. I want to meet and question a shaman for myself. While I am expecting a kind of mestizo Gandalf or Merlin, I am introduced instead to Segundo Valdera, a stout, sweaty man with a round, hairless belly framed by the curtains of his open shirt. One of the region's top shamans, he appears to be in his early thirties. He invites us into his spare adobe home that has a dirt floor and a few pieces of furniture made of rebar and plastic twine. He glances from me to my interpreter, to my local guide, and then back to me again. Even after I explain my interest in his powers, he has no idea what to make of this inquisition. In fact, he looks a little worried.

"We not only call Mount Chaparri but also Mount Mulatto," the shaman explains, "because both are like magic. They have a special force. And that force helps us in the work we do." He speaks with authority about things he believes should be self-evident. "All shamans throughout Peru call these mountains because Chaparri is a magic mountain that covered a civilization. Chaparri can be used for good or bad magic," he says. "It depends on how I wish to use it."

Valdera lets this final thought hang in the air for effect, then says he has little more to add to my understanding of the connection between bears and the spiritual world.

But what about the bear paw sword I saw up at the ecological reserve?

"You call the mountain's energy with that sword," he explains. "The bear paw is on the sword because there are bears on Mount Chaparri. It helps to have the bear paw on the sword in order to call the mountain."

At this stage—barely ten minutes since our arrival—the shaman puts his hands on his knees and looks around the room, signaling the end of the meeting. I thank him and offer to pay for his professional time. I am advised to offer a ten-sole note, which he scrutinizes with a keen, appraising eye. Peruvians are forever on the lookout for counterfeit currency and are wary of bills with the slightest smudge, tear, or imperfection. In the momentary pause, we all stare at the bill in question and I sincerely hope I have not given offense. Finally, his face brightens, he rubs his moist belly, and then reaches for my hand.

THE SUN SETS behind the mountain, split in two perfect beams by the stone heart of Chaparri. Darkness gathers around the reserve center and soon the world is reduced to the glow of fluorescent and candle light under the bamboo palapa. Beyond, the constant trickle of the nearby spring and stars in a moonless sky.

I browse the books on the handmade shelf, many featuring the photography of Heinz Plenge, who narrates over my shoulder. His specialty is wildlife, and he has been capturing images of Peru's flora and fauna for the past thirty years. I find a photo album containing early twentieth-century black-and-white images of grinning hunters holding up the spectacled bears they've just killed. A few pages in, I come to a series of snapshots taken in 1976, featuring fresh-faced young men sporting haircuts and fashions that are miraculously back in style. Behind me, Plenge strokes his graying beard as he considers the images of his younger self, and longtime friend Bernard Peyton.

During his early days as a nature photographer, Plenge found himself on assignment in Chaparri, photographing condors. At that time, he couldn't believe such a place still existed, a place with intact forests and abundant wildlife—a place untouched by mining. He was also surprised by the evidence of a healthy bear population. Soon after his discovery, he urged Peyton to come and see for himself. After a few days of walking the forest, they were rewarded with the sight of a bear.

Having grown up in Chiclayo, Plenge has always been interested in spectacled bears. Then, when his beard "began to turn white" five years ago, Plenge realized that he wanted to make more of a direct contribution to the preservation of bears and their habitat. When he began searching for a stretch of healthy, intact dry forest to preserve, he soon found that most of the forests in the Department of Lambayeque had already been ruined. Then he remembered Chaparri.

"I thought Chaparri must be destroyed because it is very near Chiclayo and Chongoyape," he says. "When I returned after twenty-eight years, it was a great surprise to find out that there were deer, condors, bears, and all kinds of animals. I discovered the reason all the animals were still here was because the people were afraid of the mountain."

Although the government does invest in forest conservation, it doesn't seem to care about the dry forest, Plenge claims. Almost all the money goes to the protection of the lowland tropical forests of the Amazon basin. He decided it was time someone did something to conserve this unique and vanishing habitat, so he bought a piece of land at Chaparri, built a small, solar-powered house, and began working with the local community in the cause of conservation.

In Peru, there is intense pressure on local communities to turn over their land for mining. The resulting conflicts sometimes end in violence. "Here, the laws are made by the mining companies," Plenge explains. "We have had hundreds of years of gold mining, and see how poor we are now." Although Santa Catalina de Chongoyape previously succumbed to this pressure and sold a tract of land (strictly for agricultural purposes) to an international mining conglomerate, the community has since committed itself to supporting the ecological reserve.

Then came a surprise. After seeing what the community was trying to accomplish at Chaparri, the mining company sent a letter announcing the donation of all two thousand acres for inclusion in the reserve.

"Protected areas in Peru have a lot of problems," Plenge says. "More than ten percent of all the land is supposed to be protected by the government, but the government doesn't have the will to take care of the land. This is the first time in Peru that community, government, environmental, and private groups have all agreed."

Plenge has plans to help make Chaparri a small part of a community-based ecological and archeological tourism circuit that links the dry forest on the coast to the Andes and the jungle in the south. In Peru, he claims, people can see more bird species than anywhere else on earth.

"In Chaparri, we have two symbols," he says, "the white-winged guan and the spectacled bear. But there are many more people interested in birds than in bears." He is referring to the legions of bird-watchers or "twitchers" as they're known, who will travel to remote regions to view exotic species. By 2015, he hopes to see one million tourists visiting northern Peru each year in a sustainable, ecologically sound industry built on intact ecosystems and communities that directly benefit from their protected lands. In the case of Chaparri, visitors pay a fee to the community, are required to hire a local guide, and travel to the reserve from the community in taxis owned and operated by local people. "Here we don't want mass tourism," Plenge explains. "We want it to be small and controlled. After all, the whole point is to save the environment."

Although Chaparri's current ecotourism marketing strategy is focused on birds, Plenge believes the future belongs to the bears. Bringing more attention to the bears, he says, is the best way to ensure their long-term survival. He cites the example of Canada's growing bear-viewing industry as a model. I decide not to mention that British Columbia's bear-viewing industry relies on seasonal superabundance of food at a fixed location, such as salmon runs in rivers or sedge in tidal estuaries. Tourists want to see wild bears in their natural habitat and they want a better-than-average chance of seeing them. At Chaparri, it would seem the smart money is on the birds.

For now, they work to stop poaching. While it is illegal to hunt bears, Plenge says, poachers don't go to jail if they're caught. "The law is very weak. Since Chaparri has been made a reserve, a few people have tried to hunt here, but the community captured them. What's funny is that most of them were politicians. They sell the skin, head, and paws in Chiclayo. Men continue to kill bears because they want to demonstrate that they are macho."

Poaching has been reduced at Chaparri, but in the north it continues to be a threat. And while the parts trade for Asian medicine hasn't been a problem so far, he suspects it is just a matter of time. Until last year, Plenge believed that the biggest threat to the survival of spectacled bears was poaching. Now he is convinced that mining is a more serious concern because it means further fragmentation and loss of habitat.

Just what is the current status of the species? No one claims to know. Plenge believes the number of bears in Peru is continuing to shrink, but with the lack of scientific data, he admits there is no way to be certain. He is convinced, however, that there are more bears in this dry forest than in previous years. He saw one only last week.

Bears have played an important role in the beliefs of Peru's indigenous people, Plenge explains. In Cusco, for instance, young men still dress up as *ukukus* ("bears" in Quechua) at the annual Qoyllur Riti (Star of the Snow) festival. An Andean tradition with a Christian veneer, the men carry crosses, dance, and chatter in high, childlike voices in a celebration of sexual maturity. They also climb to a glacier sixteen thousand feet above sea level in ritual procession, carrying down blocks of ice to bring good luck and plenty of rain for next year's crops. (Recent concern for the shrinking glacier, however, has resulted in the suspension of further ice collection.) They dress as *ukukus* because bears serve as a link between the animal and human worlds. Because bears are seen as most active at dawn and dusk, they are believed to help bridge the gap between day and night. And because bears range between the mountains and the valleys, they connect the human realm with that of the gods.

Plenge is stumped, however, when it comes to the nearly complete absence of bear representations in pre-Columbian art, which I couldn't help but notice at the Museo Tumbas Reales de Sipán. The artifacts included plenty of half-human/half-animal combinations, pairing people with fish, crabs, pumas, and frogs. He says that throughout Peru it is easy to find images of the other animals, but not bears—large, intelligent beasts that can stand upright like us. So far, there has been no serious study of what this absence means. His hunch, however, is that there are plenty of bears in traditional Moche and Incan art—the bears are simply wearing masks that make them look like people. He even suspects that *Ai-apaec*, the supreme Moche god, was a bear hidden behind a mask.

Plenge's drowsy eyes are drawn to the insects circling the light. I sense my time running out. What about the role of the supernatural in protecting Chaparri? Does he believe?

"A lot of people have disappeared here," Plenge says, as a matter of fact. He stares into the darkness, remembering. "Before this house was built, I slept here in a hammock, and then in a tent for a year and a half. At night, a man with tall leather boots would march around my tent, but I only saw him from the waist down. It wasn't a dream. It was real. I saw it with my own eyes. This would happen five times a night. I would fall asleep, then wake up and see it again . . . But this was in 1987 or 1988 when I was working with a shaman. At that time, we drank a lot of cactus juice.

"Chaparri is the most important mountain for shamans," he explains, echoing the refrain. "It is summoned by shamans throughout Peru. They also come here to look for the cactus called San Pedro. The San Pedro that grows here is the most famous. They come at night so no one can see them."

I have seen the fleshy green cactus growing wild on the hillside and noticed a pile of them that had been cut and stacked not far from the shaman's house. San Pedro, a thick column-shaped cactus that can grow twenty feet high, is known throughout Peru as a powerful folk medicine in the treatment of fever, hepatitis, and bladder infections. Because it contains mescaline and other psychoactive alkaloids, it is also widely sought for its transcendental properties. It has been in continuous use in Peru for at least three thousand years. Shamans cook up batches of cactus juice and people consume it during a ritual that often involves vomiting, hallucinations, and radically altered perception. It allows the consumer to see beyond the ordinary—colors, shapes, patterns—and deeper into one's own consciousness and soul. I'm assured it forever changes the user's relationship with possibility and existence. Unfortunately, there is none available for me to try. It must be prepared by a knowledgeable shaman and consumed as a part of a ritual. Plenge expects that at some point, the shaman's house will be used for such ceremonies.

"We have invited shamans to come and see this place and know that they are welcome to work at Chaparri," he says. "In the future, if someone wanted to have an experience with local shamans, they could do it here . . . So, consider yourself invited."

———

IN SANTA CATALINA DE CHONGOYAPE, the town hall is filled with citizens: grandmothers, grandfathers, a few deeply tanned workers, a pair of nursing mothers. They sit on low wooden benches facing the president's table, where I sit awkwardly in a chair off to one side. It is a simple room with a concrete floor and posters on the wall featuring spectacled bears and extolling the virtues of conservation. Some people glance, others stare openly, wondering just what business the gringo has with the leader of their community. Finally, a short, smiling man in a pressed white shirt enters the room to greet me.

After hearing my bumbling speech about who I am and what I'm doing in their town, President Orfillio Torres explains the relationship between Santa Catalina de Chongoyape and the Ecological Reserve of Chaparri.

"Back in 1999, we decided to take care of the wildlife: the bears, condors, deer, all these animals," he says. "Here, we say the bear is life and water. The bear preserves the plants and if the bears preserve the plants, it will rain. Taking care of the animals and plants means the rains are going to come. And this is going to be very good for agriculture. With the reserve, our health will be better. And in the future, tourists will arrive; then we will see some economic return." I survey the faces before me. Everyone seems to agree. "Two months ago, the reserve opened to tourists. Now we are seeing the first economic benefits for the community . . . But not every tourist who comes here may enter the reserve," he cautions. "It is a selective group."

"Couldn't the community make more money by selling the land to a mining company?" I ask.

The people blink, wait for the translation, then look to the president.

"We have seen that in other communities, where the mining company has entered, the people are still poor," Torres says. "And those companies have also affected the health of the people. That would happen here. And they would destroy all of the dry forest until we have nothing left. There would be no animals here. So the people said no to mining." He hopes neighboring communities follow their lead.

Other benefits of the reserve go beyond ecological health and hoped-for financial return. The people at the ecological reserve have organized an annual soccer tournament called, naturally, the Bear Cup. It was created to help spread the word about the bears and establish the animal as a mascot for the community. The popular tournament is played by men, women, and children. Winning teams receive cash prizes and the overall tournament winner takes home the coveted trophy. Torres wants me to know that they are grateful to Dr. Peyton for providing the shirts for the teams.

"It's really good for the community," Torres says, "because it brings the people together and makes them very, very happy."

I mention some of the accounts I've heard about the mountain's mysterious power. I want to know, has the president himself ventured to the mountain? Of course, he says. In fact, he has seen three bears at Chaparri and claims they are very intelligent. "Once, a hunter shot and wounded a bear in the stomach," he says. "The bear gathered medicinal herbs, put them in the wound, and survived.

"But some people are afraid to go to Chaparri," he admits. "Mount Chaparri is known for its magic. Also, two or three times a year, you may hear a brass band that appears from the mountain. I have heard it myself. That band is from Old Ferreñafe."

I ask if anyone else has stories related to Chaparri. I want to know if they've had a chance to visit the mountain and, if so, what they experienced. I am met with the mass inspection of shoes. Torres breaks the silence. "Once, there was a mining company that wanted to work on Mount Chaparri, so they sent some people to conduct a study. The people were sleeping on the back of the mountain. At midnight, they felt a very cold wind come up. In that wind was a black man riding a horse. He asked the people from the mining company, What are you doing here? They responded that they were researching the possibility of mining. Then the black man turned his horse around and quickly rode away." The people from the mining company packed up and never returned.

While it is true that most members of his community have never ventured to Chaparri, Torres says visitors should not be afraid. "The people of Chongoyape want to have other people come to visit this nice place," he says. "Our community takes care of nature because nature is the lungs of the world. We are taking care of the world by taking care of our forest."

Outside, with the president and townspeople, I grip and grin like a seasoned politician. We all squeeze in close for a group portrait. As I say good-bye, a middle-aged woman pulls me aside to say she found the conversation interesting. There was one thing, however, that did not get mentioned. Some of the women will be making stuffed bear dolls to sell to the tourists and she wants me to tell my readers to buy them. These will be no ordinary bears, she says with entrepreneurial flair. They will be little "Juan Ositos."

4

LAWS OF THE JUNGLE
Kingdom of Cambodia

TWO TRUCKS roll past squalid shacks and bordellos before lurching to a stop at the edge of a lagoon near the port of Sihanoukville. Eight armed and uniformed Khmer men spring from the unmarked vehicles and proceed down a gangplank to a café built out over the water. A pair of foreigners in civilian clothes— Brian Kennerley and I—follow close behind. We move rapidly from relentless sun into the shade of a deserted dining area, where the men lose no time questioning the shirtless proprietor.

Kennerley is in charge of this raid. A stocky thirty-four-year-old with a strawberry blond brush cut, he has encountered more than his fair share of subterfuge. In broad, New Zealand English, he announces our intentions to search the premises. After a short pause, another voice translates these words into Khmer as the men launch into action. The proprietor, a sinewy man in his mid-forties, stands with his wife and numerous children, offering nods, smiles, and pleasantries.

In back, the men rummage through plastic coolers, crates, and wire cages. They are searching for bits and pieces of Cambodia's endangered wildlife: all manner of avian, reptilian, and mammalian species, including *Helarctos malayanus*, the Malayan sun bear. In Cambodia, as throughout Asia, bear paws are consumed as an exotic delicacy. Through his interpreter, Kennerley rephrases and shuffles the questions. "Do you have any wildlife for sale? Where do you get your animals? When was the last time you sold wildlife?" The proprietor has no wildlife, he protests, and hasn't seen any for ages. He stopped selling the stuff years ago—when he was first informed it was illegal. Kennerley nods at the dark, almost stagnant water visible through the gaps in the floor. He turns to his interpreter and right-hand man, Hain Kim Chai. "Ask him again."

The interrogation continues in a respectful but insistent manner and yields much the same results. Finally, Kennerley asks for a copy of the menu. A teenaged girl offers a photocopy in a grimy plastic sleeve. It is entirely in Khmer. Hain runs a finger down the menu and translates the offending items: *Deer Soup with Spices, Hot Fried Wild Boar, Lizard Curry Thai-style*. When presented with this evidence, the proprietor looks neither embarrassed nor surprised. In fact, there is no trace of a reaction on his face. He explains that the menus are old and that he hasn't gotten around to changing them.

Two of Kennerley's men return from the backroom with a garbage bag and set it on the table for all to see. They pull out a sheet of scales that look like medieval armor or a flap of dinosaur skin. It is immediately recognizable to everyone else as pangolin, or scaly anteater, a heavily armored mammal that can range in size from three to six feet. Pangolins are not closely related to any other living mammal and their ancestry remains a question. When threatened, their only defense is to curl up into a ball with their triangular scales pointed out, resembling a giant pinecone. Highly prized for their meat, they are the easiest of prey.

Kennerley orders photos taken of both the evidence and the proprietor. An official form is read aloud, explaining that killing pangolins is in violation of the Wildlife Law, which provides for the protection of endangered species and the prohibition of trafficking in wild animals. Kennerley orders his men to round up the menus. They sit at the tables, pull out pens, and proceed to cross out all references to illicit delicacies. The way the proprietor sees it, we are interfering with his livelihood, his right to provide for his family. But he remains impassive. In this brutalized country, most everyone has learned to respect power and recognize the risks of challenging authority. Almost everyone, that is.

The man's youngest son breaks free of his mother's grasp. He looks to be about four years of age and, like several of his siblings, he wears no clothes. He stares up at me—the closest white man—with perfect, unmistakable hate. To the delight of the other men, the child launches into a series of martial art moves—karate chops, forward kicks, back kicks, and punches as he travels across the floor. Everyone stops to watch. Finally, he bends down, picks up a broomstick, and assumes a wide-legged stance. He expertly wields it with the requisite grunts and shouts. With each swing, he closes in on my knee until his mother rushes over and scoops him up from behind.

TIME AND AGAIN, I am confronted with the question: What am I doing here? I have come because Cambodia is an ark of the continent, a place of last refuge in the storm surge of human consumption. One of Asia's last bastions of biodiversity, Cambodia is also home to the world's smallest and least understood species of bear.

Adult sun bears range in length from four to five feet and their coats are short, sleek, and black. They have a loose, wrinkled brow and a short muzzle that can range in color from gray to rust. Their ears are small and round. Their crescent-shaped chest patch—which gives them their name—can be white, yellow, or the orange of a setting sun. The palms of their large paws are soft, hairless, and end in long claws, which help with the climbing of trees. In proportion to their body size, their heads are large and their teeth are massive. Their tongues can be extended up to fifteen inches and they have a reputation for aggression when surprised. Weighing in at between 60 and 140 pounds as adults, these light flyweights of the bear family are emblematic of the crisis unfolding in the jungle around them.

Remarkably little is known about sun bears, although they are believed to exist throughout Southeast Asia—from Myanmar and Vietnam to Borneo and Sumatra. Even basic questions about food preferences, range size, and reproduction remain unanswered. They are Southeast Asia's least studied, most neglected species of large mammal, and this lack of knowledge poses a serious challenge to conservation efforts. No one knows how many are left in the wild, but when compared to anecdotal stories of past abundance, the prognosis is not good. Both CITES and the IUCN list the sun bear as vulnerable to extinction. The threats facing their survival are ominous. Throughout their existing range, the relentless pace of habitat destruction and poaching could spell their disappearance from the wild in a few short years unless someone steps in and takes action.

WildAid has wedged a boot into that narrowing gap between Cambodian wildlife and its imminent destruction. Unconventional, unafraid, and highly controversial, WildAid is a nongovernmental organization dedicated to stopping the illegal trade in wildlife and the destruction of habitat by placing themselves between the animals and those intent on killing them. Simply put, WildAid believes the time for reports, gentle suasion, and the wringing of hands is over. For some ecosystems and species, it is quite literally do or die. WildAid confronts the questions: What are we prepared to do to stop the destruction of wildlife? How far are we willing to go?

Headquartered in San Francisco, WildAid has chosen Cambodia (along with Thailand, Myanmar, Ecuador, and the Russian Far East) as an area of direct action. Due to Cambodia's recent history of political and economic catastrophe, the destruction of its forests has significantly lagged behind the pace set by other nations in the region. It is a place where the jungles are still relatively healthy, a place where elephants, tigers, and bears can still be found in the wild. But this situation is rapidly deteriorating. To protect what's left, WildAid aims to disrupt the entire cycle of the wildlife trade in Cambodia, from poaching to trafficking to consumption. Part of WildAid's work in Cambodia is done by Kennerley and his men, nine in all, known collectively as the Wilderness Protection Mobile Unit, which is based in Phnom Penh. Through their Western donors, local hiring policy, and partnership with elements of the government, WildAid has the equipment, manpower, and authority to patrol and stop the illegal wildlife trade anywhere in the country. Anywhere near a road, that is.

Since its inception in 2000, WildAid has saved well over eight thousand live wild animals. Over the last seven months, the mobile unit has intercepted no fewer than ten sun bears that were destined for lives as pets of high-ranking officials, as parts for the traditional Chinese medicine market, or simply sold for their tender paws, which are removed, one by one, for orders of bear paw soup. In this last case, keeping the bear alive between amputations is the cheapest way to go. Forgoing refrigeration affords considerable cost savings in a land where electricity, when available, is at a premium.

AFTER A MORNING of rifling through kitchens and confiscating menus, we pile back into the trucks with our knees pressed against the AK-47s slung over the front seats. Dossiers are opened containing mug shots and intelligence reports on local restauranteurs and wildlife traders. We break for lunch in a tourist restaurant where the crew sits around a large table awaiting Kennerley's order.

"Ask the manager to come over."

A Khmer man in a clean white shirt approaches the table with the same forced smile I have been seeing all day.

"Are you selling wildlife here?"

"No, sir," the translation comes back. "Not any more."

Kennerley thanks the man and sends him on his way. He looks around the room and spots a pair of waitresses huddled in the corner. He gestures and the younger of the two approaches.

Kennerley considers the menu (written in both Khmer and English), then orders the braised muntjac, an endangered species of tiny, whippet-sized deer. They are hunted relentlessly. Little is known of this species, and as recently as 1994, a new subspecies was discovered in neighboring Laos. The waitress takes the rest of our nonwildlife orders and heads for the kitchen where she is intercepted by the more senior waitress, who grabs her upper arm and hauls her back to our table. Terribly sorry, we're told. There's been a mistake. They don't serve wildlife here.

"But it's on the menu," Kennerley points out. "And the other waitress said it wouldn't be a problem."

"She is wrong. We don't serve wildlife."

Kennerley shakes his head. He gives me a look that says, "See what I mean?" then orders the men to search the entire restaurant, leaving the two of us alone at the table.

Kennerley's Irish face is reddened by the tropical sun. His scowl breaks out into a transformative grin when he talks about the institutional corruption and his method for working through the madness. He is a realist, a pessimist, but a man who remains committed to action.

"Lying is rampant," Kennerley says. "The Khmer are used to accepting lies and going no further because it's their way."

Kennerley is approaching the end of his tour of duty with WildAid. He's been the project manager of the mobile unit for eighteen months. In his other life, he's a cop in Auckland where—along with tours of duty under the UN in war-torn Bosnia and Cambodia in the mid-nineties—he has learned a thing or two about the art of interrogation and the subtleties of trafficking in contraband. He is married to a Khmer woman and has a son who was born in Phnom Penh. This is what he's chosen to do on a two-year sabbatical from his work back home. He says it keeps him fresh.

"The way it works in this country is that the law is only for the poor people," he says. "I guess it's also that way in other countries, but here it is so in your face. There have been improvements in enforcement of wildlife laws over the last eighteen months, but part of me feels it will be too little, too late.

"For example, we confiscated a thousand swallows off one guy. He was selling them for meat. This was just one guy. Imagine how many others there are. How long can the wild population sustain that kind of hit?" It will take time to change the local people's attitudes, he says. The hope is that WildAid can help convict more wildlife traders in court and that this will act as a deterrent. "There are still small amounts being sold in the local markets. We've been successful in slowing down the open trade. You will never stop it. But let's reduce it to the point that the survival of the wildlife is no longer in doubt."

After lunch, we resume our tour of restaurants. Some are full-service places with plastic tablecloths, others are mom-and-pop operations on the front porch of a shack. The kitchens are a blur of wilting vegetables, steaming pots, and gore-encrusted chopping blocks. Finally, one of the proprietors admits to selling wildlife but says she doesn't keep any on the premises. When a customer places an order, she sends a runner to the nearby market. Chinese tourists and Cambodian government officials go to the fancy hotel to order their wildlife, she complains. Why can't she sell it here?

ENTREPRENEURS, large and small, are taking advantage of Sihanoukville's budding tourist trade. The port city formerly known as Kompong Som (but now named for the king) has a few decent beaches overlooking the azure Gulf of Thailand. It offers one of the cheapest sun and sand vacations on the planet. Rooms can be had for $5 or $10, and meals start at a buck and a half. Some places will even let you sleep for free on a mat under one of their huts in return for eating and drinking at their restaurant. The place attracts young, fiscally challenged Western backpackers and the kind of leather-skinned, middle-aged dropouts you find washed up on the west coast of Mexico.

Surprisingly, this is also a place where wildlife can be found. Not long ago, a family of five wild elephants (out of the estimated 150–250 left in Cambodia) came crashing out of the nearby jungle. They made themselves at home, raiding people's crops and loitering on the beaches. Although the tourists found their presence a welcome distraction, one local businessman wasn't amused. He told WildAid to come down and do something about it or he would order the elephants shot. In the time it took for the mobile unit to drive down from the capital, four of the elephants had wandered off. However, a single adolescent bull remained on a beach, surviving on handouts from tourists. The now-habituated elephant was tranquilized and brought back to WildAid's rescue center for safekeeping.

When Kennerley started, he would come down to Sihanoukville and collect 550 pounds of wildlife from the restaurants. Now, he says, they don't get anywhere near that kind of haul—45 pounds being the current average. On this day, we find plenty of wildlife listed on menus, but little in the way of evidence. Kennerley admits that while it's true that things are improving, he believes the locals have been tipped off before we arrived. He relies on a network of paid informants, some of whom he imagines are double agents. However, just when he thinks he has a handle on who is trafficking in what, the bad guys change their tactics.

"They are very clever and have their own informants," Kennerley explains. "They are well organized and have backing from some government officials. They also pay bribes to all the different departments."

Not long ago, Kennerley and his men busted a truck and

trailer with 1½ tons of tree resin. A major cause of habitat destruction, the industrial harvest of resin—used domestically for waterproofing boats and exported for the manufacture of varnish and paint—is a major threat to the jungle. In the same trailer, they also found 660 pounds of wildlife, including over a thousand turtle shells and seven hundred snakeskins. The raid was the result of a tip from one of his informants. Kennerley and his men waited by the side of the road to Phnom Penh for forty-five hours to intercept the truck. He has made a similar bust on a truck hauling over two hundred live macaques hidden in bags beneath loads of scrap metal. These wild monkeys were headed for Vietnam, then North America and Europe, where they were destined for medical experiments, Kennerley explains. In the West, primates imported for live experiments are supposed to be captive-bred, not captured from the wild. But in Southeast Asia, almost no one bothers to check—except WildAid.

When WildAid comes across bear paws, it's usually in more exclusive restaurants, not the ones we've been touring today. They recently found two bears being kept at a restaurant as "pets." High-ranking officials and businessmen consider bear meat a delicacy. The maximum penalty for selling bear meat is ten years' imprisonment, although this penalty has never been applied. To the best of Kennerley's knowledge, only two people have ever been convicted of trading in endangered species, and they received only one- and two-year sentences, respectively.

"It's more of a slap on the wrist," Kennerley says. "Really, it's a whole lot of bullshit."

There is still plenty of jungle in Cambodia; over a third of the original forest cover remains. Once he rescues a bear, is there anywhere safe to release it?

"Oh, no," Kennerley says. "*God* no! Not at all. Same for all of Southeast Asia. The best hope for animals like bears, elephants, and tigers is to collect them and put them in zoos. But for the other animals we can still release [like macaques and pangolins], their future is limited as well because there is so much illegal hunting. With all the habitat loss, there is not much future for anything. People want to make as much money as they can in the shortest period of time. They're not interested in the long term. People are just grabbing what they can get . . . Bears and tigers are great, but we should work hard to protect the less famous species so they don't experience the same fate. They're harder to get excited about.

"We are seeing changes, slowly," he admits. "We're beginning to see a change of attitude by government people. In a few years, things will be better than they are now. I'm just wondering if that's going to be too little, too late for the animals."

We finish the day at the Park Hotel and Casino where a sun bear was known to be kept with other wildlife in a private "zoo" for the amusement of the clientele. Today, we discover that the sun bear's tiny cage is empty. When queried about what happened to the bear, the caretaker claims that it was "killed by a snake." He forgets, however, where he buried the body.

HEAT, HUMIDITY and poor hydration have conspired in a blaring headache. I find my tattered room in the Marlin Hotel ($10), shut the blinds, peel off my clothes, and lie on the bed awaiting the weak, air-conditioned breeze. Kennerley chose this place because its owner is Australian and he can get *barang* food for dinner—*barang* being the Khmer word for "Frenchman" and, by default, all white-skinned foreigners, including Kiwis. After my head clears, I meet Kennerley downstairs in the bar where New Zealand and Australian flags are in evidence around the pool table. I pull up a stool and order a pint of lager.

Here in the relative privacy of the bar, Kennerley tries to explain the realities of working in Cambodia. He says everyone is on the take—police, military, military police, and ministry officials included. "It's rare to find an honest person," he says. "Money talks. It's part of the society, part of the norm. Sometimes, wildlife traders hire the police as escorts to get the goods to market."

His men are on secondment from either the Cambodian Military Police or the Ministry of Agriculture, Fisheries and Forests. WildAid supplements their regular government salary (of about $20 a month) with an extra $200 a month. Higher-ranking officers get more. Kennerley says that much of their regular salary goes as a kickback to their superiors and he suspects that the men give them a portion of their WildAid money as well. This is how things are done in Cambodia. He says he often doesn't tell the men where they're going in the morning until they are already under way. On sensitive missions, he collects their mobile phones.

"I'm pushing the men to do something they are uncomfortable doing," he says. "It must be difficult for them at times. I give them credit for what they do. But I also think I have informers, although I can't prove it."

In the past, he says, other members of Phnom Penh's sizable NGO (nongovernmental organization) community criticized WildAid as being too heavy-handed, although that criticism has now largely abated. The criticism was based on their methods of stopping the trade.

"It's controversial because it's enforcement," Kennerley says. "And if you go around arresting people, taking away their right to kill every single animal on the planet, of course people are going to be upset."

In addition to enforcement, Kennerley says it's important to give the poachers and smugglers alternatives when it comes to making a living. WildAid does this in several ways: by providing jobs, farmland, and training. Incarcerating the head of a family, he says, doesn't put food on the table.

"It's a tricky issue. We're the 'stick' and the alternatives we provide through the farming project is the 'carrot.' It's good cop/bad cop. We [the mobile unit] strictly do enforcement. We're here to apprehend them."

He chuckles and takes a deep drag on his cigarette.

"If I was only making fifteen dollars a month and had a lot of mouths to feed, and I could make a lot more money by cutting down a tree, I'd probably do that too. It's simple economics. It's survival . . . They can't see beyond the day's food. This is a country where parents arrange to sell their daughter's virginity for two hundred dollars. Do you really think they are going to care about a couple of bears? Think again. If I had the chance to make two hundred on the sale of a bear—more than a year's salary—to better the lives of my family, would I do it?

"Life is cheap here," he says, crushing his cigarette in the ashtray. "People are treated like dogs. They kill each other over the slightest thing . . . They're all smiles one minute and the next minute they change. You have to be careful to keep things from escalating."

NEXT MORNING, the team assembles at the trucks in the sting of the eight o'clock sun. Kennerley rides shotgun as we make our way back to Phnom Penh. It's a three-hour journey in what promises to be ninety-degree heat. We roll up the windows, turn up the AC, and soon the men doze to the Voice of America.

We pass dozens of pagodas, a couple of mosques, and a lone Christian church. There are countless parched rice paddies awaiting the coming monsoon. Buffalo graze on the bleached stubble in the fields and, where they can find it, wallow in the soupy mud by the side of the road. A pond of standing water is crowded with pink lotus. Above the fields are oil and coconut palms and the odd gum tree.

Depending on their means, a few people live in cinderblock houses built eight feet off the ground to avoid the yearly flood. Most live in bamboo and palm frond shacks built on stilts for the same reason. Underneath nearly every house, hammocks swing with children trying to beat the heat. Along the road, women hunch over charcoal fires.

Cambodia is a country of just over thirteen million people living in an area roughly the size of Oklahoma. It is one of the poorest nations on earth. The median age is nineteen and the life expectancy for men is fifty-five; women can hope to live to the ripe old age of sixty. The U.S. Central Intelligence Agency World Factbook is incredibly concise. It gives field operatives the quick and dirty on every country on the planet, provides useful and up-to-date statistics and data, plus a remarkable paragraph called "Background" that boils down the absolute fundamentals. The following are the four sentences that summarize the Kingdom of Cambodia:

> Following a five-year struggle, Communist Khmer Rouge forces captured Phnom Penh in 1975 and ordered the evacuation of all cities and towns; over 1 million displaced people died from execution or enforced hardships. A 1978 Vietnamese invasion drove the Khmer Rouge into the countryside and touched off almost 20 years of fighting. UN-sponsored elections in 1993 helped restore some semblance of normalcy as did the rapid diminishment of the Khmer Rouge in the mid-1990s. A coalition government, formed after national elections in 1998, brought renewed political stability and the surrender of the remaining Khmer Rouge forces in 1998.

WE PASS A lone billboard on a hill. Rather than pushing soft drinks or mobile phones, this advertisement features a painting of someone being hauled off to jail by military police for capturing a sad-looking sun bear. Regardless of literacy levels, the meaning is unmistakable. This message was brought to you by WildAid.

When asked about the role bears play in traditional Khmer culture, Hain Kim Chai, Kennerley's interpreter, says that Cambodians have a low opinion of bears. There are two kinds in his country, "big bear" (Asiatic black bear) and the more numerous "little bear" (sun bear). Simply put, Cambodians see all bears as stupid, cute, and sometimes dangerous beasts. He tells two common folktales of how easily the sun bear can be duped.

"If you are very quiet, you can sneak up on a bear that has found honey in a tree," Hain says. "The bear always closes his eyes when he reaches into the beehive to avoid the stinging bees. If you climb up behind him and scratch the tree like a bear, he will reach behind and hand you some honey because he thinks you're another bear."

The other men nod in agreement.

Hain tells a story of a man who owned a bear. The man liked his bear so much that he decided to live with it under a tree. He took the bear with him wherever he went and the bear loved him in return. One day, the bear saw his master sleeping under the tree. A fly landed on his master's nose and the bear wanted to shoo the fly away so his master would have a good sleep. The bear picked up a huge rock and crushed the fly, but also killed his master. This story is still commonly told to children.

"Bears are not clever, like the snake," he says, offering another folktale to prove it.

One day the most beautiful girl in the village went out to dig for bamboo roots. While she was digging, she saw a python moving toward her. Startled, she lost her digging stick down a hole. Afraid to return to the village without the bamboo roots, she prayed that if someone could get the stick for her, she would promise to love him. The python heard her prayer and went down the hole to fetch the stick. He returned the stick to the girl, then—looking to collect his reward—followed her to the village and into her bed. Problem was, she was already married. Later, when her husband saw that she was pregnant, he knew that it wasn't his child and grew very angry indeed. The woman ran down to the river to wash but her husband followed and cut open her stomach. All kinds of serpents came slithering out. This is the reason, they say, Cambodia has such a variety of snakes.

I'd like to see Disney take a run at that one.

"The rabbit is the smartest," Hain concludes. He explains that the rabbit is a kind of intermediary between the animal world and the world of man. "At night, the rabbit lives in the moon. Traditional Khmer culture forbids killing rabbits."

We pass legions of 70cc scooters, or "motos" in the vernacular. Some carry the driver along with a cargo of live hogs tied and flopped over the seat. Some have dozens of ducks, counterbalanced on either side, tied at the ankles and hung upside down mere inches above the road. Entire families can be seen on a single moto, the father clutching the handlebars, a small child on his lap, and a slightly bigger child standing on the running board between his knees. Mom rides sidesaddle behind with a baby cradled in her arms. Others ride packed tight, a dozen or more, in the back of a wagon towed by a slightly more powerful motorcycle.

The people wear the traditional Khmer red and white checkered scarves, made famous by the Khmer Rouge. Women wrap it around their head in a kind of turban; men wind it around their hips as a sarong—both sexes pull it across their face to act as a filter against the dust.

As in India, I am told that public displays of affection between the sexes are considered offensive in Cambodia. Instead, we see women and girls walking arm in arm and grown men riding motos side by side, holding hands.

NEAR PHNOM PENH, traffic slows to a crawl. In the flattering light of late afternoon, the city of one million people is a beautiful wreck of crumbling French colonial façades, gilded pagodas, and a few hopeful office blocks. Slums bookend stately walled villas, renovated apartments, and new grocery stores. The air is thick with dust, charcoal smoke, and the belching exhaust of countless two-stroke engines. Motos buzz between the chaos of cars and trucks as saffron monks stroll through it all with unhurried poise. Almost everyone is young.

The mobile unit stops in the center of the capital at Psar Toul Tom Poung, a.k.a. the Russian Market—so named for the Soviets who shopped there during the 1980s. Today, it is the most important market in the city, where Kennerley's wife and the wives of his men shop on an almost daily basis. The warren of stalls is stifling and rank with the smell of cardamom, body odor, ripening jackfruit, and meat. Young mothers sway in hammocks with their babies over great sides of fly-specked pork. Men gut and scale fish on the floor. Chickens, eels, and carrots are for sale, along with jeans, silk, and moto accessories. Kennerley's men find butchered, endangered turtles and confiscate the meat in green garbage bags. It won't go to waste; all confiscated wildlife is collected and sent to the wildlife rescue center where it is fed to other endangered animals. Kennerley finds that, thanks to regular spot checks and patrolling, the market is finally cleaning up its act. When he first started it was pretty much anything goes.

We end our tour at the display tables of trinkets and charms. Kennerley points out rows of carved elephant ivory (bangles and dice), fake tiger teeth (pig teeth), and genuine bear claws and incisors. All is kept under glass and the watchful, smiling eye of a gray-haired merchant. There are half a dozen other competing vendors selling similar wares. Kennerley explains that, for now, he is powerless to stop the open sale of these kinds of "value-added" wildlife products. Until the law changes, he is restricted to clamping down on those dealing in live animals and meat.

I finger through bear incisors. Some have a hole in the root to make it easy to use as an ornament or charm. There are dozens of teeth that once belonged to sun bears. One of the largest catches my eye. It likely came from a "big bear" (Asiatic black bear) and has been carved into a Buddha figurine.

"Buddhist people are supposed to protect the animals," Hain explains, wading into the obvious irony. "But they have no choice. People are poor."

IT IS NOT until several days later, as we push away from the bank and into the Piphot River, that it finally dawns on me how far I am from home. Koh Kong province in southwest Cambodia is known as a wild and unruly place. It is home to some of the poorest people in Cambodia and, until 1998, was the last stronghold of the Khmer Rouge. It also contains some of the world's best remaining sun bear habitat—and my best hope of seeing a sun bear in the wild.

The twelve-foot aluminum powerboat holds two of WildAid's uniformed MPs, my interpreter Hem Puthea, and me. Hem is a patient man with a sincere face and a delicate handshake. He impresses me with his professionalism and ability to turn out in spotless pants and shirt even in the most remote locations. The MPs carry sidearms and AK-47s. Perched at the bow is Sim Chean, a tough-looking captain in dark sunglasses and a smart blue beret. A former member of the Khmer Rouge, Sim now patrols this jungle full time for WildAid. His baby-faced comrade pilots the boat from the stern. He is skinny, barely out of his teens, and—at over six feet—is the tallest Cambodian I have yet seen. Hem and I sit sandwiched between, holding on to our hats.

This is a regular patrol in search of wildlife and precious tropical hardwood—both are being poached and transported out of the province. As the last village fades into the distance, the jungle grows thick from the banks to the tops of rolling hills, which, I'm informed, are actually the Southern Cardamom Mountains. Due in part to the work of WildAid, a logging moratorium was declared in this region back in 2001. Other than one or two huts on shore, there are few signs of human presence in the uninterrupted green.

In this jungle, the most serious threat to sun bears and other wildlife is the invasion of human beings, which has been facilitated by the completion of the road. Not only are newcomers hunting bears and other species to the edge of extinction, they are also chewing up habitat at an alarming rate. Desperately poor and largely illiterate, these newcomers practice destructive slash-and-burn agriculture techniques, and chop down yet more trees for charcoal. Bags of this jungle fuel are sold to villagers and can be seen piled up on the side of the road throughout the region. WildAid aims to disrupt and eventually end the wildlife trade, the hardwood trade, and creeping "land encroachment." All these activities are illegal, and I have come to witness the enforcement of the law.

A slim, open sampan has been spotted near the shore. Sim signals to his partner and our boat swings hard to starboard. An old man and two young boys drift in wait of our arrival. When we pull up abeam, Sim's smile turns sour and he tells the fishermen that he's coming aboard. The boys wear only shorts; the old man is missing an eye. Sim lifts floorboards and looks through bags and nets on the narrow, wooden craft. When he's convinced they have nothing of interest, he jumps back on our boat and shares a joke in Khmer with the old man. Everyone laughs but me and we continue on our way.

This scene repeats itself a half-dozen times. We discover no hidden bears or timber, only a few skinny fish. A few miles upstream, the river and shore seem completely pristine and primeval. Sun bears are uniquely adapted to lowland tropical hardwood forests. They are built to climb these trees to find fruit and to tear open trunks to extract insects, larvae, or honey. Their physical structure is unique among bears, and yet they are the least-known member of the bear family—both to science and to the general public. Almost nothing is known about how logging and deforestation affects them. Although I am well aware that the odds of seeing a sun bear in the wild are incalculably small, I relentlessly scan the shore. I am rewarded with a view of a big, black hornbill perched in a tree above the river.

I spot a thin trickle of smoke just around the bend. We make our way to the offending site and tie up to the trunk of a tree. Sim marches straight up a small path followed by the kid with the machine gun. We find an acre slashed and burned, the embers smoking still. There are no signs of shelter. Sim pulls out his GPS and notes our coordinates and then captures the destruction with a digital camera. Finding no one to charge, we return to the river.

The farther upstream we travel, the deeper my anxiety grows. Aside from Hem, I had only met these well-armed men a few moments before stepping onto the boat. They smile at me and point out wildlife along the river. I notice a recent and dangerous pattern in my judgment, weighing the risks and dangers of a given situation only after it is well under way.

We land near a small collection of palm frond huts and I am grateful for the promise of shade. This is the first encampment we have seen for miles. My companions clearly know their way around this site and we walk unannounced between the structures.

Hem explains that the people who live out here are the poorest of the poor. Many have a hard time finding enough to eat. We pass semiclothed and naked children who don't seem surprised to see us. A man in his thirties acknowledges our presence with a wary glance. Stripped to the waist, he chops at a huge, felled banana stalk with a machete and tosses the shreds to a nearby pig. A toddler, presumably his son, hugs the far end of the stalk and gets a kick out of the vibration. Sim asks a question in Khmer and the man points down the path with the machete.

We enter a clearing near the riverbank where a shack has been built of palm fronds and rough-hewn planks. Eight children, ranging in age from toddlers to late teens, are playing or squatting in the shade. One barefoot young man gets up and leads us across the clearing to three earthen kilns that are used for making charcoal. One is out of commission and we are here to destroy another. This last one will be left as a concession while the family finds some other way of making a living. By this time all the children have gathered around to observe the proceedings. While the faces of the younger ones are grimy, the adolescent girls appear remarkably well-groomed.

Back at the hut sits the matriarch of this clan. She says she's forty-two but looks much, much older. Her husband died a few years back, leaving her to provide for her family with only the help of her older boys. She sits on the plank floor and runs her hand over her smooth, gray hair, which is tied at the nape of her neck. As Sim explains again why the kilns are illegal, she stares into the middle distance.

The woman protests that she doesn't have food to feed her children. She owes rice to her neighbors and there is no way to pay them back except through the proceeds of the charcoal kilns. Sim has heard this all before. He pulls out some documents and presents them in a polite but official manner. She cannot read the papers herself so the details are read aloud. She must sign her name, promise to destroy the final kiln within thirty days, and never again make charcoal from this jungle. She pauses, staring. Then, with great concentration, she touches the ink pad with her thumb and slowly makes her mark.

As I stand there in my bright shirt, nervous sweat, and pale, February skin, I feel ashamed. I marvel at how far I am from home and just what it is I am doing in a jungle where armed men stand between the poor and their means of survival. What are we willing to do to protect wildlife? Just how far are we willing to go? I briefly consider what's in the balance: bears, tigers, and all the other creatures this jungle supports. But mostly, I think of the plight of this fellow human being, this mother.

Sim wants to make a more thorough search of the area. Hem and I wait near the widow's house, with her smiling, curious children. I ask what will become of this woman and her family. What will she do?

Hem says she fishes with her sons. There are other ways of making a living. They have chosen charcoal-making because it is the easiest thing to do. He says he is very sorry for this woman, and that, as a city boy, he feels like an outsider here. It is difficult work, he says, enforcing the wildlife and forestry laws. But someone has to do it. Hem explains that his own grandfather worked to protect Cambodia's forests back in the 1970s, before Pol Pot. And as we stand on the riverbank in the shade of coconut palms, watching the children play in the dappled light, he tells me what happened to him when he was a boy some thirty years ago.

"The young kids had guns and were told to kill their fathers and mothers," he says. "This was part of their training and education: only to do bad. My grandmother was scared because my grandfather was the chief of the Department of Forestry. They investigated and killed whole families. My grandmother thought that if she was still alive they would kill our family, so she [committed suicide] by hanging herself in a tree. They also got my uncle. I remember these bad times.

"The Khmer Rouge divided the people into two groups," he explains. "Those coming from Phnom Penh were called 'New People,' the ones living in the villages they called the 'Old People.' They wanted us to be like the Old People. They threw some of the little boys up in the air and stabbed them with bayonets. I saw that. I saw them kill whole families. It was 1975. They chased the Americans out and they chased a whole lot of people from the town. People with engineering or training. You see the movie *The Killing Fields*? Exactly. [Thumbs-up.] The real one.

"When the Khmer Rouge came with the jeep and the guns, they said to my mother, 'Your husband must go to retraining.' My mother wanted to stay with the baby, so my father was going to take me with him to the training school. One of the Khmer Rouge said I was not allowed to go with him, so they took me out of the jeep. And that was the last time I saw him. The Khmer Rouge lied to my father. He went to the meeting where they were shooting and chopping people with axes. In 1977 and 1978, I saw a lot of people killed. Every day they killed and sometimes I saw it. I hate them very much. We were happy when the Khmer Rouge was over . . ."

I stand with my back to the river and nothing left to say. No reference point from which to begin to understand.

"These are much better times for Cambodia," he says. "Development, and no war. It's good."

As if on cue, Sim, the former Khmer Rouge, returns from the clearing and I know I will never forget this day. We gather our gear and wish the people good luck. The widow is speechless, but her children laugh and play. As we push off and slip into the current, I look over my shoulder and see her sitting there with her cheek propped on the heel of her hand.

AFTER TRADING our patrol boat for a truck, I find myself returned to the river's edge. Here, the dirt road empties onto the loose deck of a waiting ferry. Out of the truck steps Hem Puthea, Delphine Van Roe, Oran Shapira, and me. It has been a long, hot day and we turn our back on the blood-orange sun. Compared to northern climes, night falls fast in the jungle. There is little time to linger or prepare for the darkness to come.

The ferry is composed of a couple of sampans lashed together under a deck of wooden planks. It is powered by an enormous old truck motor that has been bolted to the back with a prop at the end of the drive shaft. A wisp of a man steers the contraption with ease.

Delphine Van Roe, assistant to the WildAid country director, was born in Phnom Penh to a Cambodian mother and a father of Swiss extraction. Her family fled the advancing Khmer Rouge when she was a child. Educated in Europe, Van Roe speaks English, French, German, and more than a little Khmer. She has a delicate, dark complexion, raven hair, and big chestnut eyes. She could have modeled for Benetton. She alternates between aloofness and official friendliness as she describes her organization.

"I want to contribute to Cambodia," she says. "That's why I came back."

She announces straight away that there are things she wants to see improved—like more of a focus on human development. "WildAid used to be perceived as an extremist organization," she explains. "We were called neocolonialists—the ayatollahs of conservation. But an evolution has taken place in WildAid . . . In 2002, the government approached our director to help protect the Southern Cardamom Mountains." She believes WildAid is making a difference.

However, the new road has become a major problem. It facilitates the shipment of wildlife out of the forest and allows people to move in and damage the land. WildAid's focus is on enforcing the law and protecting the wildlife and habitat that remain. Its ultimate goal is to see the Southern Cardamom Mountains declared a national park and, together with a series of other national parks, form a 3.2-million-acre area of contiguous forest cover. Eventually, they hope it will become recognized as a World Heritage Site—which would bring international profile and added resources for protection. It is, she claims, the last big forest in Southeast Asia.

"Koh Kong is a lawless place," she says. "It's a center for trafficking and smuggling between Thailand and Cambodia. We end up going into an encroachment area and dismantling the houses of poor family farmers. They just end up building it over again. That's why we have to find alternatives and must explain why the farmer cannot rebuild. What we need is community outreach and education at all levels of society . . . The military is our major threat. They buy people off and pay them to hunt the wildlife. We are trying to work with them, trying to negotiate with them to make them change."

Van Roe recounts an incident last December when the

WildAid team caught some men in the jungle making resin for commercial use. They turned out to be military. The next day, they came back in force and assaulted the WildAid station. They roughed up an MP and stole some machine guns. WildAid reported the incident to the government and publicized it to anyone who would listen.

"We don't want our people to be under threat," Van Roe says. "The local people are scared and we are trying to build trust."

WE ARRIVE after dark in the village of Chi Phat and walk between rows of shacks along either side of the dirt road. We pass an open-air restaurant full of men cheering on the heroes of two different martial arts movies on competing TVs. The houses are in rough shape, little more than a roof and a couple of flimsy boards as shelter against the rain. Inside, girls nurse babies, women prepare meals, and old men in hammocks scratch themselves and yawn. They all take a good long look as we move farther into the darkness.

Shapira has arranged for us to stay in a guesthouse owned by the chief of police. It is a sturdy wooden structure with several bare rooms upstairs. Just as we settle in, the village generator shuts off, so we fumble around for candles instead. The karaoke, however, has only just begun. Somewhere out there, someone has a significant set of batteries.

Cambodians have a habit of illustrating how thick something is by grabbing their calf with both hands. I have seen this several times. Where North Americans would say, "It's as big as a breadbox" or hold their hands apart to show the length of a fish, Cambodians use their leg to illustrate width. This is especially telling on someone like twenty-eight-year-old Shapira, whose calves are nearly as big around as my thighs. Built like a wrestler, he is also thick through the neck, shoulders, and arms. Below prematurely gray hair, he has an intense but handsome face and glacier-blue eyes that dare me not to look away. As if the armed soldiers under his command weren't enough to secure his status as alpha male, he unconsciously presses his considerable physical advantage. His previous gig was as a soldier with the Israeli army's counterterrorism unit, and he leaves little doubt about who's in charge around here. He is unsure, however, of what to make of me.

The four of us sit on the balcony sharing stories by candlelight, piecing together the reality of living and working in this jungle. Shapira, who has been in Koh Kong for seven months, knows bears have been trafficked through this village. To prove it, he jumps up to fetch the man who owns this house. Five minutes later, he returns with a small, dark man hardly visible in the shadows. Shapira says this man knows a lot about bears and trafficking. Go on, he says. Ask him some questions. I say I would prefer to do this alone with Hem.

"Go on," Shapira says in his thick, Israeli accent. "It's no problem. Ask him."

"All right," I say at last. "How much is a bear worth in this village?"

Shapira waves his hand and stops Hem from translating. He shakes his head.

"I don't know how they do it in America, or Canada, or wherever," he says. "But here you do not ask such a direct question."

Clearly, he and Brian Kennerley come from different schools of interrogation. Fully convinced that he has unmasked me as a fraud, he looks around the room at Hem and Van Roe as I feel myself sinking into the floor. I suggest that we excuse the good chief of police and call it a night. I thank the man for his hospitality and time.

"I know there is trading," Shapira says, after the man leaves the room. "People don't want to give info. They're changing tactics. We are making their lives difficult, for sure. They use radios and all kinds of techniques to deliver the wildlife. They put wildlife in backpacks . . .

"The species we deal with mostly are muntjac and pangolin," he says, ranging around the room. "In the last seven months, I've had information on three tigers and one bear. Many times we will get false information that the trader will sell himself. So we will be in the wrong place . . . We never see the traders. You will never catch them." He spreads out on the opposite bench. "Traders never, never get their hands dirty with wildlife. They pull the strings, they make the connections. The same with the logging operators and managers. You will get the deputies but you will never get the traders, just the poor people working for them. Unless you catch him with something in his hands, there is nothing you can do."

And what of illegal logging? These trees are a critical part of the environment upon which sun bears and other animals depend.

"It is very much like the drug trade," he says. "They provide the villagers with chain saws and the villagers must pay with the wood they cut. The traders will give them food and other stuff in advance . . . These villagers get caught in a cycle that never ends. They always owe the trader so they just keep on cutting. They will never pay off the debt."

He says the only way to get at the traders is by making them lose money. So he and his men confiscate or burn the wood. As with the poachers, the first time he catches a logger he gives him a contract and explains the law. If he catches him again, he threatens an impossible $100 fine. The traders make a relative killing. Exotic, tropical hardwoods are in demand around the world as a status/luxury item. Secretly cut and smuggled out of the jungle, five cubic meters of second-class timber (half a cord) can go for over $1,200 in the capital.

"You must understand that these people are poor and that the law is new," Shapira says. "They pay the poor people to keep the animals or the wood at their house so the traders themselves won't get in trouble. You get the wood but not the owner of the wood. They are not stupid."

Faced with such a seemingly impossible task, why not simply pack up and go home?

He glances at Van Roe. "It's a good question," he admits with a smile. "It's a frustrating job. Law enforcement is not nice, especially when you are doing it to poor people. And some of these people have nothing. Absolutely nothing."

I tell him about the widow I saw on the river. He's all too familiar with the case.

"It's not easy . . . I mean if someone gets into a position where she has to borrow rice to feed her children?" He scratches his head. "So when I can, I try to tolerate, or advise that we should tolerate. It depends on the case, of course. There is a difference between a trader and a poor lady who has to borrow rice to feed her children . . . When I was in the military in Israel, I had to destroy houses," he says. "And here I am doing it again in Cambodia."

It must be surreal, I say, trying to save wildlife in a country dealing with the effects of genocide and thirty years of war.

"Especially when you are trying to enforce a forestry law on a widow with children who only have half a shirt," he says. "And she's crying at you and tugging on your arm and begging for mercy. It is very hard."

Shapira admits that it feels as if he's making some progress and he hopes to someday see ecotourism in the Southern Cardamom Mountains. Done properly, it can benefit the local population and give them a reason to protect the wildlife.

"The thing that frustrates me most is that I know without strong support from the government, we are only delaying," he says. "And that's a painful truth."

Van Roe, who tries to hold a more hopeful view, says goodnight and disappears down the hall.

Hem thinks we are missing the bigger picture. He reminds us of the catastrophe of the Pol Pot years to illustrate how far his country has come. That was the worst time imaginable. It's difficult for outsiders to understand. Then, remembering his audience, he says that, of course people have suffered in other countries—but at least it was at the hands of an outside enemy. Hitler didn't kill his own people, after all. He killed the Jews. Pol Pot—"Brother No. 1"—killed his own people and this was far worse.

Shapira sits up from his reclining position. He considers Hem with a mix of understanding and patience. "No," he says in a calm, assured tone. "There is no 'worse' in killing. Killing is killing."

On a bed of boards, I unroll a plastic mat and pull the mosquito net around me. Below our building, a pack of dogs is engaged in what sounds like mortal combat. I try to remember what it was that brought me to this jungle. In the off-key wail of Khmer Karaoke, the dream of seeing a wild sun bear succumbs to the fear that I am only chasing ghosts.

WELL BEFORE any hint of dawn, the village stirs to life. Roosters rouse the lazy to enjoy the coolest part of the day. Shapira and Hem have left to gather men and supplies. I wander downstairs and across the road where an old woman sits besides strips of cool green banana leaf and a glowing charcoal fire. She makes it known that this food is for sale and I hand over the thousand riels (twenty cents) requested. Inside the bundled banana leaf is sticky rice and cooked sweet banana.

Four men have been hired for this expedition to serve as both bodyguards and drivers. They mount motorbikes with AK-47s slung over their backs. We climb on behind—the now-familiar machine guns sandwiched in between. We head through the still morning air into the heart of Koh Kong on the remnants of an old logging road. The jungle has reclaimed much of the strip that, outside the village, seems to dwindle to little more than a path. The road weaves into darkening forest, a place where sun bears, tigers, elephants, and poachers are said to roam.

We ride across "bridges" that consist of little more than a few narrow planks placed across a ravine. The owners of these planks, who live in adjacent shacks, wave us through. Since this is the only way in or out of the jungle, they will collect their toll from us on the return trip.

Now and again the trail breaks out into a clear-cut, where commercial logging took place several years ago. We pass smoldering fields that have recently been cleared for planting, and the new houses of "land encroachers"—the awkward euphemism for poor migrants who move deep into the jungle. The group stops to take pictures and record the location. The exasperation on Van Roe's face is unmistakable and she wonders aloud how they'll ever stop the destruction.

Although the problem stubbornly persists, WildAid can chart some success. In 2001, WildAid recorded 401 cases of land encroachment. The following year, the number of cases was down to 147. Similarly, the number of fires recorded went from up to forty a month down to three or four. Shapira says he will return to this site another day, with his men, to confront whoever's responsible.

We stop for a lunch of rice, pork, and Israeli coffee spiced with native cardamom. The incessant wail of motorcycle engines is soon replaced by the distant call of gibbons. The jungle reveals its beauty in deep green shadows, placid pools, and the velvet teal and aquamarine wings of tropical butterflies.

Thirty hard miles in, we arrive at the village of Chay Araing. Where Chi Phat was gloomy and foreboding—a ragged way station at the end of the world—Chay Araing appears as a memory from another, better time. A time when the jungle was a garden well able to provide for the needs of its people.

Our base is a smart wooden house near the river where women are busy washing clothes. The home belongs to an acquaintance of Shapira, another acting chief of police, who is somewhere out in the jungle. We are welcomed by his wife and told to make ourselves at home in the shade below. In this, the hottest time of the day, there is little to do but rest.

A YOUNG ROOSTER is pulled from underfoot and butchered in the yard. We enjoy a dinner of fried chicken, fish, rice, green tomatoes, and papaya in the fading light. The buzz of cicadas reaches a crescendo, then suddenly falls silent as if someone had thrown a switch.

Word is sent throughout the small village that I am looking for information on bears. We are met with a polite silence. I try to imagine how this looks to them: Outsiders (including two white men) show up with four armed guards and immediately start asking questions about wildlife. It's a wonder they don't run us out of town.

Hem decides to strike out on his own and goes from house to house. At Van Roe's suggestion, he tells the people we're collecting traditional stories about animals for a children's book in hopes that this will seem less threatening. He returns with the promise that one of the elders will answer my questions in exchange for a bag of tobacco.

Soon, a shadow approaches our party. In candlelight, he appears darker than the other men, nearly black from decades in the tropical sun. His hair has gone gray but his eyes are still clear and bright. Mi Yam is seventy-seven and says that the bears of this jungle are well-known for their drunken behavior. Ordinarily gentle creatures, bears become violently drunk on termites. When a bear is drunk, it becomes crazed and every animal, including man, must take care to get out of its way. He tells the story of a fellow villager attacked by a drunken sun bear that jumped on the man and bit his face. The man luckily kept his eyes but lost skin from his cheeks. His nose was broken and torn. Ordinarily, bears are afraid of men.

He himself was attacked by a bear when he was twenty years old. He was out working in the forest and the bear snuck up from out of nowhere. He heard a whooping sound and turned around to see a bear running straight for him. He grabbed the lid from a pot to use as a shield, but tripped and fell. The bear slashed him, bit him on the hip, and then stood on his back and bit his buttocks. At this point, Mi Yam stands up and pulls down his shorts. A small battery-powered headlamp is hanging in the rafters above and someone switches it on for a closer look. He runs his index finger along a series of white scars and a quarter-sized gash where the flesh was ripped away. He invites us to do the same. He counts himself lucky and says only one in ten people survives such an encounter. His explanation for the attack? Extreme inebriation.

The area around this village is prime sun bear habitat. When he was young, Mi Yam would meet bears in the forest every day. Now, he says, there are maybe one or two left, which makes him sad. Bears, elephants, and tigers have all but disappeared because of the war, hunting, and logging. He admits that he killed his first bear when he was fifteen but is reluctant to say more because of all the wildlife people hanging around.

I offer two pouches of tobacco and thank him for his stories. He rolls a cigar with a leaf plucked from a nearby bush and inhales with satisfaction. As he walks away, the dancing ember fades into the night.

"In Cambodia, if you speak with an old man in the mountains, you can be sure he's telling you the truth," Hem says. "He's not lying. In the town, you can't tell if people are telling the truth or lying but here in the jungle, they keep the traditional culture and you can be sure what they say is true."

One by one, our team drifts off to sleep in hammocks under the shelter of the house or between nearby trees. The owner of this home, thirty-four-year-old Sim Sous, arrived almost unnoticed and has been sitting quietly by himself, listening. The acting chief of police is a slight man, even by Cambodian standards, yet he is frank and fearless.

"I saw a bear recently," he says. "About twenty kilometers from here."

He has nothing to gain by talking to me. He either senses that we are no threat to him, or simply doesn't care. He explains that he is a former poacher but has since left the trade because the animals became so scarce. In his relatively short career, he captured thirty-six elephants. He declines to say just how many bears and tigers he's killed. Now he works for an American NGO, Cat

Action Treasury, and walks the forest noting the presence and habits of animals. He signed a contract promising to stop poaching and hunt only snakes and wild peacocks for his family. In return for this pledge, and the regular information he provides, he receives a salary.

I wonder who else might be willing to pay for this information, but refrain from asking.

In the last four years, he claims to have seen hundreds of bears trafficked through this area. They are sold for their gallbladders, which fetch $700 in Phnom Penh. A live bear goes for a thousand. Tiger skin is worth $350 per kilo. China is the ultimate destination for most wildlife. These days, he rarely sees these large animals, only tracks, and new hunters are coming into the area from the adjacent province of Kompong Speu. Bears like to live high up in the trees where they make their homes and find honey, he says. Now that the big trees are disappearing, so are the bears.

He claims to have been a successful poacher; the proceeds of his work built this house. He often went hunting bears in the dark, using the battery-powered headlamp hung on the beam above—the very one I've been using to make notes.

In the distance, the thump and whine of karaoke cranks up for the night—even out here in the dark heart of the jungle. Hem's eyelids droop and his voice is getting hoarse. He has been translating for hours on end and it's beginning to wear him down. I find a mat upstairs under images of Buddha and delicate Cambodian beauties cut from magazines. There is a luminous poster of happy, cartoon people reaching toward a ballot box bathed in light—overt propaganda extolling the joys of democracy.

THERE ARE FEW more encouraging sights than a plowed and planted field waiting for the rain. All at once it speaks of industry, patience, and hope. Especially in a place like this.

A dirt road runs down the center of the huge tract of land in the new village of Sovanna Baitong. The jungle presses in at the fringes. Every few hundred yards or so is a tidy new one-room shack with a bright green vegetable plot out front. Behind these homes are the furrows of recently tilled earth. In the distance, the first tractor I have seen in Cambodia. Perhaps best of all, a redbrick schoolhouse is rising from a solid foundation. This is no refugee encampment; these people are putting down roots.

This community of sixty families was created from scratch by the residents themselves with the vision, help, and money of WildAid. Another fifty families are on their way and WildAid hopes to accommodate eight hundred people before year's end.

The people come from the surrounding jungle. They are former poachers, land encroachers, Khmer Rouge, or all of the above. They have little or no schooling; most cannot read or write. Their slash-and-burn farming style previously resulted in the destruction of one hectare of land per family, per year. After planting rice in the ashes of the trees, they would gather one or two harvests before moving to another part of the jungle to start the process all over again. Here, they have a settled life with access to clean water, rudimentary health care, and agricultural instruction. The school will be completed this year.

Yoav Staretz, an agricultural supervisor, gives Hem and me the grand tour. The gaunt twenty-eight-year-old Israeli is soft-spoken and deeply tanned from working in the sun. He towers meekly over us all. Although Staretz was born and raised on a kibbutz, this project is not based on that model. "The kibbutz didn't work in Israel," he says. "It doesn't work anywhere."

The people here will work together during harvest and planting time, but each family has its own plot roughly one hectare in size. After rice in the rainy season, the main crops are those that do not require much water: melons, cassava, and zucchini—which Staretz recently imported from Israel. No one had ever seen zucchini before. The people made soup from the leaves and declared the plant a rousing success. When they discovered that it also produced a tasty squash, they were over the moon.

"I want these people to be self-sufficient by next year," Staretz declares. "Some NGOs take a few people and make them millionaires. They give them a house, everything they need. They put so much money into a small number of people. Our idea is to find the cheapest way to make them sustainable. Once we get the project model, we can do it many times. We study our mistakes. We see what crops are suited to this place and what we can grow. After one year, the people must manage themselves; buying fertilizer, marketing, transporting the yield. And we have a micro credit scheme. We introduce them to companies to which they can sell their yield directly, not to a middleman." Here people get their yield and keep the profit. In the nearby village, the people live on someone else's land and get the equivalent of fifty cents a day for their labor.

We tramp across the soft earth to a humble shack near the edge of the forest. The family spots us coming and snaps into action. As we approach, I see the woman of the house rushing to make her children presentable. Some pull on shorts, others shirts—few have both top and bottom covered. The naked ones stand behind the others.

In the shade below I meet Kung Serot, surrounded by his large family. He is known simply as "Hunter" because of his success at his former trade. At fifty-four years of age, he is making a new start. He has never been to school. Before casting his lot with WildAid, he hunted deer, wild pig, and gibbon. He'd rather not talk about hunting bear, tiger, or elephants out of respect for WildAid, and because he still fears the penalties under the law for killing these species. He was also a land encroacher.

Before becoming a poacher in 1990, Kung spent twenty years as a soldier in various armies. In 1970, he fought for the U.S.-backed government of General Lon Nol in his offensive against the North Vietnamese. Five years later, he joined the Khmer

Rouge and spent three years fighting for Pol Pot. In 1978, he ended up with the army of the new Vietnamese-backed Cambodian regime. He stuck with them for a dozen years.

Kung holds a squirming baby boy who wears nothing more than a pig's tooth tied around his neck with fishing line. The boy clearly wants to get as far from me as possible. Kung's ropy arms are covered with intricate, blurred tattoos that date from his days with the Khmer Rouge. He says he got them for protection. If someone shoots him, he says, the bullets won't hurt and if he finds himself in a malaria-infested jungle, he will not fall sick. I ask him if it works. He says, "So far, so good."

Staretz confirms the prevalence of such beliefs among the people. In fact, a few days before my arrival, they held a ceremony. A pig's head was paraded through the farm—which, along with some chicken heads, was sacrificed to the gods to rid the place of evil.

Soun Theavy, Kung Serot's wife, is some twenty years his junior. She smiles but studiously avoids eye contact. With her left hand, she covers the stump where her right used to be. It was blown apart by unexploded ordnance twenty-five years ago. She says living here gives her freedom. Here, it is not illegal to farm, and when the school is built, her children will have a chance at an education—a chance she never had. She doesn't miss living in the jungle because life there was very hard. They lived alone and never had any company. Now they have neighbors, friends, and plenty of human interaction. She even has a chance to see motorcycles and trucks now and then.

I speak with other farmers who tell much the same story. Although they owe a debt to WildAid and choose their words with care, they seem genuinely grateful for the help. They show me their homes and gardens with an irrepressible pride. I try to imagine their initial reluctance when, yet again, someone is offering them a chance to partake in another social experiment. From French colonialists and missionaries to the communists and Khmer Rouge, someone always has a plan.

The people I spoke to do not care about habitat destruction or the fate of the sun bear, elephant, or tiger. They care only that they have a safe place to live, food in their stomachs, and a chance at a better life for themselves and their children. And this seems like more than they could have dared to dream only a few short months ago.

MY FINAL STOP before leaving the jungle of Koh Kong is the WildAid station near Chi Phat. Out front are piles of precious tropical hardwoods fading and warping in the sun. The wood is left as a warning to poachers of what will become of their contra-band and as proof that WildAid does not sell confiscated wood for profit.

A substantial building with room enough to house a dozen men, the station's porch holds powerful dirt bikes for speeding through the jungle—plus half a dozen portable Chinese band saws and heaps of old chain saws seized in the protection of the jungle. Inside, the place has the look of an old Vietnam-era mili-tary barracks from the pages of *Life* magazine. Tacked on the wall are the Cambodian flag and portraits of their majesties, King Norodom Sihanouk and Queen Norodom Monineath Sihanouk. Below, a couple of desks and a row of empty hammocks. In the cor-ner are wall maps, a radio, and a rack of Kalashnikovs—vintage specimens from China, Russia, and North Korea. The MPs and Ministry of Forests men under Shapira's command range in age from around eighteen to fifty. They have spent an enormous amount of time patrolling some of the best sun bear habitat re-maining in Southeast Asia. I ask if they have ever come across a sun bear roaming wild and free. Only one man raises his hand.

Their boss, Sim Chean, enters the room buttoning his shirt. He is glad to see me. He has changed into his best uniform and wonders if I want to take a picture. He leads me to the backroom to show me the evidence he has seized from poachers. The nets, snares, crossbows, and guns all seem antique, homemade—the spoils of an archaeological dig. He would like to show me more but he must travel to Phnom Penh to give evidence in court against the military for their recent assault on this station. As it turns out, he was the one who was beaten. If he's the least bit anxious about facing his attackers again, he doesn't let it show. After all, he's been in far tighter spots. In fact, after years of fighting for the Khmer Rouge, they threw him into prison. He spent a year in dark, solitary confinement before escaping to join the other side.

Sim wonders what kind of bears we have in North America and if they are in danger too. He says he is usually shy around foreigners but wants to make sure whoever reads this book understands that, despite all the problems, some Cambodians are trying hard to save the bears and other wildlife. They are doing the best they can.

"DRUNK ON TERMITES?" Matt Hunt exclaims. "Where'd you hear that one?"

Hot wind whips our exposed skin. We stand in the back of a flatbed truck, speeding along the parched road out of the capital. We pass oxcarts, old motos, and shiny new World Food Program SUVs. We're en route to the Phnom Tamau Wildlife Rescue Center with a load of food for the inmates. Hunt is one of two British animal husbandry specialists who have been hired by WildAid to oversee the operation.

"Bears eat fruit, berries, pretty much anything they come across," he says. "If a bear finds a nest of honey, it will become totally obsessed with it. I could see how people would see them as aggressive if they were protecting a source of honey. They will spend ages just going for it, right to the last drop." Plus there's the supreme aggravation of all those stinging bees. But drunk? He thinks not.

Hunt has been working at the rescue center for two years now. The locals love him; he's forever teasing and cracking jokes. The freckled twenty-seven-year-old has a roguish smile and speaks Khmer well enough to hold a conversation. I am impressed and tell him so.

Between us in the bed of the truck are piles of long green grass and vegetables, along with shrink-wrapped chicken from the local supermarket. The only live animal we have on board is a tiny muntjac deer traveling in the safety and shade of a cardboard box that once held a color TV. Its legs are as thin as breadsticks; it barely comes up to my knees. Rescued from poachers, it will spend some time in recovery before being released.

Hunt began his career working with bears in a zoo back in England. He first arrived in Cambodia as a volunteer with Free the Bears, an animal welfare NGO that aims to live up to its name. Free the Bears founder, Australian housewife Mary Robinson, has launched a worldwide effort to "protect, preserve, and enrich the lives of bears throughout the world." When his volunteer contract expired, he was offered full-time employment with WildAid.

"I always fancied working with sun bears in particular because they're like the little Jack Russell Terriers of the bear world," he says. "They have so much character to them."

While most of the bears that end up here are former pets of rich and powerful Cambodians, some were bound for restaurants. One little emaciated sun bear was found tied to a stick waiting to have his paws cut off. A few were brought to the rescue center by local people who saw them for sale in the markets. They know they shouldn't pay money for wildlife but say they can't stand seeing bears being mistreated so they buy them and bring them in. So far, only one rescued sun bear has been the victim of bile farming.

When I declare that I am excited—at long last—to be laying eyes on a real, live sun bear, Hunt has words of warning. "Even though most of the bears were pets, you can't trust them," he says. "No matter how good they are, I would be wary of getting in a cage with an adult bear." It's a thought that hadn't crossed my mind. "The youngsters play and have a good time but they're still strong and stubborn," he continues. "They don't always want to do what you want. And they can win, so respect that."

He refers to the pink scars on his leg below the hem of his shorts, just above the knee. The puncture wounds are similar, but over fifty years fresher, than the last ones I've seen. "This was from a youngster," he says. "We were building the enclosure and had them out playing. We were trying to dig a hole and she got down into it with us. She's usually docile as anything but I think she found a bone." He rolls his eyes, remembering.

"Believe me, you don't want to get bitten by a bear, even a sun bear," he says, to clear up any confusion. "They just grab hold. They're not like a cat that will bite and then let go. She just bit and chewed and her teeth just went further and further into the leg. It was fairly bloody and it got nicely infected. It sort of collapsed the muscle." Here he offers his other thigh for comparison and I can see what he means. "I forgave her," he says.

PHNOM TAMAU Zoological Gardens and Wildlife Rescue Center cares for over eight hundred animals of eighty-six species, over half of which are globally threatened. Owned by the Cambodian government and operated by WildAid, the former zoo has evolved from a sad menagerie of tropical animals into a last chance for some of Cambodia's troubled wildlife. The place has become an attraction for locals and tourists alike, and employs about fifty Cambodians full time, most of whom live at the center. Unfortunately, visitors are steering clear for fear of infection. Avian flu has been flaring up throughout Southeast Asia and has recently been found in some of the center's animals. The government has placed aviaries under quarantine and most people have decided to err on the side of caution.

We, however, unload the food and the frightened muntjac—which goes straight into an isolation pen to calm its shredded nerves. Matt takes me to a pen where black-faced pileated gibbons are kept; they go bonkers as soon as they see him. He invites me in to meet his favorite, a goofy-looking, wide-eyed specimen that is suspected of having Down's syndrome. It throws its arms around Hunt, who proceeds to tickle it until it laughs. That's right—an unmistakable, raspy laugh out of a broad, smiling face. I didn't even know it was possible.

We pass Asian wild dogs, crocodiles, mynah birds, and otters. Egrets and storks pick gingerly through the pond. Macaques and gibbons are eager to hold our fingers and get scratched behind the ears. We stop and greet the once-wild elephant that was rescued from Sihanoukville. He holds my arm and then sucks at my hair with his dexterous, inquisitive trunk. A baby elephant enjoys having its tongue stroked and I am to happy to oblige. Eventually, we stop in to see the tigers.

In Southeast Asia, tigers are at the top of the food chain. Unlike most of the northern hemisphere, where bears are the monarchs of the forest, here the sun bear must always watch its back. Hunt speculates that sun bears have even evolved a defense mechanism in the baggy skin around their shoulders and neck. If a tiger pounces and grabs hold, they are able to twist, turn, and (hopefully) escape.

There are several tigers at this facility, but we have come to check up on an adolescent male recovering from the bird flu. He was hand-raised by Hunt's boss and fellow Brit Nick Marx who, at fifty-three, is built like a Navy SEAL. The two men slip into the tiger's cage and I ask if I can join them. They exchange glances, shrug their shoulders, and I follow them in.

They get down on all fours and each in turn rubs his face against the tiger's muzzle in the preferred feline greeting. The cat issues a noise that I'm told is a purr but sounds like an outboard motor. Finally, the tiger makes its way over to me.

In Cambodia, as throughout their range, tigers have faced a precipitous population decline in recent years. Prized even more highly than bears for their value in traditional Chinese medicine, they are quickly disappearing from the jungle. The situation is so perilous that even these tigers must be protected by armed guards at night. No one knows how many tigers are left in Cambodia and any estimates that are offered are easily politicized. Marx does not profess to know but says there are "very, very few. I'd say perhaps less than fifty, spread out. Not a viable population over the long term."

I crouch down and the tiger comes right up to my face but does not present his whiskers to me. Instead, he bats my knee with a paw the size of a salad plate—claws retracted for now. As I look into his huge round pupils, feel his breath against my face, I hear a little voice coming from deep inside my lower brain stem, a voice in a language from so far back in the mists of evolutionary time I can hardly make out the words. But the body remembers; it knows to run.

"He's testing you," Marx declares.

How does one pass such an exam?

"Take off your hat," he cautions. "He doesn't like the look of it."

I remove my silly hat and the tiger bats my knee again, only this time a little harder. He is trying to get a rise of out of me. Then suddenly he walks around behind my back.

"*Oh,*" Marx declares. "No self-respecting tiger would walk around behind you and let you get away."

This observation does not comfort me. Suddenly, the tiger gently gnaws on my shoulder—then lets go. I slowly stand up and ask what to do. The tiger answers by grabbing my shirt in his teeth and giving it a good yank. I check my companion's faces, which have clouded with concern. Suddenly I've got that feeling again—that act first, think later regret that hits me once it is too late. Marx quickly moves between us. Foolishly, I ask what he would do if the tiger came at me again. Would he raise his voice, gently kick him in the ribs?

"Oh, I wouldn't do that," he says. "This cat is my friend and we have developed an incredible trust. I wouldn't want to do anything to change that."

Easily distracted by the shrink-wrapped chicken, the tiger follows Hunt into the corner and hunkers down to lunch. I slip outside the cage and into the company of the wide-eyed Cambodian staff who work with these cats every day. They tell me they would never, ever step into the cage as I've just done. The boys and young men gaze at me with awe, unsure whether I am incredibly brave, incredibly lucky, or both. The older men regard me warily as yet another reckless foreigner who, through astonishing ignorance, is a danger to himself and others.

THE SUN BEAR population at Phnom Tamau is twenty-nine and counting. Their enclosures are paid for by Free the Bears and staffed with volunteers. Here, rescued bears are fed and housed in a safe, clean facility while they become acclimated to close proximity with other members of their species. Eventually, they join one of three general populations, which are divided into males, females, and sub-adults. Some of the bears were purchased from their captors; some were stolen; others were "voluntarily donated" at gunpoint. At the moment, all are under the care of Free the Bears volunteer Nev Brodis.

Despite his fair complexion, Brodis is not afraid of the sun. Stripped to the waist, he pulls his long blond hair back into a ponytail. At twenty-three years of age, he's looking forward to a few adventures before settling down. He's recently arrived from Clyde, Scotland, to spend six months looking after these bears with the help of the Cambodian staff. This morning, he's busy trying to feed a new arrival inside the quarantine building. Aural, as he's known, is a big, aggressive 140-pound male who recently lost his paw in a snare. I poke my head around the corner for a look. When he sees me in the shadows, he roars, lunges at the bars, and strikes out with his nonexistent paw. The stump is pink and white but I'm told its healing nicely.

"I try and get him used to me," Brodis says. "We're slowly making progress. He's definitely showing less aggression than he did a month ago."

He unhooks the electric fence at the juvenile bears' enclosure. These bears are between two and three years old—three being past the retirement age from their brief careers as pets. While juvenile sun bears are playful and somewhat manageable, all that changes when they reach adolescence and starts throwing their weight around. Once we're inside, Brodis opens the cage and five young bears come bounding out into the open.

The bears pounce on the fruit scattered throughout the yard. They roll around at my feet and climb their jungle gym. The bear nearest me is about the size of a large bulldog. He picks up a lychee in his paws and rolls over on his back. He expertly palms it back and forth between hind and forepaws in a kind of game, then punctures the ripe fruit with the long claw of his index finger and dangles it down to his mouth.

I bend down and present my hand to a young male bear, who gives it a thoughtful sniff. I run my hand down his short, black fur and he doesn't seem to mind. He stretches his muzzle up toward my face. I gently blow into his nostrils and he scrutinizes my breath. Eventually, he rolls over on his back and scratches himself in the dirt. I reach out and touch the paw that he's holding up in the air. The palm is cool and soft; the naked skin remarkably like a human hand. He pauses for a moment—returning the touch—then rolls over and bounds away.

After half an hour amid tumbling, climbing, and wrestling cubs, I visit the adult sun bears. The males roam around their enclosure like beefy convicts—avoiding, confronting, or greeting each other as their social hierarchy dictates. In the wild, bears are solitary creatures, associating only for the purposes of mating and, in the case of females, to raise cubs. But bears are nothing if not adaptable. As they learn to tolerate each other's presence, they establish relationships that make living in a confined space possible. They become habituated to the presence of other bears, humans, or most anything else.

"I don't know if any of these bears will ever be released into the wild," says Brodis. He is skeptical that there is any place safe from poachers. "But in the meantime, it's a place to bring them."

It's also a good place for Cambodians to learn about their endangered species. Nearly 200,000 people visited the center in 2004. The hope is that young people who see the animals here will remember and perhaps be moved to preserve them and their habitat once they become adults.

Scientists believe that, after the giant panda, sun bears are the most likely to become extinct. Unlike the panda, with its worldwide profile, the sun bear is a relative unknown. In fact, it is feared they may disappear before the public knows enough to care or before science has had a chance to study them. How is it possible that such an incredible beast still exists in this world with so little known about its life, history, or behavior? Sun bears are already extinct in many parts of their former range. The lack of knowledge about sun bears, combined with increased poaching and habitat destruction, creates "an ominous situation," according to renowned bear biologist Christopher Servheen in his 1999 "Sun Bear Conservation Action Plan," Part of the IUCN's comprehensive *Bears: Status and Conservative Action Plan*. He warns that it is likely the species will disappear from many areas before its existence has even been documented.

It is approaching the hottest part of the day and most of the other refugees have wisely opted for shelter. But not this curious bear. A fine, muscular specimen, he sits down across from me on the other side of the fence. He sits on his backside and lets his belly relax, like a construction worker taking a break for coffee. His sleek black coat shines in the sun and his creamy chest patch spreads in a distinct U across his wide neck. His prodigious testes hang down nearly to the grass. He considers me for a while, then hides his face in his paws. He peeks out at me, then covers his face again. Tiring of this game, he yawns and his pink tongue comes sliding out and down to his knee. Finally, the bear reclines on his elbows and fixes me with an almost challenging gaze.

In the political disaster of the 1970s, the Cambodian people were turned out of their cities and towns and forced to survive in the jungle, the sun bear's natural habitat. Perhaps it was inevitable that these forest exiles would end up here, behind bars, near the capital of a nation consumed with forgetting.

Watching this beautiful bear, I can't help but think of cakes with files baked inside and other Hollywood jailbreak routines. I have the sudden and compelling urge to open the gate and run.

5

WAITING FOR WINTER
Manitoba, Canada

ONE STEP out of the Lazy Bear Lodge and the cold wind wants to shove me over. I stand my ground and cinch the hood of an impressive new parka. Clad in the latest high-tech fibers and the down of countless birds, I walk north along Kelsey Boulevard—the main drag of a town without a stoplight. At the end of the icy road loom the concrete towers of a granary, the most imposing structure in Churchill, Manitoba, Polar Bear Capital of the World.

A pair of Arctic foxes skulk across the windswept road; their fur the very definition of white. These catlike canines are found throughout the circumpolar world, usually near the coast, and are valued chiefly for their winter coat, which in summer can turn a less marketable gray-brown, chocolate, or bruised blue. They make a good portion of their living by following polar bears, scavenging leftovers out on the ice. One of them halts its trot to see if I have anything tasty to offer, then continues on its way.

I pass a few streets of single-family homes and businesses fronting Kelsey, but for the most part this town of eleven hundred souls is contained in rows of townhouses and low-rise apartment blocks that stand bravely against winds that blow across the surrounding tundra and in from Hudson Bay. Satellite dishes sprout from every building, gray ears cocked to the southern sky.

While waiting at the Winnipeg airport for my connecting flight north, I overheard an American woman say that visiting the polar bears of Churchill is definitely on the "list." By *list* she meant the world's peak wildlife-viewing experiences—like squatting among blue-footed boobies in the Galapagos Islands, walking with the elephants in Kenya, or sitting with the chimps at Gombe. Although this woman had done all this and more, she was looking forward to finally ticking the polar bear box. She is not alone.

Churchill is a mixed community of people of European descent, as well as Metis, Cree, Dene, and Inuit. Most locals move about in pickup trucks; it's mainly tourists who brave the ice and snow on foot. We shuffle between the gift shop (polar bear skin: $4,800)* and the Eskimo Museum, dressed in similarly thick, expensive garments. Living as I do in a mild, Pacific clime, I own no proper Arctic clothing. I was forced to borrow this parka from a friend. No ordinary coat, I am told that it retails for $800. I suppose it's revealing to admit that I have never owned a suit worth half as much, but there it is. It is an excellent parka, it keeps me warm, but I am afraid; afraid I will soil, snag, or somehow besmirch this garment. Mostly, I hope it won't give the wrong impression.

As I pass pedestrians on the frozen road, I catch a few words of German and French—and the unmistakable twang of Dixie. Recognizing that this is not the best way to meet the locals, I make a beeline for the Legion.

Social club of that disappearing species, the Canadian war veteran, branches of the Royal Canadian Legion can be found in most communities across the country. An estimable service

---

* Prices in Canada listed in Canadian dollars. At the time of writing, one Canadian dollar was worth approximately $.80 U.S.

organization for those who served their country, it is an institution undergoing a transformation. Now only a fraction of its members are vets. A cousin to the U.S. Veterans of Foreign Wars clubs, the Royal Canadian Legion has become a social hub for anyone who appreciates the virtues of cheap beer, meat draws, and the company of those attracted to same. Because I am not a member, the barmaid asks for volunteers—John Repay kindly signs me in.

Churchill's Legion is unnaturally clean. There are, of course, the requisite billiard and shuffleboard tables, dartboards, and video lottery terminals, but this place shines with a suspicious newness, like a movie set for "bar, circa 1978" that's still tacky to the touch. I order a bottle of beer and claim one of the many empty tables. Before I have a chance to remove the parka, I am invited over to Repay's table at the center of the room. This is where the action is.

"I saw you were going to sit by yourself," he says. "We don't let people do that here."

Repay, forty-four, and his friends extol the virtues of living in Churchill; the friendly people, the wilderness, the absence of big city pretensions. Many of the men around the table migrated up from large urban centers when jobs were plentiful, back when the military ran the show. Since the government pulled out thirty years ago, it's been tough finding steady work. Still, there's the railway, which links Churchill with the prairie provinces and their amber waves of grain. Churchillians take jobs with the granary, the port, the government, or part-time in tourism. They manage just fine.

Polar bears, I'm told, have always been a part of life in Churchill, Manitoba.

"They have as much right to be here as we do . . . Or more," says Repay. "I had my cabin broken into one time and the bear was still asleep inside when I arrived. We ended up scaring him more than he scared us," he says, smoothing his thinning hair.

"Some people get really upset with the bear damage, but you have to realize where you are."

Churchill is literally and figuratively at the end of the line in northern Manitoba. However, the price of alcohol is the same as in Winnipeg, Brandon, or any other city in the South. The provincial liquor board sets one price for the entire province. Consequently, a beer in the Churchill Legion costs about $2.50. A gallon of milk at the store, however, can set you back eight bucks.

One of Repay's friends, Manford Bussell, has worked for the Town of Churchill for the past twenty years. He has long, graying hair and a smile that invites company. He's lived thirty-nine of his forty-seven years in Churchill and has no plans to move. Recognizing the make of the parka hanging on the back of my chair, he guesses it cost at least $600. "Writing must pay well these days," he says.

Through his job with the municipality, Bussell has been getting gigs working in Churchill's emerging film "industry." Churchill and its environs have been used in a few feature films, including 2003's *Snow Walker*, based on a Farley Mowat short story, and a 1984 Timothy Hutton vehicle called *Iceman*. Bussell acts as a locations scout, cultural liaison, and general troubleshooter for production companies working out of Churchill. In all those years poking around the tundra, he's had his fair share of polar bear encounters—dating back to childhood.

"I remember my mother making egg salad sandwiches," he says. "The window was open and all of the sudden a bear stuck his head in to have a look. My mother had to smack him on the nose with a spoon."

But enough about bears. Although Churchill is internationally famous for its polar bears, he says there's plenty more to see, including beluga whales, caribou, and migratory birds. The six-week bear-viewing season has about reached the saturation point and he wishes people would pay more attention to the other attractions—especially whales—and help build a more diversified tourism industry. This opinion has earned him the sobriquet "Beluga Manny."

Across the table is the Resident Drunk, a tall, dark man who is also a civic booster, although he's not on the payroll. "Yeah," he says. "Fuck the polar bears. You should tell people to come up and see the whales." He's been offering witticisms since I sat down. When the nicotine itch overtakes him, he stands and makes an announcement for the benefit of everyone present—but especially Repay who, as it turns out, is the president of Churchill's Legion. "I hear you can go into a shop in Vancouver and buy your pot [marijuana] over the counter," he says, referring to my notoriously laidback hometown, a.k.a. Vansterdam.

"And you can't even have a cigarette in the Legion in Churchill." He shakes his head at this injustice, jabs a cigarette between his lips, and shuffles toward the door.

Another fiftysomething drinker with a faded, hard-rock haircut says that around here, you can still live cheaply, especially if you hang your hat just outside of town in "cottage country." He leases a chunk of Crown land for $75 a year, bought an old house for a loonie (one dollar), and hauled it out to his spread. He's not worrying about retirement savings plans as he lives "off the grid."

(Since we're on the topic of money, to the best of my knowledge, Canada is the only country that sports a polar bear on its currency. A "toonie," the two-dollar coin, features a handsome specimen.)

What about firewood? I ask. There aren't many trees around and the ones I've seen are little more than spindly, waist-high spruce. Although Churchill is situated on Arctic tundra, just eighteen miles south of town there are plenty of decent trees, they say, the same trees used to build the Lazy Bear Lodge. These forests fill the stoves of many of the homes and cabins in and around Churchill. The returning Resident Drunk concurs. "After I finish watching *Jerry Springer,* I can drive down and cut enough firewood for the entire winter before *Maury Povich* is on."

He wants it known that, although he supports tourism, he's not interested in encouraging more Americans to visit. "Do you know how many I've met over the past twenty-four years that I'd classify as human?" he asks. I'm sure I don't know. "Eight," he says, without missing a beat.

Bussell's eyebrows rise, just for a second, then he orders us all another round. Not all the tourists are American, he says, but some of them are ignorant and he has genuine concerns for their safety. "I live on the edge of town," he explains. "Once, when I was in my garage sharpening my chain saw, I saw tourists wandering around in the dark. I told them, 'You don't know what you're dealing with.'"

Bussell has developed a deep respect for polar bears. He was on the scene when the last person was mauled in Churchill back in 1983. A local man had been scavenging through the remains of a burned-out hotel and filled his pockets with meat from the freezer. The bear attacked from behind. The man was still alive when they found him, but died of his wounds in the hospital.

"It's just a matter of time until it happens again," he confidently predicts. "And next time, it will be a tourist."

DAWN PATROL, 7 A.M., and the sun is still a rumor. Natural Resource Officer Kurtis Kline, twenty-three, has graciously consented to let me ride shotgun on his first patrol this Halloween morning. He's a big, blond, apple-cheeked man who clearly loves his work. He's not too keen on the media relations aspect of his job, but is happy at least that I'm not toting a video camera.

The men who work for Manitoba Conservation on the Polar Bear Alert Program have to contend with all kinds of foolishness this time of the year. It starts as soon as the bears arrive in the summer and reaches a fever pitch around Halloween. It seems all the world has come to cover a story I have heard about only in passing.

Churchill is located directly on the migratory path of the

Western Hudson Bay polar bear population, which consists of approximately twelve hundred individuals (outnumbering the town's human residents by a hundred). They spend the winter and spring out on the ice pack, but are forced ashore in the summer to await the return of the ice. Generally, the males stay close to shore while pregnant females and mothers with cubs head farther south. By late summer, there are plenty of bears around. The Polar Bear Alert Program helps keep bears and people apart during bear season, usually July to December. If anyone sees a polar bear in town, they call the Bear Alert Hotline (675-BEAR) anytime, day or night. Six conservation officers live in the Bear House just up the street from the Lazy Bear Lodge and take rotating on-call and active duty shifts. Response time is three to six minutes. The men of the Polar Bear Patrol also coordinate the Halloween night operation, which is designed to secure the town's perimeter and ensure that no hungry polar bears are wandering the streets. This morning's recon is part of that stepped-up effort.

"You have to do it," Kline explains. "The kids are wandering around with big bags of sugar and bright, fancy costumes. If a kid gets taken by a bear, it's high times for no one, really."

Kline takes me past the nine traps they've set up around town to catch intruders. Made from sections of metal culvert, these bear traps on wheels are baited with fragrant seal meat and stationed at strategic locations. This morning, the traps are all vacant, which is a bit of a surprise. He says they are overdue for a capture.

Although this is only his second season in Churchill, Kline has already amassed considerable experience with polar bears, which he can compare and contrast with his black bear knowledge from southern Manitoba. Polar bears can be twice as large, he says, and their temperament is markedly different. Where black bears usually run away when confronted with a loud noise, polar bears often remain unfazed. In his opinion, polar bears can be far more aggressive. North American black bears (*Ursus americanus*) rarely attack humans. Although brown bears (*Ursus arctos*) attack people more often than polar bears, they generally maul their victims, then leave them alive as if to spread the word. Polar bears have been known to stalk and prey on humans. In the end, however, researchers say the style and severity of a bear attack is often the result of a complex set of circumstances and has more to do with environmental considerations and an individual bear's history than its species. (Witness Chhattisgarh's sloth bears.) But as in any physical confrontation, size matters.

"There is nothing cute and cuddly about a polar bear," Kline says, scanning the snow and bushes. "People want to pet them [captured bears] and I tell them they would lose a hand. A few of the bigger brutes bite the bars and can claw their way through quarter-inch steel plate."

Polar bears are also famous for their curiosity which—owing to their power and size—they are able to indulge with abandon. Because any unusual feature on the tundra might yield something good to eat, it is always worth investigating. Where black bears run away from vehicles, polar bears often approach. Same with buildings. "Black bears will only break into a cabin if they can smell food inside," Kline says. "Polar bears will break in just because they can. A polar bear will bust down the door, tear everything up, and then take out a wall."

If I'm ever confronted with a bluff charge from a polar bear, Kline offers this advice. "Make yourself look large, stand your ground, and make a lot of noise. As soon as you start to run that bear will be all over you. They're that quick."

The biggest member of the bear family and the world's largest land predator, adult male polar bears can reach eight feet, nine inches long and weigh between 770 and 1,500 pounds. Quick mental image: A large polar bear skin could cover a small car. Females are about half the size of males. Incredibly, most polar bear cubs are born weighing just over a pound. Polar bears are not the fastest bears, but can move across the snow at thirty-five mph, when motivated.

It is important to keep people and bears safe and separated, Kline explains, but not only for preservation of life and limb. Back in the old days (the 1970s), they'd shoot any polar bear that wandered into town. Now, polar bear viewing is one of the most important industries in Churchill, contributing between $6 million and $10 million to the economy each year. As an economic generator, it is surpassed only by the port and the regional health authority. Because locals live with three hundred to four hundred polar bears wandering past (or through) their community each fall, they are fairly "bear aware." Kline spends much of his time worrying about the fifteen thousand tourists who show up for polar bear season. While polar bears are found throughout the circumpolar world, during a six-week period every fall, Churchill offers the most accessible and reliable base for seeing them.

"Tourists are pretty ballsy. They'll go past the warning signs and go right out there on the rocks," he says, referring to the shore. "We can't pull them off. They don't think anything will happen to them." He has a hard time believing anyone could be so oblivious to the danger, particularly people who are otherwise so well-traveled and worldly.

"The best is when they recognize you in the bar," he says. "You tell them that you just rode in on a polar bear. You say, 'Yeah. It's just tied up outside if you want to come out for a ride . . .'" He shakes his head. "Jesus. The ignorance of some people. We shouldn't wind them up but we do sometimes. It gives us a bit of fun."

Kline is called away to another job and I'm passed off to Natural Resource Officer Syd McGregor, who is pleased to show me the dump. Before jumping into his truck, I prod the stiff Arctic fox in back—its eyes partly open and lips frozen in a snarl.

Once I'm inside, McGregor lights up a cigarette and considers me through the smoky haze. He tells me he's had more than a few media types on ride-alongs recently. They often end up disappointed because most of the bear action is at night. He just had a television crew yesterday and they came up empty-handed. There's usually some activity out at Churchill's city dump, however, so he ends up taking the media there to ensure they get a shot. Halloween is often the busiest day. While he tries to accommodate all media requests, public safety comes first.

When I ask if, in his opinion, the Halloween Patrol is effective at keeping bears at bay, McGregor claims his three-year-old son will be out in costume tonight. Spider-Man. I say this sounds like the ultimate vote of confidence.

"Last year came off without a hitch," he says. "It's more of a precautionary thing, really. Some people think there are over two hundred fifty bloodthirsty bears circling town waiting to grab a little trick-or-treater. But that's not the case at all."

As we approach the dump, I spot a polar bear mother and cub bounding between garbage piles away from the flash of what appears to be cameras. A loud crack is just a second behind, announcing a shotgun blast. McGregor's fellow conservation officers are busy chasing bears. The dump is full of good things to eat this time of year, due to the huge influx of tourists. The scent of partially consumed meals from hotels, restaurants, and tundra tours attracts bears throughout the region. There is a plan afoot to close the dump and open a recycling depot and waste transfer station. Conservation officers are ambivalent about whether or not this will be a change for the better. Some think the lack of frozen snacks at a convenient location will encourage the bears to continue up the coast; others think they will simply move into town for the fresh stuff.

A voice calls out over the radio and McGregor grabs the mike. A bear has been spotted back in town and it's making its way down the beach near the hospital/recreation center known as the Town Complex. This is not good. We fly through the dump and hit the road at high speed. I don't have the presence of mind to time us, but I'd say we cover the distance in well under six minutes. We slow down in town but move with purpose toward the last reported coordinates. We can't see the bear, just a short woman in a red snowsuit and a tall man with wild shaggy hair. A German television crew has beat us to the scene.

I spot the bear moving along the boulders parallel to the shore. Other than in zoos and the far-away glimpse at the dump, this is my first good look at a polar bear. I keep an eye on him as McGregor loads the twelve-gauge shotgun and kicks open the door. The bear pauses as if divining our intentions. Behind us, the Germans jog along with a video camera and a fuzzy boom mike.

"You're very lucky to get this kind of action on a ride-along," McGregor says, firing off a shot. "So far, you're the first person to get it this season."

As he loads and fires a second round of cracker shells, the Germans scramble to set up their shot. However, this bear will not wait around for a focus pull or color balance. It bounds away, rock to rock, giving shoulder checks now and again. Finally, after a cracker shell explodes in its general vicinity, the bear leaps into the water and paddles out into Hudson Bay.

The fugitive makes good progress. With slightly webbed toes and massive paws, polar bears are the champion swimmers of the bear family, easily earning their Latin name *Ursus maritimus*, or "sea bear." McGregor watches for a few minutes, then grabs a pistol and loads a "screamer." The Germans are a flurry of hair and tripod legs, setting up next to our truck. McGregor says hello, lets them get into position, then fires off the spiraling red flares out over the gray and gloomy sea.

"He's not swimming in the right direction," McGregor observes. "I need him to head farther up along the coast." The next screamer produces the desired course correction.

The cameraman steps back from the viewfinder and gives his

hair a flip. His partner pauses for a moment with her hands over her earphones, listening. Finally, she smiles and flashes a thumbs-up.

HALF AN HOUR LATER, I arrive at a Quonset hut fortress on the south side of town. The boys like to call it D-20, an old designator left over from its days as a military depot. As far as everyone else is concerned, it's known as the Polar Bear Jail. Inside, Kurtis Kline and his partners are busy anesthetizing three of the eighteen inmates. Outside, the place appears abandoned except for a Japanese television crew who've been waiting in the aching cold for nearly three hours. They got an early tip about the "Bear Lift" and need to get this shot. I opt to wait inside the heated truck.

Problem polar bears are incarcerated for up to thirty days and are fed only water and snow. This is not cruel and unusual punishment as they regularly go four months without a substantial meal at this time of year. In addition to their confinement, they get a lip tattoo and an ear tag for research identification and to keep track of repeat offenders. Over 80 percent of the polar bears in the Churchill area have been handled at least once by humans. In 2004, 151 polar bears were flown across the river by helicopter at a total cost of $114,000. This is the program's biggest expense. After that (and staffing costs) the next most costly item is Telezol, the drug used to anesthetize the bears, which costs $40 per vial. Last year, total expenses for the bear program came in at $265,000. Although a few bears find their way back to town or the dump, most get the message and stay between the North and Seal Rivers, waiting for the ice to form.

Three buses arrive and offload camera-toting tourists. Soon the crowd grows to sixty people. Everyone stands behind a yellow rope designed to give men and machines room to work. Half an hour later, Kline drives out on an ATV hauling what looks like a snowmobile trailer with a polar bear sprawled on top.

The conservation officers do this on a regular basis, but only when the place is full and they can make the most efficient use of helicopter time. Unfortunately, the jail is only half-full. Be that as it may, a second German television crew (let's call them Unit Two) needs the shot and they are willing to pay to have the bears flown out. Cost: $1,500. While this is but a pittance for the Germans, it's solid cash for the bear program. A classic win-win. I abandon the warmth of the truck and stake out some territory as close to the action as possible. Soon, I am politely asked to shift down to make way for the sponsors of today's event—who've just arrived in plush new three-quarter-length parkas.

Kline is busy helping lift one large and two medium polar bears onto the nets spread out on the ice. Because these bears have had an extra five weeks hunting seals out on Hudson Bay this year, they are in much better shape than usual. The giant male, perhaps twelve hundred pounds, is lying on his back with a forepaw in the air. When Kline turns his back to straighten the net, the massive paw begins to move, as if batting a fly away. One of his colleagues points out the offending claw, and an additional injection of anesthetic is administered. When the bear is well and truly down for the count, one of the conservation officers hoists a toddler from the crowd and carries him over to one of the smaller, sleepier specimens. He leans down and lets the kid get a close look at the immobilized bear. With a tiny, bare hand, the boy reaches out and touches the creamy fur for one thrilling moment before being whisked—wide-eyed and grinning—back to flashing cameras and his mother's outstretched arms.

Finally, two helicopters arrive and the men begin securing the line. One helicopter will transport the bears while the second contains yet another television crew who will get the angles from the air. Kline and associates make sure paws and snouts are not tangled in the nets and that the bears are positioned for a comfortable flight. Finally, the first helicopter lifts off and the bears ascend into the heavens, one by one, cradled in separate hammocks. The *whump, whump* of the blades drowns out the endless barrage of shutter releases as every lens turns in unison, following the furry payload across the sky. The increased windchill factor is impossible to estimate, but when the downdraft from the second helicopter is added in, I can feel my body begin to reject my nose and cheeks.

I escape to the truck and wait for a ride back to town. The others shuffle back into their buses and soon all is quiet again. Then, a good twenty minutes after the last sightseers depart, an old periwinkle bus pulls up and parks precisely where the bears were launched. A fresh group of tourists wander out for a look around, happily taking pictures of the silent metal building. Satisfied, they file back in and the bus rolls away.

As NIGHT FALLS on Churchill, a helicopter lifts off and slowly circles town. Below, a mobilization of men, women, and children. Emergency medical staff, firemen, Royal Canadian Mounted Police, Manitoba Conservation officers, Canadian Rangers, and Parks Canada personnel—they're all out on the street in trucks, vans, and SUVs, looking for danger. Down on the frozen ground, costumed kids go door to door, looking for treats.

Some Halloween Patrol volunteers creep slowly along their appointed rounds while others are stationed at specific hot-spot locations watching for any sign of movement. Kids roam in clusters and groups. Wherever anyone goes, the paparazzi are close behind.

I ride along in a big blue Suburban with Park Warden Melissa Gibbons, a woman in her early twenties who—with slight build and delicate features—at first might seem an unlikely candidate for long-term survival in this environment, let alone a career in wildlife management and enforcement. But this is the North, where first impressions hold dubious value. Gibbons works at Wapusk National Park, which is located twenty-eight miles south of Churchill. *Wapusk* is the Cree word for "white bear," and the park encompasses over 4,200 square miles of polar bear denning habitat. Gibbons has volunteered to let me tag along with her to-night as I play out my role in this twenty-fifth anniversary edition of Churchill's Halloween tradition.

We're supposed to be scanning for flashes of white fur in the dark, but I am distracted by the colorful trick-or-treaters caught in our headlight beams. Gibbons stops so I can jump out and ask some questions.

"We're not afraid of bears," announces a ten-year-old girl, who is disguised as an angel. Her younger sister is a cat. Or a mouse. "I know a kid who saw a bear while he was out trick-or-treating [a few years back], but no one freaked out. They're just like another dog, but bigger."

Up at the corner, a stationary fire truck keeps an eye on the proceedings. Inside, the guys are enjoying a large pizza and the odd can of beer. They will be spending four hours on this very spot and say they wouldn't miss it for the world.

Next block over, I see the German television crew (Unit One) setting up a shot with a couple of kids. They want the trick-or-treaters going from house to house on a small sled, but the kids don't feel like making the effort. The tall, long-haired guy jumps out from behind the tripod and slowly pulls the sled (off-camera, of course) as his partner gets the shot.

I find a mummy and witch with bags of high-fructose corn syrup. The mummy is distracted, trying to adjust his glasses with bandaged hands, but the witch is media savvy. This will be her second interview of the evening. She puts her hand on her hip and patiently answers the questions we all seem to be asking.

I stop the ambulance and speak with yet another volunteer who's giving up four hours of her night to keep Churchill polar bear–free. As a mother herself, she's especially keen to ensure this Halloween holds no surprises. In fact, she has a daughter out there making the rounds. Although tonight is quiet, she says that last year was a little scary because the patrol spotted five bears in and around town.

Wouldn't it be easier to call off Halloween, or at least move it all inside the spacious (and warmer) Town Complex?

"This is one night our kids get to be like all the other kids Down South," she says. "Besides, we've done it so long now, it would be hard to take it away from them."

Halloween marches on as Gibbons and I monitor the radio. It seems that the coast is clear.

We spot the Japanese in their rented SUV and twice more pass the German crew (Unit One). Because they are doing TV, they are highly conspicuous. I can't help but wonder how many other writers are out there keeping a low profile, getting a fresh angle on this story that apparently suffers little in the retelling.

Gibbons spots another Parks Canada vehicle and introduces me to Bob Reside, who's volunteering for his third Halloween patrol. He seems relaxed and in good spirits. When I ask how many times he's been interviewed today, he smiles and rolls his eyes. Most of the media interest comes from overseas, he says, and it's standard to have several Japanese television crews milling about, as well as Germans, Australians, and the BBC.

"We were attending the organizational meeting [for the Halloween Patrol] on Friday afternoon," he explains. "As soon as we walked in the room there was a camera in our face. This was an entire week before the event. They want to know all the players . . . Emergency medical services, RCMP, fire department—everyone was there. The people who've done this before were talking to each other like they would normally, and the new people were looking at the camera dumbstruck because they weren't sure what they were supposed to say or not supposed to say. Every year it happens. We get a lot of people coming through. The UK has sent people here for sixteen or twenty years now. A crew came in from Japan two years ago. They were going to do a [single] show—they ended up doing a miniseries and staying for over a year. Now there're back for more. Same company, but they thought they'd look at it from a different angle. The French and Italians were in the other night . . ." The media used to show up unprepared for the cold, he adds. Now they have premium boots, the latest high-tech garments, the best money can buy.

I nod, thank him and Gibbons, and wish them all a good night. I decide to walk the rest of the way back to the hotel.

It's only half past nine and already things are starting to wind down. Fewer and fewer kids are out braving the cold, the cheap candy, and the possibility of a sudden, violent death. I can see that most of the foreign correspondents are retiring to the warm glow of Gypsy's Café to compare notes over beer. I cinch up my hood and trudge back to the Lazy Bear Lodge, wondering what it would be like to have the budget for my very own Bear Lift and chase helicopter. At least I have the parka.

IF MEMORY SERVES, there is a ride at Disneyland where families can hop in a plastic boat and travel down a sluice built to resemble an African river. Charismatic megafauna jump out, broadcast recorded noises, and spew water with animatronic reliability. Even as a kid, all it did for me was whet my appetite for a real wildlife safari. Now, as our oversized school bus lurches across the tundra, I realize I'm living a childhood dream come true.

I'm traveling in what's known as a Tundra Buggy, a custom-built vehicle for conveying tourists along the polar bear route some eighteen miles east of Churchill. I count up to eight more of these white monstrosities in view at any given time; all slowly wending their way across the frozen landscape, pausing for good long looks at the bears. My forty fellow travelers and I see wild polar bears aplenty. Some doze in snowdrifts or amble through stunted willow twigs; others loll on their backs pawing the frigid air.

The vehicles themselves are feats of engineering. Easily the largest land-based passenger vehicle I've encountered (barring trains), they move across the tundra on huge, underinflated tires to minimize wear on the terrain. Built atop a fire engine chassis six feet off the ground (with windows another five feet up), they are tall enough to keep polar bears from reaching inside.

We stop and watch a full-grown male stride across a frozen pond, the fur of his paws flaring out like bell-bottom corduroys. He observes us out of the corner of his eye, then alters course in order to cut us off. As he walks straight up to our vehicle, there is a collective intake of breath from the passengers. Windows slide open, lenses are focused, and the polar bear sits back on his haunches. He looks left, then right down the length of the vehicle, surveying the faces staring back. He extends his snout in our direction and takes a good long whiff, deciphering what's onboard. Finally, he stands on hind legs, reaches up the side of the vehicle, and fixes his gaze on a woman leaning halfway out a window. They meet face to face in a moment of direct, interspecies connection. Finally, he lowers himself and the woman leans back inside with the stunned and grateful expression of someone who's just had a brush with celebrity.

Windows are closed as sandwiches, apples, coffee, and cookies are doled out inside the warmth of the vehicle. At the start of the tour, we were warned of the dire consequences if anyone dares feed the wildlife. The penalty, we were told, was a $15,000 fine. A bear accustomed to getting handouts from humans is headed for no end of trouble. This kind of bear poses a grave threat to people and will likely be destroyed. A fed bear, they say, is a dead bear.

After lunch, we see a mother and yearling cub, and watch a bear roll over on its back to writhe and scratch on the ice. We see a small bear face off with a much larger opponent and succeed in chasing him away. I shoot more film in the next two-hour stretch than at any other time in my life. I'm unsure what's come over me. Beyond the close proximity to these bears, it seems that our curiosity and fascination with them is—for the most part— reciprocated. And they are incredibly easy on the eyes: long, muscular neck and legs, Roman nose, massive paws, and relatively small ears. There is grace in their silent, swaying gait. Their creamy fur cloaks them in a kind of symmetry with their environment that seduces artists far beyond the circumpolar world. Their hair is actually translucent. It allows solar radiation to travel down the shafts where it is absorbed by their thick, black skin. Their shape is as pleasing as any form in nature. Even the filthy ones, the ones who've been sleeping on top of rotting seaweed or have been rummaging though the dump, cannot obscure their beauty. Perhaps that's what helped save them.

In 1973, the five countries that comprise the polar bear's range (Canada, Denmark, Norway, the USA, and the former USSR) met in Oslo, Norway, and signed the Agreement for the Conservation of Polar Bears. At the time, the main threat to the polar bear's survival was overhunting, and it is a credit to the signatory nations that a management plan was worked out to help keep the threat of hunting in check. Polar bears are still hunted throughout most of their range—primarily by indigenous peoples—and a system of quotas is in place. By and large, this has been a successful agreement and has helped ensure the survival of the species. In Manitoba, there is a complete ban on polar bear hunting.

Another threat to the health of the global polar bear population soon appeared—one that has not been so easy to address. Because polar bears are at the top of the Arctic food chain, their bodies concentrate many of the chemicals that waft up from the industrial South and contaminate this once pristine ecosystem. Scientists have been tracking increasing levels of pollutants in tissue samples of polar bears for years now. Dangerous levels of chlorinated hydrocarbons (like DDT), PCBs, and other contaminants show up in polar bear flesh, organs, and milk. This symptom—the contamination of polar bears—speaks to the larger, more troubling disease of industrial pollution that plagues the entire planet.

On the horizon, a mobile outpost comes into view. My home for the next five days, the Tundra Buggy Lodge is actually five white trailers on massive wheels hitched together at the edge of the bay. At this moment, it occupies the world's premiere spot for viewing polar bears. When we arrive, there are a half-dozen specimens wrestling in the snow. The "lodge" consists of two Pullman-style sleeping cars, a lounge car, a dining car, and a car for staff. With its oversized tires, satellite antenna, and stark surroundings, it looks like a mockup for a moon colony.

As our buggy backs up to "dock" with the mother ship, the woman next to me says she couldn't imagine staying out here overnight, let alone the better part of a week. She's already seen enough polar bears this afternoon to last a lifetime. I smile and wave good-bye as they secure the door and rumble across the tundra back toward the parking lot and—eventually—civilization. I stow my bags and take another thirty-six exposures.

Soon it's time for cocktails and a chance to get acquainted with the rest of the group, who arrived the day before. Among the fifteen guests aboard is an eighty-three-year-old shipping magnate from New York, a twenty-six-year-old IT professional from London, a radiologist from Montreal, a gentleman farmer from Texas, retired teachers from Ontario, a bureaucrat from Vienna—animal lovers one and all. Most are wealthy and some have made their way well through the "list." Wandering among the penguins in Antarctica seems to be a hit.

In the dining car, I end up sitting across from a newlywed couple from Madison, Wisconsin. Both nurses in their early thirties, they've saved for this experience and are wide-eyed with the wonder of it all. It's snowing outside and the sky is free of stars. Directly below our window, the orange glow of the spotlight reveals a hundred yards of tundra and three polar bears staring back at us, noses raised, working to decode the exotic aromas emanating from our direction. An Arctic fox and a pair of ermine flash through the ring of light and we toast our good fortune.

After dessert and a slide presentation, I retire to my bunk. Each bed compartment has its own reading light, a small window, and a curtain that can be drawn for privacy. I stretch out to scribble illegible things while outside two bears take turns sitting up on their haunches, peering in at me.

Small, terrier-sized carnivores that were recognizable as bears first appeared about twenty million years ago. Over time, they developed into much larger animals and ranged over different kinds of terrain. Polar bears are the newest bear species, evolutionarily speaking. Closely related to the brown bear (*Ursus arctos*), polar bears are thought to have evolved into a distinct species only 100,000 to 200,000 years ago, specifically to fill a previously unexploited ecological niche in the Arctic environment. Seals were able to haul out on pack ice and nurse their young in complete freedom—until a brown bear noticed them and decided to investigate. Scientists speculate that this took place somewhere along the coast of Siberia. The descendents of that bear came to depend on the seals and developed into the white bear we know today.

Like the innovative brown bears before them, Paleo-Eskimos left behind their familiar territory in Siberia and ventured out to the polar regions of North America about four thousand years ago. Once they determined how to exploit this new, unoccupied environment, they spread quickly from Alaska to Greenland—encountering polar bears all along the way. To these people, and later Dorset, Thule, and Inuit cultures, the polar bear was a creature of huge significance in their religious practices and ceremonies. The Inuit people hunted polar bears for clothing, bedding, and food, and a number of rituals and taboos about the hunting of bears (mostly to do with respecting a bear's spirit) endured to modern times. But the environment that first attracted and sustained both bears and humans is showings signs of rapid change.

As I watch these polar bears on the shore of Hudson Bay, some 2,200 miles away a gathering of the world's foremost climate and Arctic scientists is taking place in Reykjavik, Iceland. They've convened to finalize and deliver their Arctic Climate Impact

Assessment, which incorporates the work of over three hundred scientists and the world's top polar research centers. It was four and a half years in the making. Scientists concluded long ago that rising carbon dioxide levels from human activities are turning up the heat on the planet. But this group's findings are particularly bleak. Contrary to corporate disinformation campaigns and censored government environmental reports, climate change is an observable fact; a fact that has compelled 156 nations to commit to the Kyoto Protocol to limit the production of greenhouse gases. The United States, however, the world's biggest polluter, has turned its back on the agreement.

Arctic temperatures are rising twice as fast as the rest of the globe. Over the last half-century, the average winter temperatures in places like western Canada and Alaska have risen by five to seven degrees Fahrenheit. By century's end, temperatures are expected to continue to rise by at least as much again. There has already been a dramatic reduction in the Arctic Ocean's summer ice pack, which is 20 percent smaller than it was in the 1970s. It's expected to continue to decline at a precipitous rate with the most dire predictions showing the virtual disappearance of summer ice by the end of the century. This will have dramatic effects on animals throughout the Arctic ecosystem, including the Western Hudson Bay polar bears, loitering outside my window.

For polar bears, it's all about the ice. They prefer ice that forms fresh each year adjacent to land. Although they have been spotted as far north as latitude 88°, polar bears avoid the multiyear ice because this environment is far less productive for their favorite food, ringed seals—which they can smell up to forty miles away. Polar bears hunt seals where they congregate at the ice's edge, at breathing holes in the ice, and in snow-covered haul-out lairs where seals hide their pups. Why don't the Hudson Bay bears simply move farther north? Because the polar bears already there have no interest in sharing with southern refugees. Besides, they too will feel the heat. Scientists predict that by the end of the century, the changes in the north may be so profound that the entire species (currently estimated to be between 22,000 and 27,000) could vanish—along with the environment that shaped them.

It is too depressing to wonder how the end will come. Will there be a few stragglers left here at Polar Bear Point, waiting for the ice that never forms? Will they lie down on the warming tundra and starve? Or will they turn back on Churchill and make their last stand at the dump? Will someone read this after I'm gone and view it as some kind of small, sentimental sketch of what it was like to be near them? In Inuit legends, polar bears are actually people when inside their dens and only transform into bears when they don their hides to go out into the cold. Perhaps polar bears will have to leave their fur coats at home.

For over an hour, I watch polar bears watch me until finally the generator shuts off and the spotlight fades to black.

WATCHING POLAR BEAR bouts while enjoying a hot breakfast is a privilege I never considered possible. And yet here I am each morning, loading up on porridge and coffee as they go at each other like overgrown adolescents.

It's mostly adult and sub-adult males picking "fights" with their nearest neighbors. Keeping in mind that these are ordinarily solitary creatures, their playfulness—and restraint—is remarkable. It often goes like this: Bear #1, a large adult male, is lounging on the snow. Bear #2, a medium-to-large adult male, comes over to see if he can get a rise out of Bear #1. This procedure often starts with sizing up each other's teeth. They open their jaws as wide as possible, exposing the upper canines. This is often followed by squaring off, circling, and then one or both rising up on their hind legs. Once up, they shove each other with forepaws, not unlike schoolyard bullies. A bear hug often ensues in which one or both bears get a good lock on the loose skin of his opponent's neck. This dance usually lasts only a few seconds, then down they come to start all over again. Although plenty of opportunities arise for inflicting damage, this rarely takes place. More often than not, the bears fall together, exhausted, and rest side by side. Eventually, one will take a swat at the other in order to resurrect the game.

Each day we climb aboard our buggy to explore and take more photos. Our feet never touch the ground as we are perpetually in the elevated safety of the lodge or on the buggies. To be caught below on the tundra with a polar bear could mean a swift and violent death. Our only exposure to the environment is on secure viewing decks or through small, open windows. This lofty perspective soon seems natural.

On our way south, we pass a watchtower that was once used by the military. Now it is occupied by members of an environmental NGO. They're here to find out why polar bears, who haven't eaten for months, would spend their precious energy wrestling with one another. In the animal kingdom, play behavior between adult males is exceedingly rare, yet these bears congregate in groups of two to fourteen individuals and spend much of their time play fighting—and providing an irresistible attraction for tourists. Is it to establish social ranking so real fights can be avoided out on the ice when food and mates are at stake? Or is it a chance to hone skills in a low-risk situation that can be used with lethal force when needed? Volunteers are spending long hours in the towers, in tundra vehicles, and at the lodge to observe and record their findings. They hope to solve the mystery of adult male play, and see what effect our presence has on their behavior. In other words, they're watching us watch the bears.

In general, females keep their distance from the big males gathered up near the lodge. As we travel farther south, we get a better look at mothers with cubs. Polar bears mate out on the ice sometime between March and May, but females delay implantation of the fertilized embryo until late September or October. When pregnant, they make their way farther south to denning sites and give birth anytime from November to January. (Polar bears do not hibernate. Dens are only for maternity purposes.) Cubs stay with their mothers for about 2½ years for protection and in order to learn hunting and survival skills. As with other members of the bear family, it's thought that male polar bears kill cubs to bring females into estrus and to destroy the offspring of competitors.

We stop after having spotted a distant female and cub snuggling atop a drift. As we fine-focus on the pair with telephoto lenses, the mother gets up and leads the cub in our direction. The cub is no bigger than a golden retriever and is lurking behind its mother's haunches. As soon as she moves, the cub moves in her shadow. When she stops, the cub puts his mother between himself and our vehicle. Finally, the mother sits down directly beside us, as if introducing her cub to this curious find. Eventually, the cub ventures out from behind its mother and slowly, confidently, approaches to a barrage of flashing cameras. Its body movements belie the fact that it is torn between indulging its curiosity and returning to the protection of its mother. This dilemma is solved when the mother gets up and saunters away.

We encounter other mother-cub combinations, including a family group with two cubs almost as large as their mother. They rove around like a gang, confronting an adult male and ultimately chasing him away. One sow has a yearling cub and a nasty gash on her shoulder, which she spends much time rubbing in the snow. It's clear that she has been called upon to defend her cub. Above the bright red wound is a white leather collar with a plastic box which records detailed information for yet more interested observers.

The flow of days at the edge of Hudson Bay is punctuated by a series of distinct bear encounters. As the hunt for the perfect shot heats up among our group, we travel farther and farther afield looking for new bears in still more flattering light.

We get a visit from a polar bear mechanic. A curious sub-adult male, he proceeds straight up to our vehicle, ignores the occupants, and disappears under the chassis. We can hear him rooting around below, looking perhaps for oil, radiator fluid, or some other taste of the exotic. Finding little to his liking, he departs out the other side of the vehicle with grease marks on his shoulders and head.

Other bears stretch up the side of the buggies hoping, wishing they could only reach the small open windows. Back in 1982, when the tundra vehicles were smaller, this actually occurred. A photographer had the flesh ripped off his arm by an unseen bear when he stuck his elbow out the window to help steady his camera. From the vantage point of the bears, we must look like brightly colored seals popping our heads out glass air holes—albeit on a new ninety-degree plane. One such bear stands up and looks directly at me. When I stick my head out the window for a closer look, I feel (and hear) my friend's parka snag on the window frame. I wince, then get lost in the dark brown eyes staring back at me. We're no more than six feet apart. The unmistakable curiosity reminds me of a dog's hyperalert expression just before it cocks its head in thought.

One day, it appears as if the ice is firming up, the next it all blows away. Other than looking for sparring partners and nonexistent food, there isn't much for a bear to do but wait. Naps are common. As is scratching. Sometimes the latter is accomplished with a claw, but more often than not it is carried out on an unfortunate shrub. Females in particular seek out twiggy willows and drag their undercarriage low, back and forth across the unsuspecting bush.

Driven by hunger, a few bears have developed a taste for seaweed. One in particular is constantly seen on the beach pawing through the snow for this dark, rubbery snack. He even rolls around in it to spread the salty smell all over his fur. Polar bears are the most carnivorous of all the bear species. Their diet consists mainly of ringed seals, although they will also eat bearded seals, young walruses, narwhals, and belugas. When stranded on land, they browse kelp, grass, berries, and the odd dead whale.

Occasionally, they kill and eat each other. These bears also like the gray water runoff from the lodge. Although all other waste products are carefully collected and removed to the dump, the gray water drains off the dining car and into the tundra from a large, metal pipe. The coffee, shampoo, and dishwater soup is a popular attraction.

Each day, buggy loads of bear lovers arrive. They usually end up near the lodge in the afternoon when the resident bears are putting on their best show. There are sometimes four or five different buggies surrounding the same sparring pair, the bears seemingly oblivious to the hundreds of photos that will be taken of them over the course of a single day. These bears are almost constantly observed. When the (other) tourists are gone and even we are tucked into our bunks, a specially equipped "Polar Bear Cam" vehicle roams around collecting real-time polar bear photos and uploading them to a Web site. It's all a part of a network of images and information available to anyone who wants to subscribe. If only the sloth bear, the moon bear, the sun bear, and the spectacled bear had such a publicist.

Does all this attention help or hinder these polar bears? It has certainly made a difference for the Western Hudson Bay population, which were regularly shot as pests before the tourists started coming. Has it inspired direct action to help save the environment upon which polar bears depend? The creation of Wapusk National Park to protect polar bear denning sites would be one tangible example. But what about changes Down South? Will urbanites forgo their gas-guzzling SUVs in favor of public transit? Will voters stop electing politicians who are contemptuous of science and international cooperation? Will polar bear watchers take steps to change their lives or will this exclusive experience become just another anecdote for the cocktail circuit? The fact that we've burned so much jet fuel to visit the polar bear's environment itself poses a moral question. Allowing people to see polar bears in their natural habitat can be a powerful force in helping to protect them, but there is an underlying profit motive at work. There's an *industry* here. And this isn't necessarily a bad thing, as long as we clearly see it for what it is. Churchill's polar bears are prized as a natural "resource" over which scientists and tour operators compete for access—along with TV producers and writers wishing to sell their stories.

ON MY FINAL MORNING at the lodge, I walk through the sleeping cars to the rear observation deck before the day-trippers arrive. Half of our group is out in the buggy getting sunrise shots and the other half is in the dining car lingering over coffee. I have the place to myself.

For protection, the open platform consists of a metal floor, waist-high metal walls, plus a door that can be opened and closed during "docking" procedures. Below are four polar bears, including one very aggressive and confident adult male. He is thick and well-muscled; his coat is rich and white. Once my presence is generally known, one of the lesser specimens makes his way over for a look, but is summarily dismissed. In fact, all the other bears in the immediate vicinity are deemed too close and are chased away—along with any doubt about who's the boss. Suddenly, I have become a resource worth fighting for.

Ownership established, he circles back to me on the platform. Although I'm still over six feet off the ground and well-protected, my confidence begins to fail. The bear rises up on his hind legs and reaches all the way to the level of my boots. His claws clink against the metal as his paws spread out and up, trying to reach even farther. We look into each other's eyes and I become aware that his head is wider than my shoulders. He has a black scar just below his left eye and a small amount of bright red blood on his left ear—no doubt from a recent bout. Studying my scent, he inhales short breaths through his nose and mouth, exhaling in more audible snorts. He begins moving his head from side to side trying to find a seam in the metal.

I stare directly into his eyes and begin to speak. I ask what he thinks he's doing and gently taunt him with the fact that he can sniff all he wants but he won't be able to get me. The look of curiosity I've encountered in other bears is missing; it is replaced with frustration and determination. I recognize that I'm being viewed as prey. He begins banging on the side of the platform with both paws and the full weight of his upper body. I feel the floor shift below me and competing reactions from within. The first, the gift of instinct, encourages me to cower in the corner. The second is the unmistakable urge to reach out and touch his broad, black nose. The urge to *pet* the polar bear. And there, it seems to me, lies the absolute miracle of our species' survival.

I snap a few photos as he excitedly sniffs and snorts. Other bears gather around to watch. He shoves the wall again, and sways his head back and forth. Suddenly, I kick my side of the wall. Stunned, he drops on all fours and takes a few bounding leaps away. From the safety of fifteen yards and the company of his associates, he considers me anew.

RELUCTANTLY, we bid farewell to the lords of Polar Bear Point and find ourselves returned to Churchill's airport. With snow and wind buffeting the ground crew, I wonder about the wisdom of attempting flight. And yet I know that, up here, such weather is taken as a given. Surveying a few of the hundred or so travelers waiting in Churchill's one-room airport, I can see that I'm not alone in my apprehension.

Our group gathers in a corner, awaiting the signal to walk outside and across the tarmac. Having spent all our time either aboard the buggies or in the lodge together, this morning marks the first time in five days we've stood on solid ground. Over that time, we've become a kind of extended family born of shared experience.

Once we've all checked in, our guide gathers us near a stuffed polar bear encased in glass. The specimen stands on its hind legs affecting a menacing pose—in a faux, taxidermic kind of way. It is here we're told, in a hushed voice, that there was an "incident" involving a member of our group and a "spontaneous feeding" of wildlife. It seems that someone threw an apple core at a polar bear. As we have been told time and again, encouraging bears to associate with humans with food will ultimately cost a life—almost always that of the bear. This sort of activity can also cost the tour operator its license. If any of us has anything to report on the matter, or wants to come forward to claim responsibility, we should do so now, or anonymously at the hotel in Winnipeg. The incident was captured on video by a researcher and the footage will be used to help identify the offender.

We steal suspicious glances at one another, wondering who the idiot could be. It seems no one has any leads. I flash back on the memory of an earnest young woman marching purposefully through the lodge with a notebook and then wonder if I've made any careless mistakes. We are assured that the situation will be dealt with in due course. The ground crew cracks the door and waves us out into the great wide open. Hoods are donned as we hustle across the frozen ground, up the stairs, and into the south-bound plane.

BACK HOME, my subsequent investigation into the apple-core incident is beset by roadblocks. First, no one seems to be following up. There is a rumor that said apple core might have actually been a snowball (a less important infraction). As the weeks and months go by, no one seems to care. Fair enough. But for some reason, I can't let it go.

While I was in Churchill, I heard that they once pulled an old lady off a buggy for feeding a bear. She was flown out on helicopter at her own expense. I want to determine if such diligence is the rule. I decide to follow up with the researcher who purportedly had the video footage of the alleged incident. Perhaps she will be able to put the matter to rest. After a series of phone messages left unanswered, my curiosity deepens.

When her phone line is finally disconnected, I try other means of tracking her down. It is then I discover the startling truth: Less than two weeks after I departed Churchill, this young woman became the first person attacked by a polar bear in the region in over twenty years. Official reports in the *Winnipeg Free Press* and the *Hudson Bay Post* say that she was knocked to the ground by a juvenile polar bear as she walked from a helicopter to the lodge. Thanks to the quick thinking of her companions, she escaped with only a minor shoulder injury and was back at work the following day. Through the well-established Churchill grapevine, she lets it be known that she isn't interested in reliving the story for me or any other member of the international press corps, and no one else is willing to talk. It seems the polar bear community is circling the buggies. Glad that the incident resulted in no lasting physical harm, I let the matter rest.

Still. If only I'd placed a wager with Beluga Manny back when he confidently predicted that the next victim would be a tourist. The odds were with him, of course. Although she wasn't a tourist, she certainly wasn't a local. Perhaps bear researchers deserve their own category. Better yet, I wonder what kind of spread the boys at the Legion would offer on writers.

6

A SHEPHERD'S TALE
Lazio & Abruzzo, Italy

THE CROWD SWELLS up the well-worn steps and out through a passageway once known as a *vomitorium*. Gathered in clusters on the stadium's lower tier, we lean in close to our guide. Over her shoulder are the redbrick ruins of the Flavian Amphitheater, a soaring structure that once held 45,000 spectators. This most imposing of Roman antiquities is strangely modern and familiar. Nearly two thousand years after its construction, it is still the foundation of stadium design. In the center is a maze of passageways and cells formerly concealed under the arena's sand-covered floor—*arena* being the Latin word for sand, sand being the medium used to absorb the endless flow of blood.

The facts and legends surrounding the human drama that took place here during the days of the Roman Empire scarcely need retelling. The festivals of violence, the glorious death of countless gladiators, the fortunes won and lost are well documented and widely known. I am not here to wonder about the improbable rise of a clever and fearless slave who became the most famous celebrity of his time, nor have I come to dwell on the martyrdom of Christians. I am here to take a good long look at the site of history's most notorious mass slaughter of wildlife solely for the purpose of entertainment.

Untold thousands of animals—crocodiles, elephants, giraffes, lions, boars, stags, and ostriches—were transported here to die for the amusement of the crowds. The human carnage, while endlessly fascinating to the citizens of Rome, was in the end too expensive to fulfill the demand. As far as sheer numbers of lives are concerned, animals paid the highest price in Roman arenas and circuses. Especially in the Flavian Amphitheater, which the Venerable Bede rechristened the *Colosseum* in AD 730.

The weather is bad. Rain spits from a lowering sky. Amid the throngs outside, costumed "gladiators" brandish swords and pose for souvenir photos. Inside, the dim ruins are abloom with brightly colored tourists and the sparkle of camera flash. None of this manages to diminish the experience.

Because of the tendency of modern and imperial historians to inflate numbers for reasons of shock or pride, it is impossible to know with any certainty how many animals met their fate here. However, it is believed that nine thousand were slaughtered for the amphitheater's dedication in AD 80; eleven thousand were killed in Trajan's games of AD 108–109; and three thousand more died in AD 281 during Probus's games. While most people are familiar with the fact that lions were used in Roman spectacles, fewer know that bears were among the most popular "man-eating" beasts to appear in the Colosseum. Their images are preserved in graffiti, frescoes, and reliefs from the time. Countless bears were collected throughout the empire by special troops of the Roman army, known as "hunters," who were skilled at capturing animals alive. These men spent their careers roaming all over Europe and the Middle East in search of wildlife for use in the Colosseum and other imperial amphitheaters. Special corporations were set up for the transportation and distribution of wildlife. Mosaic advertisements for businesses specializing in the trade can still be found in the Roman port of Ostia.

A great many animals died en route to the Colosseum or due to heat exhaustion while simply waiting their turn in the arena. The corpses of bears would be thrown into the street where, according to the Roman mason Habinnas, "The common people, having no other meat to feed on, and forced by their rude poverty to find any new meat and cheap feasts, would come forth and fill their bellies with the flesh of bears." Bears that survived capture and transport would find themselves held starving in dark cages below the arena where the footfalls of men, the smell of other dangerous beasts, and the roar of the crowd could be heard overhead. Finally, the cage would be brought into position below a trap door, which would suddenly spring open to the sky. If unwilling to move through the passageway, the bear would be prodded out into the light. There, enraged or confused, it would face the disorienting jeer of thousands, and the attack of armed *bestiarii*—highly trained men who specialized in fighting animals. Other times, it would be set loose to maul a common criminal.

One of the problems with featuring bears in the arena was that, if given the chance, bears prefer to avoid confronting humans. Ingenious Roman entertainers overcame this challenge by specially training them to chase people, and by starving them before an event. Whips and fire would be used to urge them to attack, but this wasn't always reliable, as even the most fearsome beasts would often become disoriented and cower.

Emperor Claudius was said to delight in watching not only men kill each other, but also in seeing animals kill and dismember people. He drew the line, however, at consumption. The sight of animals eating human flesh—even though a crowd pleaser—was deemed unworthy of Roman eyes. Commodus, son and successor of Marcus Aurelius, disgusted both his contemporaries and posterity by "hunting" in the arena from a specially constructed platform located well out of harm's way. From this comfortable perch he speared hundreds of bears. Before the Romans were through, elephants, lions, tigers, and hippopotami had all been routed from their natural habitats across the known world.

The meat of beasts slain in the arena also made its way to the finer tables of Rome. This became fodder for a challenge by the early Christian theologian and apologist Tertullian of indirect cannibalism on the part of Romans who ate arena meat. "[What of] those who dine on the flesh of wild animals from the arena, keen on the meat of boar or stag. That boar in his battle has wiped the blood off him whose blood he drew; that stag has swallowed in the blood of a gladiator. The bellies of the very bears are sought, full of raw and undigested human flesh." This was Tertullian's comeback for the assertion that the Christian Eucharist was itself ritualized cannibalism.

The bloodbath didn't end until AD 524. Soon after, the arena fell into disuse and was eventually stripped of its marble to build the ostentatious cathedrals of the new Holy Roman Empire. Throughout the rise and fall of subsequent regimes, however, the Colosseum endured as one of the world's most famous tourist attractions.

After a brief reprieve, the rain falls again on our multiethnic group, releasing the scent of sweat, perfume, nicotine, and hair products. We begin to drift and scatter. As a parting thought, our tour guide announces that archeologists are still picking bear teeth (and that of other animals) out of the bowels of the arena below where, as it happens, a thin black cat prowls among the damp weeds, engaged in mortal combat with a mouse.

FORTY-TWO LEAGUES (126 miles) from the Roman Colosseum, I sit down to lunch with Mario Posillico in the picturesque village of Villetta Barrea in Abruzzo National Park. The cavernous dining room, which has little to recommend itself by way of ambiance, is designed to accommodate tourists in season, which is still two months away. We would have had the place to ourselves, if not for the busload of boisterous schoolkids who seem to have timed their arrival with ours. Surprisingly, my host recommends this place. Although my blood sugar level plunged hours ago and I can hardly remember breakfast, I keep my expectations in check.

Posillico and I have been corresponding for months. A forty-year-old doctor of natural sciences, his dissertation at the University of Naples was on *Ursus arctos marsicanus*, the Marsican brown bear. A subspecies of the European brown bear, the Marsican brown bear's last stronghold is Abruzzo National Park, Italy's first and most famous national park. In Roman times, the bears from Marsica—as this part of the central Apennines was known—offered some of the closest, freshest, and least expensive bears for the spectacles in Rome.

Posillico works as a biologist on contract with the Ministry of Forests, which works in concert with Abruzzo National Park. One of only five bear biologists in Italy, he has been directly involved in the recent brown bear work in Abruzzo. He is a genial man with a round, trustworthy face. He is intrigued that anyone outside the country has heard of or is interested in the fate of Italy's native bear.

He orders an array of regional dishes along with a jug of red wine. When the first pasta course arrives—handmade gnocchi—he explains that it is flavored with orapi, a native herb that is a favorite of both bears and humans. The people have always shared the resources of the region with bears, he says, and orapi is an excellent example. A kind of wild spinach native to Abruzzo, it tastes of artichoke and nettles. By the time the second pasta course arrives—ravioli with local ricotta served in a tomato sauce—I no longer notice the children shouting at the adjacent tables.

At one time, brown bears (*Ursus arctos*) ranged throughout much of the northern hemisphere. Today, they exist in isolated pockets in Western and Central Europe, the Middle East, Asia, and across large tracts of Northern Europe from Scandinavia to the far reaches of Siberia. New World brown bears are now confined to Western Canada and Alaska, and in remnant populations in Montana, Wyoming, Idaho, and Washington State. In North America, *Ursus arctos* is represented by two subspecies: *Ursus arctos horribilis*, which is commonly known as the grizzly; and *Ursus arctos middendorffi*, the Kodiak brown bear, which lives on Kodiak, Afognak, and a few other islands in southcentral Alaska.

Ursus arctos is the most widely distributed bear species. While stable in some regions, its population status is unknown in many jurisdictions, or is believed to be in decline. The biggest threat to its continued survival is the ongoing loss of habitat and poaching. The Marsican brown bear is in the final stages of this unrelenting pressure.

Before traveling to Europe, I had read official estimates—published by Abruzzo National Park—that reported between seventy and one hundred bears remaining in this genetically isolated population. Perhaps five more brown bears are thought to exist in Trentino in northern Italy. Numbers are important. When it comes to bears, I was under the impression that the number sixty was the minimum threshold from which a population is thought to be able to recover. Maybe the numbers have improved slightly, I say. Is there a chance there could be more than a hundred?

Posillico shakes his head. "There are only thirty bears left," he says. "Hopefully." He apologizes for having to deliver the bad news. Sadly, he doesn't hold out much hope that the Marsican bear will survive.

This isn't going the way I had planned. I had envisioned a good news story of a wily and tenacious bear population, small but secure in their habitat near the heart of the old Roman Empire. I had it all figured out.

"So you're a realist," I say, "not an idealist."

Posillico smiles politely and tells me he learned his English in Australia. There, he not only got a grip on the language, but also developed an admiration for Australians' "direct way of speaking." Here in Italy, people don't speak directly, he says. The Australian method better suits his character.

The waiter delivers the third pasta course. Fettuccini with wild Abruzzo mushrooms. Although it too is excellent, my appetite is on the wane.

"I hope the bears survive," he says, "but there are many challenges. At a minimum, two point five bears are expected to die every year. This represents between eight and ten percent of their population. No one really knows their rate of reproduction . . . My personal feeling is that the animals always surprise us. For example, after World War II, there were just twenty or thirty Abruzzo chamois left; today there are almost six hundred fifty in Abruzzo National Park. We sent some to other parks for a reintroduction program. So, in a relatively short time, the population recovered."

Now he's starting to sound like an idealist.

"Obviously, the brown bear has no such reproductive rate, totally different habitat use patterns, and so on. But genetically, it is possible that they can recover," Posillico says, dismissing my earlier assumptions. "Consider the case of the Kodiak brown bear. The Kodiak brown bear population has less genetic variability than the Marsican population. But there are an estimated three thousand Kodiak brown bears, not thirty. That is the main point. The Marsican brown bear is in an emergency situation—probably worse than it has have ever been. But at least there are no genetic reasons telling us that they are not able to mount a rebound. This is a good point in itself.

"Everything the bear does surprises me," he says, topping off my glass of wine. "This work has given me the opportunity to see the mountains through their eyes. I try to get into their thoughts . . . I've seen the bears. Not so often, but I've seen them. I just move behind them, discovering the signs of their presence, the way they use their food, the way they move. It's really impressive."

The main course arrives. Pan-fried lake trout cooked in white wine—the village's signature dish. I have suddenly and inexplicably run out of questions—except what could possibly keep him motivated when the prospects look so bleak.

"I've always been fond of the mountains since I was a boy," Posillico says. "And these were my first mountains, so I have a deep sense of love for this place. It's an emotional attachment."

He is not alone. The people who remain in these Apennine villages do so for tradition, quality of life, and a chance to live closer to "nature." In Western Europe, virtually all the landscape has been touched by human hands. Over the rise and fall of civilizations, nature has been molded and remolded to suit human needs. Since before recorded time, shepherds have grazed their flocks in these mountains and, consequently, bears have developed a taste for sheep. But over the course of just one or two generations, this way of life has all but disappeared from the Apennines, removing a significant food source for bears. In addition, bears have long made use of orchards and cultivated fields—an even more important food source. Unfortunately, now that agriculture in the high mountain passes has become economically unattractive, fewer and fewer acres are under cultivation.

These mountains have always been famous for cheese, Posillico says, some of which we've just enjoyed. Local shepherds, whose goats and sheep produce the milk, know these mountains intimately and have always had the most direct contact with bears.

He dispatches a cup of espresso in one smooth move. "Perhaps you'd like to meet some?"

As the world's first national park (Yellowstone) was being established in the Territory of Wyoming in 1872, a small royal hunting reserve was set aside in the central Apennines to protect two increasingly rare species, the Abruzzo chamois and the Marsican brown bear. Bears were considered the property of the king, and any damage they caused to livestock or crops would be compensated by the royal house. Fortunately for the bears, the king never found time to hunt. Fifty years later, in 1922, Italy's first national park was established on the land and the park soon expanded to cover 75,000 acres.

It wasn't long before the park fell on hard times. During the fascist regime and postwar period, it endured a prolonged period of neglect. When economic prosperity finally returned in the 1960s, a rash of private construction took place—including homes, villas, roads, and ski slopes—until 10 percent of the park was lost to development. Although the park grew again in the 1970s to 100,000 acres, the following decade is remembered as a period of conflict with hunters and developers. Another 10,000 acres were added in 1990, and for a time, the park enjoyed a reputation throughout Europe as a model for other parks and protected places.

The task of carving a national park out of central Italy bears little relation to establishing a national park in the wilds of western North America. Granted, it's all about setting aside large tracts of land for preservation, but in the case of Abruzzo, human settlement had taken place here in the Upper Paleolithic (between forty thousand and ten thousand years ago), which means that an ongoing accommodation has to be made between the residents and their historic use of the land. In the case of Abruzzo National Park, this includes twenty-two villages, twelve thousand permanent residents, and the vestiges of an agriculture-based economy.

Today, Abruzzo National Park encompasses 110,000 acres in the heart of the Apennine range, where dolomite peaks reach 6,500 feet. Surrounding the park is a 150,000-acre Outer Protection Zone of forest and cultivated valleys. The park's medieval mountain villages are for the most part unspoiled by the excesses of industrial tourism found throughout much of the country.

Barrea, Opi, Civitella Alfredena—there are nearly two dozen medieval set pieces. Many are perched atop mountains and hills; all are well out of reach of franchise-modernity. The winding, cobblestone passageways and well-preserved stone houses and churches are as much of an attraction as the forests and fresh air.

Here, people dwell in the heavy permanence of their history. To this outsider, they seem as characters in an enduring, classical play. They must be ever-mindful that countless predecessors have trod the same stage before them, living out similar scripts, and that countless more will pick up their roles in the future. How different it is in my young city (118 years old), where buildings disappear and are replaced with astonishing speed. So intense is the velocity of change, that—after an absence of a mere six months—a stroll down a once-familiar Vancouver street can be a disorienting experience.

People come to Abruzzo National Park to see how it used to be. Whereas North Americans go to Yellowstone to marvel at the sublime and astonishing natural world, many older Italians visit Abruzzo wishing to get closer to an Italy they remember from long ago, while younger generations who visit end up feeling nostalgic for a way of life they never knew. Meanwhile, the old traditions slowly fade away.

MAURIZIO CARFORGNINI smiles from behind the wheel of a Land Rover, the color of which matches both his ranger's uniform and his olive-green eyes. He wants me to ride up front with him—Posillico can sit in back. And, we're told, there will be no need for Posillico's help in translation. Carforgnini spent four years in Canada back in the 1960s. Unfortunately, he says, his family moved to Montreal where he was "forced" to speak French. So he apologizes in advance that he won't correctly pronounce all the English words. He didn't think much of Montreal (other than the beautiful women). He couldn't wait to move back to Scanno where his family roots go back countless generations.

We climb the steep cobblestone lanes in first and second gear. Scanno, a small town that has remained much as it was in the Middle Ages, was made famous by photographer Henri Cartier-Bresson in the early 1950s. His portraits depict stern, dignified women in traditional Scanno costumes—black wool skirts and hats. Men wore conspiratorial expressions and black wool capes. All were framed by narrow stone passageways. Today, the set is little changed. There are still a few dark matrons milling about, and old men in wool sport coats, but the vast majority is middle-aged and dress remarkably like their counterparts in other parts of Italy and the Western world. The few young women I see are clad in designer jeans; young men favor tracksuits.

From Scanno, which is just outside the park's Outer Protection Zone, we take rough back roads through typical bear habitat, which include steep slopes of beech and black pine, and valleys of fields, meadows, and orchards. Carforgnini has been a forest ranger in Abruzzo National Park for twenty-eight years. A big man with an expansive personality, he exudes boundless enthusiasm for both his job and his native Abruzzo. He says, in halting English, that he knows all there is to know about the bears of this region and spends his days outside, in the forest, looking for animal signs.

"In North America, you have grizzly bears, black bears, and polar bears," he says. "Our Italian brown bear is something different. If we take your bear to Italy, maybe he won't be able to survive. Because here the environment and the bear changed together. So this bear is very unique, very smart—that's why he survived."

Barely. At one time, bears were widely distributed throughout the forested regions of Italy, but by the sixteenth century, they were extirpated from most of their range. Although Abruzzo's bear population has long been a small one, its decline accelerated in the late 1970s. Several events conspired against the native bears at that time, including the introduction of wild boars to the park by hunters. The wild boar population exploded. Boars compete with bears for acorns and often chase them away. Hunters set up wire snares to catch boars, but caught and killed many bears instead. "And these are the known mortality figures," Carforgnini says. "Imagine how many were killed that are unknown."

In the 1980s, there was a "crash" in the bear population. Because so many were killed in a five-year period—due mainly to poaching—it has been difficult for the population to recover. The park responded with a bear feeding program consisting of a regular supply of apples, carrots, and carcasses left at remote stations. The bears made heavy use of this food source until the late 1990s, when the program was abruptly discontinued. Bears had begun to lose their fear of humans and associate our scent with food.

At the edge of a field, Carforgnini stops the Land Rover and shows me a tree where a bear broke off a branch while feeding on apples. This happened thirty years ago. The trunk has healed over completely but the memory is fresh in Carforgnini's mind. He gestures with both hands at the tree and asks why, why haven't any bears returned to feed on this tree since?

It is late April and we travel through sunny slopes and valleys suspended between seasons. Yesterday's snow is gone, but last year's grass is still pressed down with the weight of winter.

"In Italy, especially in the mountains, agriculture is dying out," Carforgnini says as we descend into a quiet valley. "It's expensive and the return is small. Once Scanno had four thousand people and everyone got their wheat from this valley. Now Scanno has fifteen hundred people and we get our wheat from Bulgaria."

Carforgnini's older brother Liborio is a shepherd, farmer, and *formaggiaio* (cheese maker). He greets us warmly and invites us into his ancient stone farmhouse. On the wall inside are several soft-focus photographs of small bears taken on this farm. Adult Marsican brown bears weigh between 147 and nearly 500 pounds and measure fifty-three to sixty-nine inches from snout to tail; these appear to be at the lower end of the scale. Liborio says he is turning part of the farmhouse into a bed-and-breakfast for tourists who like to spend a quiet week on a farm in bear country, away from the circus that is Rome. "Have you heard of agri-tourism?" he asks.

We sit around an old wooden table. Several bottles of moonshine appear, including *genziana,* a bitter brown liquor made of the root of an alpine herb; *limone,* an opaque, bright yellow concoction made of lemons and sugar; and a sweet, store-bought liquor made from chestnuts. I am carefully watched as I sample each one before my glass is filled again. The conversation becomes more animated and the gestures grow in size and grandeur.

The first time Liborio saw a bear was while tending sheep alone near Scanno when he was fourteen years old. He remembers being interrupted while reading a book. His dog began to bark and then a bear came bounding straight at him. He ran to get his father who was busy making cheese. While he was gone, the bear attacked the sheep.

Farmers and shepherds in the region receive government compensation when bears or wolves attack their flocks. After an inspection and some paperwork (and sometimes a lengthy delay), they are paid the market value of any animals killed. Before the compensation scheme was in place in the late 1970s, shepherds were left to do whatever they could to protect their flocks. Although shooting bears was illegal, it was sometimes necessary to quietly dispatch problem bears, whose haunches would often resurface as bear prosciutto. In all his time in this valley and the surrounding mountain pastures, Liborio reports having seen bears on only seven occasions. The last time was six years ago.

He pours another glass of sweet-sour limone for me, and one for himself. He takes a drink, then looks me in the eye. "The people of Abruzzo have never had the bear as an enemy," he says. "But now the bear comes into town to kill chickens. This never happened before. It's because there is no more livestock in the mountains. No more food for the bears. Before, this valley was full of grain. Now nobody farms because it's too expensive to bring in machines to cut the wheat. This is why bears have problems."

He invites me to return and have dinner on his farm. Better yet, I can return in the summer and stay for a week. He won't let me go without a gift. After filling my glass yet again, he disappears into a cellar only to return with a large, five-pound cake of *pecorino* cheese. It is a gorgeous thing, creamy white with tapered edges decorated in textured lines that meet in the center on top. He wraps it up and presents it with both hands.

I meet shepherds in their fifties, sixties, and seventies who are too old or too stubborn to change, men convinced that although it is impossible for any normal man to make a go of it here in the new global economy, they can still survive somehow. For the most part, their sons have no interest in shepherding. They all have stories of encounters with bears—some of the peaceful variety; others involving the loss of livestock. These stories are relayed with passion and pride. It adds an element of drama and perceived danger to their work, the romance of which they clearly relish. While they all speak of a respect for the bear, little of this sentiment is extended to wolves, whose numbers have rebounded dramatically and pose a greater threat to their flocks.

In fields, barns, and kitchens throughout the park, I hear historic tales of bears preying on sheep and goats. Events that took place in the 1940s are relayed with the detail and clarity of this week's gossip. One shepherd tells me he used a castrated ram with a bell around its neck to lead the flock. Once, when he was eight years old, a bear killed his ram in the night. The bear hauled the carcass away but because the flock was conditioned to follow the sound of the bell, sheep followed the bear into the forest—where it killed seven more. The young shepherd approached the bear and said, "Okay. You have the sheep. But please leave the bell so no more will follow." Recognizing the reasonableness of this request, the bear dropped the bell and disappeared into the forest.

As we travel through the mountains, we meet shepherds in

barns, fields, and forests. Virtually all of them are old. It soon becomes clear that I am documenting not only the dying days of an animal unique to this region, but also a way of life that has existed here for hundreds of generations.

THE FOLLOWING DAY, we arrive at the end of a wet gravel road and the home, farm, and *caseificio* (cheese factory) of Gregorio Orotolo. He's in the stainless steel production room helping his father, Luigi, separate curds from whey. An imposing man with a ten-day beard and dark shadows under his eyes, he extends a thick hand.

Gregorio Orotolo has been tending sheep since he was six years old. Now, at forty-three, he's the keeper of a family tradition of which he is fiercely proud. "We are not frightened of bears, wolves, or hard work," he says, with a cigarette dangling from his lips. "We are frightened of paperwork." He echoes what we've been hearing all along, that as the number of wild boars increase, the number of bears decline.

Wouldn't it be easier for shepherds if all the bears were gone?

"We feel we have a strong role in preserving wildlife—especially the brown bear and the wolf," he says. Orotolo is the first shepherd I've met who has anything kind to say about wolves. "I love this place. It's a hard life but it's worth living. It's worth trying to get money from the stones of these mountains. And because we love this place, we try to work hard and work intelligently—to make it as productive as possible with nondestructive methods to give the wolf and bear a chance to survive."

Orotolo's nephew, twenty-eight-year-old Dino Sila, enters the room. He says that, despite it all, he sees a future here for himself in his family business. So much so that he went out and got a diploma in agriculture to supplement the family's considerable experience. As a young man intent on keeping this tradition alive, he is a rare exception.

All the while Luigi, the senior Orotolo, listens, stirring the goat milk and sieving out the cheese. When I ask how long he intends to work before retirement, he laughs. "Don't ask me about retirement," he says. "My pension is only worth four hundred euros [$477.80] per month—which isn't enough for anything. I will work forever." He adds a few stories of bear encounters in the now-familiar refrain—boy meets bear, bear grabs goats, boy runs back to town.

His son brings out five cakes of cheese. Abruzzo is famous for its ricotta and pecorino varieties, and I am presented with sizable wedges of each kind made by the family. It is clear that to decline any of the huge slabs proffered on the point of a knife would be a serious affront. After four such servings, I pinch the air between thumb and forefinger, indicating a smaller slice. This is met with pursed lips and a slap on the back. We all eat a meal of cheese, which ranges from creamy and mild to solid and salty. The final piece, which is reminiscent of asiago, is a cheese Orotolo has named for his family. Although all are excellent, I say, this is the best of the bunch.

Outside, the sky has cleared and we are surrounded with a view of the sleeping valley and snowcapped Apennines. Gregorio Orotolo wants to show me the secret to protecting his flocks. A shaggy pair of white Abruzzo sheepdogs nuzzle up to his hip. Relatively unknown outside the Apennines, *il Cane da Pastore Maremmano-Abruzzese* is one of the oldest breeds in the world, described in literature as far back as the first century AD. Large, powerfully built dogs, they have a bearlike head and thick, white fur. They share a common ancestor with other breeds that spread throughout Europe and the Middle East.

"These dogs are proven to be the finest for guarding sheep," he says. "Not for herding the sheep, but for protecting the flock from bears and wolves. They are fearless, and if a shepherd has enough of them, he will be able to protect his flock from danger."

Proof, if I need any, can be found in the time he was asked by a shepherd in Norway to bring some dogs to help him. The man was having trouble with bears. Orotolo brought some of his Abruzzo sheepdogs north where they had great success in guarding the flocks from the more numerous Norwegian bears.

"These dogs are the best," he says, flicking his cigarette butt into the air and exhaling in a satisfied stream.

Back in the Land Rover, I say that I've encountered the same story about the superiority of the sheepdogs in Greece, not two weeks ago. In fact, I visited a breeding farm for rare Greek sheepdogs in the village of Aetos, in Greek Macedonia. There, the finest specimens from a dwindling stock of genuine Greek sheepdogs are being bred to give to local shepherds for protecting their flocks from bears and wolves. These are the finest guard dogs in the world, they say, claiming that there are even statuettes of the dogs dating back to the time of the ancient Greeks. They are famous for their fearlessness. I roll up my sleeve and show him the bite mark on my forearm to prove the veracity of their claim.

Carforgnini shrugs. "Maybe they have good dogs in Greece, but ours are the best in the world!" He offers a few more anecdotes defending the honor of the breed. "But I must tell you," he says. "Once, in Villetta Barrea, a bear found a huge white Abruzzo sheepdog on a chain and ate it. I have pictures of this. When he started to eat the dog, it was still alive. He ate it from behind, the hindquarters first. It was a very cold spring and there was nothing left to eat."

We make frequent stops where Carforgnini jumps out to focus binoculars on some distant stump or tussock. He is concerned that I will be disappointed if I don't get a glimpse of a Marsican bear. With only thirty left, I am under no illusions. He offers to take me to a surefire spot where we will be able to lure one out into the open with honey. I politely decline, not wanting to resort to bait.

He grows quiet and reflective. "I saw a bear this year," he says. "My work is to preserve the bear. But when I meet my chief, I say we cannot do it. It's too late. The bear is finished. Last year I saw a bear with two cubs. I was happy. I said to myself, Maybe we can do this. Maybe we can save them. It gave me hope. I also saw cubs in 1999, but I had gone ten years without seeing cubs . . . Now, when there are signs of bears, they send me to see if it's really a bear. Because other people—even forest rangers—are not able to deduce the signs."

WHEN I MEET Ricardo Lanerioni outside his barn, I am distracted by the view. Framed by mountains and a leaden sky, Scanno is an illuminated manuscript come to life. I am told that Lanerioni is one man who has no trouble discerning the signs of bear or other wildlife in these mountains. He has always been a shepherd and farmer here, and at the age of seventy-two, he has seen a few changes. He is pleased that someone has taken an interest in Abruzzo's bears, sheepdogs, and shepherds.

Chairs are pulled from the corner of the barn and arranged in a circle. We sit in the chill air sipping bottles of a bittersweet aperitif, listening to Lanerioni's stories of working and living in Italian bear country. He wears track pants over trousers and suspenders, a button-down shirt, and a *copolla*—the felt cap ubiquitous among local men his age. He smiles with his entire face and Sinatra-blue eyes as he recounts tales that, surprisingly, aren't from the mists of time.

Lanerioni speaks with his body, gesturing with shoulders, arms, and hands. He jumps out of his seat to act out parts of the story. I catch only every tenth word, but it is easy to tell he is reliving a bear encounter from a moonlit night that involves a chase and the capture of sheep. The tale goes on for some quarter of an hour without interruption. Besides faithfully reenacting the bear's movements, he also re-creates the astonished look on his own face. Everyone laughs. I see Posillico trying desperately to find a break in the account in order to provide translation, but he cannot. Only when Lanerioni is back in his seat and nods does the translation begin. Posillico does his best to recount the details, but it is abundantly clear that he won't be able to capture the drama and suspense I saw reflected in the faces around me.

The simple facts of the story are as follows. Once, when Lanerioni was with his sheep on a nearby mountain, he heard a bear entering the flock's enclosure at one o'clock in the morning. Shepherds in these mountains have long kept their animals inside pens at night. When he went to investigate, the sheep came toward his light. Then he saw a bear pick up a sheep "as easily as a tennis ball," put it under his arm, and escape. Lanerioni followed the bear with fifteen Abruzzo sheepdogs. The dog pack split and tried to fight with the bear, but it jumped over a six-foot-high stone wall and began eating the sheep. By the time the dogs finally made it around the wall, the bear had picked up the rest of the carcass and carried it away. Lanerioni will always remember the bear's eyes. They glowed red, like coals in a fire.

I have heard this twice before during my time in Abruzzo: that a bear's eyes turn red when they are hungry. I ask for clarification on this point and am told that it is not only true, but commonly known. His father saw it too. Posillico delivers this last bit of translation with a straight face, and an almost imperceptible wink. Lanerioni says he has seen a bear as recently as 2002, but reports that there has been a dramatic drop in the signs and sightings of bears since he was a boy.

Lanerioni's father was known as the bear hunter of Scanno. If shepherds had problems with a bear, they wouldn't take matters into their own hands; they would call a specialist instead. "I remember when I was a boy and my father would come home late because he had to protect a flock from a bear," he says. "I asked him, 'What is the first thing you do when you meet a bear in the mountains?' He replied, 'I do the fascist salute.'"

The other Italians laugh awkwardly and tilt back the last of their drinks.

"The bear has something supernatural," he observes. "It is beautiful and gives you a sense of what man is and what nature is.

I want to preserve bears, but something in the environment has changed. Something is broken."

Shepherds like Lanerioni are practitioners of one of the world's oldest professions. The history of transhumance (moving livestock from one grazing ground to another with the seasons) goes back at least eight thousand years to the Fertile Crescent. The sheep was probably the second animal domesticated by humans; only the dog has been a part of our societies longer. In much of the world, shepherds and farmers have the most to lose by the continued survival of bears because they must endure attacks on their animals and crops. Are these shepherds trying to pull the proverbial wool over my eyes? Wouldn't they rather have their mountains free of bears? I don't believe it. These men are the last of their kind; they have nothing left to prove. They have lived their entire lives in these mountains and genuinely believe that the bear's decline is linked to their own demise. If they truly wanted the bears to disappear, it would have happened ages ago.

That night, in my room back in Villetta Barrea, I seriously reconsider the offer of luring a bear with honey. As I make notes, I am distracted by the giant cake of cheese I was given several days ago. It crowds out the surface of my desk. Since arriving in the Apennines, I have consumed my body weight in cheese. I can't imagine taking another bite, and yet it is a great responsibility. Finally, I cut a small sample for myself (mild and earthy), then carry the rest downstairs with a note in phrasebook Italian that says, "Good cheese, please eat," and set it free in the communal fridge.

THE SUN SHINES bright on the heart of old Pescasseroli, the administrative center of Abruzzo National Park. Mario Posillico and I walk through the quiet cobblestone streets at nine in the morning. Pescasseroli is a blend of ancient mountain village and

1960s ski resort that has seen better times. As we pass through the empty streets, a shopkeeper flips over his *aperto* sign as a woman sweeps the sidewalk. We are on the way to the home of Armando Petrella, a retired park ranger. When we approach the door leading to his second-floor apartment, Posillico points to the key left in the lock. He says this is an old village custom, a holdover from a more innocent time.

An eighty-one-year-old gentleman greets us in pressed slacks and a smart red sweater over shirt and tie. Petrella invites us into the formal dining room, which is furnished with dark wood and framed prints of eighteenth-century hunting and pastoral scenes. Along with the vintage reproductions are two photographs of bears.

As a young man, Petrella worked as a shepherd. The life of a shepherd is a difficult one, he says. When he was in his early twenties, he tended flocks in the mountains near Pescasseroli, where he remembers a bear prowling around his flock every other night. The pressure was wearing him down. Since this was just after the war, and there were plenty of weapons lying around, he decided to bring a gun to protect the flock. When the bear returned, he raised the rifle and fired. The bear remained still for a moment, as if nothing had happened, then ran away. Petrella followed and found it lying in a gully. He cautiously approached, then reached out and touched the bear. It was still alive. He backed off and listened to it whimper and wail. It wasn't until after it stopped breathing that he allowed himself to consider the consequences. He ran down the hill and found two younger shepherds to help bury the body.

Remorse and paranoia drove him to seek the counsel of his uncle, who just happened to be a park warden. Upon hearing the story, his uncle slapped him hard across the face. The young Petrella had brought serious trouble to the family. The flock he was tending belonged to the park's director. To make matters worse, the other park officials had been planning to go up into that exact valley the following morning to oversee construction of a sheep fence. Go back to the scene of the crime and dig up the bear, his uncle said. In the meantime, he would try to call in some favors. The problem officially went away, as far as the authorities were concerned, but Petrella became known as a poacher. The park officials ended up feeling sorry for him. The best thing to do, they concluded, was to make him one of their own.

There were an estimated one hundred bears when he started working at Abruzzo National Park in 1954. In those days, he found bear sign everywhere and it was clear there was a healthy population. There were also plenty of claims for attacks on flocks. Back then, there was abundant food in these mountains, provided by the agricultural nature of the community. But by the late 1970s, both farming and the livestock industry were in decline. Petrella noticed a parallel decline in the amount of bear sign from month to month, year to year. He believes the main cause of the declining bear population is the abandonment of the mountains by shepherds. The next biggest problem is poaching.

Petrella's wife Angelica enters the room bearing chocolate and espresso in fine china. As soon as we finish, she quietly retrieves the cups and saucers, washes them, and carefully returns them to the hutch.

One day, Petrella says, the park director decided it would be good to have a couple of bears in the park's small zoo. In March, he sent his rangers out to find some cubs and Petrella spotted a winter den. Like other brown bears, Marsican bears hibernate during the winter. After returning with a lamp and a couple of colleagues, Petrella crawled inside and encountered the sleeping mother bear. His colleagues immediately pulled him out by his ankles. Later, they returned and tried again. This time, the mother was absent and they were able to grab the two healthy cubs. He returned the next day to check on the mother and found the den torn apart and the earth overturned all around the site. It fell to Petrella to bottle-feed the cubs on goat milk until they grew too large. The experience made a significant impact on his life and changed the way he viewed both bears and the natural world. He became emotionally attached to the cubs, like a parent, he says. Finally, they were placed in the park's small zoo—where they soon died.

Petrella excuses himself from the table and returns with a framed certificate. It honors his work in the park from 1954 to 1988 and his dedication to the cause of nature. It is a cherished possession.

"I hope there will be bears in the future," he says. "But I'm not sure. Since the old times, everyone knew that they had to coexist with bears, so they had a few extra sheep in their flocks for them. The shepherds who used to have confrontations with the bears will be sad. They will miss that."

Posillico and I walk back through the center of Pescasseroli. Although there are few people milling about, the shops are open and stocked with bear honey, bear candy, bear T-shirts, beeswax candles in the shape of bears, and Abruzzo teddy bears. Inside the zoo's gift shop is a stuffed Marsican brown bear and more bear souvenirs. The bear—monarch of the Apennines—has always been the mascot of the park. The park's logo features a cartoonlike bear sitting down on its rump, facing right, with a dazed expression on its face. Its image is everywhere. Posters and a diorama depict the bear as an integral part of this well-functioning forest environment. Children come by the busload to learn about their mountains, their bears, and how all's well in Italy's premier national park. The fate of Italy's bears is in good hands.

Where are there the ringing alarm bells, alerting visitors to the fact that this environment's umbrella species is about to fold? Shouldn't there be a huge red banner out front that screams FINAL DAYS FOR ITALY'S BEARS! What about roadblocks where leaflets are distributed, informing park visitors of the looming extinction? In short, where's the passion?

We follow a path through several small enclosures with animals endemic in the region—including Abruzzo chamois—that were orphaned, injured, or otherwise unable to live on their own. When we reach the bears, we both become silent. In the first pen is a brown bear from another part of Europe. He has about a hundred yards of space to roam. A few weeks ago, this bear, which is known as Abele, had had enough of schoolchildren taunting him through the fence, so he bit off a kid's finger. In an adjacent and smaller pen is a much smaller bear, Lauretta, weighing perhaps two hundred pounds. A native Marsican brown bear from Abruzzo National Park, she was "rescued" in May 1994, after having lost contact with her mother. Lauretta has remained imprisoned in her tiny enclosure ever since, observing school groups come and go, endlessly pacing back and forth like a mental defective. Bears, wolves, apes, canaries, and humans all have a tendency to exhibit this type of repetitive action when caged for long periods of time. Biologists refer to it as "stereotypic" behavior. It is an indication of psychological disturbance.

"It's sad, I know," Posillico says. He didn't want to bring me here.

FOLLOWING MY TOUR of the zoo, I am ready to meet the new director of Abruzzo National Park. In a rumpled gray suit and slick, black hair, Aldo Di Benedetto invites us to sit down in his dimly lit office, which smells of pomade and sweat. Boxed files are on the floor as if in preparation for an audit. Like the boss, the place seems a little, well, scattered. Posillico, who interprets for me, says Di Benedetto is a very busy man and his time is limited. He is busy cleaning up a fiscal mess and I am lucky he has agreed to meet me. I already have lots of background information, I say. I promise to keep my questions direct and concise.

"Why are we failing to save these bears?"

"Maybe what we are failing to do is translate our sense of love of nature into the way we manage things." Di Benedetto leans on the right arm of his high-back office chair. If he feels broadsided by the question, he doesn't let it show. "Maybe there are some historical or cultural reasons. In other parts of the world, people act more directly. If you recognize there is a problem, you focus on the different aspects of the problem—the reasons the problem is there—and try to fix it. Things are not so straightforward here."

"Why?"

"Maybe it's the culture of the people, in my opinion. We are not used to acting directly."

"Don't Italians care?"

"Maybe, as a people, we are not used to directly managing and respecting our own natural heritage. Maybe we have lost too much . . . Too few people are awake to the problems. Most of the people who live and vote in cities are too far from here to feel such a loss. People vote for politicians who ignore [the situation] and people profit off it. Often, they miss the point that cultural heritage and natural heritage are really joined." Here, he knits his fingers.

Di Benedetto admits that the bears are in crisis and says that his department is doing all it can, given the financial troubles—troubles left over from a previous administration. He doesn't want the bears to disappear, particularly on his watch, but there is only so much one man can do.

Somehow, he warms to me and expresses genuine interest in the state of bears in other parts of the world. Soon, our time is up. Although I don't read Italian, he presents me with a handsome, hardcover, limited-edition copy of the original park history, written in 1926. It was reissued by the former park director on the occasion of Abruzzo National Park's seventy-fifth anniversary. On the cover is a beautiful color plate of a Marsican brown bear. He must like me, Posillico says. These books are hard to come by.

Outside, we agree that a hike might clear our heads. Posillico drives me to one of his favorite spots and we walk in silence though the beech trees along a decommissioned road. A red fox crosses our path—alert to the possibility of a snack.

Eventually, I ask why Italians seem to care so little about the fate of their last bears. Why the denial, the numbers games, and the universal shrugging of shoulders? A significant part of Italy's natural heritage—an animal that has somehow managed to survive despite *bestiarii*, shepherds, poachers, and widespread indifference—is about to disappear. When the bear is gone, will Italians know enough to care? Even as I ask the question, I know it could be asked in countless regions across Europe, North America, South America, and Asia.

"I'm more optimistic when you share something with other people," Posillico says. "You have to. It is much more difficult to hide the truth. You have to have the courage to criticize yourself and recognize that you are wrong. This makes the difference. You have to change strategies, change ways. As you go up in the hierarchy, you will start to have to deal with much more politically oriented attitudes, which means they control what we are saying. Also, we are not used to journalists who put the facts in front of you, like the real number of bears. It is something that journalists usually do not perceive. Here, their unstated mission is making publicity for nature, showing how beautiful these mountains are for holidays, rather than going into detail about wildlife conservation. They gave constructive criticism in the 1980s, but they shifted. They let people believe everything is going well."

The road ends and we walk along a forest path littered with copper leaves. Up ahead, a humble waterfall and a crystal pool.

"The former administration of the park would show photos of people doing radiotracking and say, 'Look, we are doing research. The bear is healthy and there are plenty of bears.' They were so offensive as to claim that there was as many as one bear for every ten square kilometers. Nobody knows how they succeeded in firing the former park director . . . There were a lot of very well recognized things going wrong, but nobody moved to make an investigation."

Finally, they did. An investigation was launched into the disappearance of four billion lire (almost $2.5 million) from the park's coffers. Although the former director was replaced, the effort to recover from the ensuing economic crisis is all-consuming. There is little money to pay staff—not enough even to buy new boots for park wardens, let alone launch any meaningful protection strategies for the few remaining bears.

"He must have had friends in high places," I say.

"He should have had more than friends. Too many political things happened. Many, many big things. I hope nobody will be killed for this," Posillico says, laughing.

———————

THIRTY MILES AWAY, in the village of Cérchio, an engraved print hangs in the living room of Dr. Giorgio Boscagli. Titled *Il Ballo dell'Orso in vicinanza della Fontana di Trevi alle falde del Quirinale* (The Bear Dance at the Trevi Fountain at the foot of Quirinale Hill), it was printed in 1830. In it, a bear wears a bridle and chain, stands on hind legs, and rests its right paw on a walking stick for support in front of perhaps the most famous fountain in the world. The faces of the gathered spectators show curiosity, fear, and amusement. A musician plays a bladder pipe while the bear's master tugs the chain with one hand, and holds a large club in the other. He encourages the bear to "dance."

Boscagli was born in Rome in 1952, but has lived in Abruzzo for thirty years. He worked at Abruzzo National Park from 1978 to 1994, followed by a stint as the director of Sirente-Velino Regional Park. Today, he is on contract with Foretse Govienesti National Park in Tuscany. Boscagli has been working on the cause of Italian bear conservation as long as anyone. He found the *Ballo dell'Orso* for sale in a Roman flea market some years back and keeps it around to remind him of his country's relationship to bears.

There are concentration lines around Boscagli's eyes, reading glasses tethered around his neck. His faded denim shirt and jeans seem perfectly suited to his thick gray hair and beard. When

I explain my confusion about the number of bears left in Abruzzo National Park, he nods. "There are two different approaches," he explains, "the political and the scientific. For the political approach, they say, we have a large number of bears. This is not the real situation."

Because researchers need fresh November snow and plenty of volunteers ready at a moment's notice, he says, it was only possible to estimate the number of bears on three occasions in the past century: 1928, 1932, and in 1985. Boscagli was the organizer of the last bear census in Abruzzo National Park.

"We estimated thirty-nine to forty-one animals at that time. Moreover, it was possible another twenty to thirty animals *could* exist, but very dispersed in the surrounding area outside the park. I printed these results at an international conference on bears in 1986—and this was the first moment of conflict between myself and the park administration. Although I worked for the park, I needed to report the real situation, not the political approach."

Boscagli wants to make it clear that no one ever directly asked him to change the numbers. But while he published the results of his research in small scientific journals, park authorities reported in one of Italy's largest circulation dailies, *La Repubblica*, that there "could be" twice that number. Technically, they weren't putting out false information, just unsubstantiated optimism that lacked foundation in fact. Because there are currently no reliable scientific studies being done, he says, it is impossible to say with any certainty that there are even thirty bears left alive.

What is certain is that there are very few bears remaining, and the park created to preserve them is itself on life support. For Boscagli, this question of numbers leads to some very personal regrets. For twenty-five years, Abruzzo National Park was considered a leader in the conservation of nature, he says. In fact, many of Europe's national parks were built on the model and experience of Abruzzo.

"The former director of the park was an extraordinary person. I had an excellent rapport with him and the rest of the group. Unfortunately, in the early 1990s, this rapport was broken and the situation in Abruzzo National Park completely imploded. When I think of the situation today . . . When I think about what Abruzzo National Park was and what it is today—really, I want to cry. Why did this happen? We could spend two years discussing this question . . . It concluded in a bad, bad way. It is a pity for Italy and for Europe.

"Today, the approach of the present government in Italy, when it comes to national and regional parks, is not the protection of animals, trees, and nature. Today, parks are the center of the economic interest of tourists. This is the approach of the present government."

Abruzzo National Park has profound economic problems, a situation that Boscagli calls "self-injurious and tragic." As far as he is concerned, no one is consistently working on the problem of bear conservation as they did twenty years ago. The allies of bear conservation in the park, NGOs such as WWF and Le Gambiente, experienced the same "implosion," he says. The environmental consciousness and passion that was present in Italy in the 1960s, and gave birth to these organizations, is gone. He says Italians are living under a false impression.

"Italians say, 'We have protected ten percent of our land. We are the first in Europe!' Abruzzo has thirty-five percent of its land in parks or natural reserves. Officially these areas exist, but are they for conservation or the promotion of tourism? Or is it for the promotion of local products, like meats and cheeses? Or beautiful pictures? The Italian people don't have a scientific approach to life; they have a humanistic approach. We have a large patrimony of humanistic culture and we have a very poor naturalistic patrimony."

When I ask about the proposed construction of a new ski village at Monte Greco—which is inside the park's Outer Protection Zone—he pauses and pulls on his pipe.

"The administration of Abruzzo is working to build this. If this occurs, it means that they would completely and absolutely disrupt the genetic continuity of this group of bears. If this happens, perhaps in twenty years there will be no more bears in Abruzzo, or maybe just one or two bears as there are in the Alps at Trentino where the same thing occurred. I remember in 1970, the province of Trentino, WWF, and local organizations of hunters joined together to save the last bears of the Alps. There were five bears and ten organizations trying to save them. The bear was not saved. They built roads and ski lifts and tourist villages in the center of the most delicate bear habitat, the most important region for dens. Today, they find one lone bear in one area and say they are happy because they still have bears. No. You don't have bears. You have the *last* bear in that area, and way over here we have the *last* bear in that area. This could be the future of the Abruzzo population in twenty or thirty years."

Boscagli's current work involves wolf conservation. He is much more optimistic about the future of wolves, which have a greater reproductive rate and overall adaptability. "Thirty years ago, we had one hundred wolves in Italy. Today, we have maybe six hundred. They recolonized very large areas where they were extirpated in the last century.

"You've come to Italy in a very difficult time in the life of this park," he says. "I can say that in the past, Abruzzo National Park tried to produce the maximum efforts to conserve the bear. Today, that direction does not exist. They have no money. This means it's difficult to focus on the real problem of conservation of nature . . . There is no longer an ecological study center. I remember we worked with them on the daily war against the poachers. Today this no longer occurs. With this situation, it is very difficult to succeed in the conservation of nature.

"Twenty years ago, it was impossible to think there was an authority in the Abruzzo region or the central Parliament that would consider building a ski lift and tourist village on Monte

Greco, because Abruzzo National Park would mobilize the world. We would ask Canada, the USA, the Soviet Union to rain down articles and media coverage on the issue. I remember when this happened with the bears in Spain and France. This made an enormous difference. Today, this is absolutely impossible. There is no one to do this today. Conservation groups are very, very poor compared to twenty years ago. And Abruzzo National Park was the leader of this and now it is completely destroyed.

"I spoke in the National Congress. I asked them, 'What is more important? The conservation of the brown bear or the conservation of the Colosseum?' The Colosseum is the most important monument of Italy. If it collapsed, it would be possible to rebuild the Colosseum. It is absolutely impossible to rebuild the genome of an animal species. This is the problem . . . Maybe if the Colosseum was in trouble, the Italian people would go out in the streets and demand that Parliament save the Colosseum, but it's very difficult for this to occur for wildlife."

I slump back in my chair.

"I'm sorry if you are not very happy with this picture. I see your face. For me it is very, very sad. I am not happy to say this after thirty years' work on this front. I continue because this is my work. I am a biologist. But . . . I have a son. Tancredi is his name."

He points to the picture of a seven-year-old boy on the mantle.

"When I was young, I had a wonderful sensation from nature. This is a romantic approach, not a scientific approach. But I shall be very happy if my son will have this same feeling I had . . . This is a very strange experience for me because for years I was against the idea of having children. After his arrival, my point of view in life changed dramatically. And I think it is very important that we have the same opportunities for all the children of the world. The brown bear is a small part of nature, but emotionally it is extraordinarily important. If we destroy this, the world could be much poorer compared to today.

"If we want to save the rainforest in Brazil or the last bamboo forest for the giant pandas in China, well, we need to pay for it. We need to understand this at a planetary level. I don't like the approach of the USA; the excess standard of living of American people is not sustainable. They don't accept the Kyoto Protocol . . . But it's also true for the Italian, Canadian, French, German, English, and Spanish people, because if we want to conserve wildlife, we will have to pay for it. Pay with money."

7

THE SKULL CHAMBER
Ardèche Gorges, France

ON DECEMBER 18, 1994, a team of three seasoned cave explorers found themselves with some time to kill on a crisp, Sunday afternoon. They decided to try their luck at a place called Cirque d'Estre at the edge of the Ardèche Gorges. It had already been a long day, but the weather was inviting; the tall limestone cliffs and scree slopes were bathed in dazzling light. The team was familiar with the area but had passed it up many times before in favor of more promising locations. Eliette Brunel Deschamps, Christian Hillaire, and Jean-Marie Chauvet had proven instincts. They had already enjoyed astonishing success in finding caves, including twelve of the region's twenty-eight Paleolithic painted caves discovered during the twentieth century. Something told them it was finally time to take a closer look at Cirque d'Estre.

The cliff overlooks an ancient bed of the Ardèche River and, at this time of year, a dormant vineyard. The gentler slopes are covered with evergreens and bare oak trees. The team hiked into dense vegetation and located a narrow cavity in the cliff. After passing through a ten-by-thirty-inch gap, they found themselves in a small, cramped vestibule. A slight draft was emanating from the darkness (a sign of a subterranean gallery or shaft), so they pressed on. They squeezed through another narrow gap, then sensed that they had arrived in a large chamber. To measure its depth, they called out and listened for their echoes, which seemed lost in the chasm before them.

In order to proceed, a ladder was required so the team was forced to retreat to their van at the foot of the cliff. By this time, both night and exhaustion were upon them and they contemplated abandoning further exploration until the coming Christmas weekend. But this would leave the possibility of someone else discovering the opening and becoming the first to explore the cave. They rallied their determination and hiked back up in the dark and cold.

Inside the chamber, they unrolled a ladder over the precipice. Jean-Marie Chauvet was the first to reach the floor, where the damp air had the odor of clay. In the arc of his headlamp beam loomed immense columns of calcite.

Aware of the fragility of the environment, the team proceeded with care and passed into a new, larger chamber. There, they were met with countless skeletons littering the floor. Among the piles of thick bones were dozens of craters in the earth—wallows made by long-extinct cave bears bedding down for an Ice Age winter. Then red ochre lines appeared on the wall. Drawn by human hands, they clearly depicted a mammoth. Overwhelmed, the team wandered among images of lions, rhinoceros, bison, and cave bears. They soon realized that they'd made the discovery of their lives. What they couldn't imagine is that they had found the cave that would change the shape of history.

ACROSS THE GORGE from Cirque d'Estre, I roll to a stop beside an empty road in a rented Citroën. When the hum of the engine fades, I hear sparrows in the branches above. On the far bank of the Ardèche, pale limestone cliffs plunge into the languid river.

The entire scene is dominated by Pont d'Arc, a dramatic natural bridge carved out by the river some half-million years ago.

I have been dwelling on extinction of late, and have arrived in a country where fewer than fifteen brown bears (*Ursus arctos*) remain. These last holdouts live in the Pyrenees where—to all but the most hopeful conservationists—it appears they seem certain to expire. Truth be told, I'm surprised to find that any bears survive in France at all, and by the time you read these words there may be next to none. But that's another story. I have come to pay my respects to a breed of bear that vanished ages ago.

From the moment I first saw the photos of Chauvet Cave in the pages of *National Geographic*, I vowed to travel here. I can't recall the last time I felt so captivated by a series of images, those charcoal and red ochre drawings of extinct mammals expertly rendered by people who lived so many thousands of years ago. And now here I am in the Ardèche Gorges, tantalizingly close to Chauvet Cave—that series of subterranean galleries so ancient and extraordinary it has forced us to reexamine our understanding of both the evolution of art and human intellectual development.

Chauvet Cave is recognized as perhaps *the* artistic find of the twentieth century. About twice as old as the more famous painted caves at Lascaux (France) and Altamira (Spain), the images at Chauvet have been dated at 32,000 radiocarbon years (or 35,000 calendar years). It is a cave filled with over four hundred paintings and etchings, most depicting large mammals—bison, horses, mammoths, megaceros (the largest deer that ever lived), lions, rhinoceros, musk ox, and hyenas. Since its rediscovery, Chauvet Cave has opened a portal into the distant past that is redefining what we thought we knew about ourselves. And yet for all its importance to our understanding of the flow of human history, Chauvet was first and foremost a bear cave.

I step out of the car, walk to the edge of the slope, and survey the far gravel bank. The modern eye still beholds the massive stone arch as a place of wonder. I try to imagine it as it was in the time of the people who first visited Chauvet Cave—just a few thousand years after anatomically modern humans first appeared in Europe. Surely, they would have seen this as an extraordinary place. At that time, the environment was a cold, semi-arid grass-land with fewer trees. I conjure up a vision of a mammoth dip-ping its trunk into the cool water as a maneless lion watches silently from the shadows. I imagine an ancestor standing beside me on the bank, and wonder about his sense of fear, reverence, or hunger observing the same scene. Then, without warning, a woman in a plastic yellow kayak floats silently beneath Pont d'Arc, awakening me to the present. Although it has been thou-sands of years since mammoths and cave bears disappeared, the river, the arch, and the cave still endure—as do we.

In the corner of a parking lot five miles away, Dr. Philippe Fosse sits in front of his laptop in a dim prefab building, clicking through digital images as he listens to U2's *Joshua Tree*. The low ceiling and thin walls bring to mind the portable classrooms rou-tinely plunked down next to overflowing, cash-strapped public schools across North America. I did my fair share of time in buildings like these.

It's almost midnight and several people are still hard at work here at Base Départementale de Loisirs, the part-time home of the research team studying Chauvet Cave. Some review notes made in the cave earlier today; others stare endlessly at maps and grids. To fortify the late-night researchers, a bottle of cognac is making the rounds.

Philippe Fosse is one of the world's preeminent cave bear re-searchers. He wears wire-rimmed glasses, an untrimmed beard, and an expression of careful scrutiny. Both a paleontologist and a zoo-archaeologist, he is kind enough to spend the evening giving me a private tutorial. Fosse explains that—in a subterranean art gallery whose walls are covered with magnificent images—he focuses mainly on the floor. "We have four thousand bones on the floor that we can see, but we cannot touch them," he says as images of cave bear skulls, scratch marks, paw prints, wallows (beds), and bones flash across the screen. "It's important because if you excavate, you destroy the floor. If you don't touch it, you preserve it . . . For us it is not so easy to work this way, but we decided to preserve all these things. And so we have to find something through observation." In addition to digital images, Fosse works with maps, 3D representations, and sonar that allows him to sense what's below the surface.

One of the images on the walls above the bones is a haunting red ochre painting of a cave bear consisting of just a few sinuous, suggestive lines and shading. It shows perspective. The bear is caught in motion, traveling right to left, with the head-down gait seen in brown bears today. This image, along with hundreds of others in the cave, was rendered by a skilled artist, someone who had observed these animals in close proximity. Because of the cave's miraculous state of preservation—due in part to the prescience of the cave's discoverers—the floors are as valuable in their way as the art on the walls. Researchers still follow the original footpath that Chauvet and company first took through the cave in 1994. And there are parts of the cave that remain beyond reach—left for future generations to explore.

"When I first came here, I was really amazed," Fosse says. "We have four thousand bones lying on the floor. Not *in* the floor but *on* the floor!"

In other caves throughout Europe, cave bear bones are found in layers, built up over the millennia. If history is a guide, what is visible on the surface at Chauvet Cave is likely the tip of the paleontological iceberg. Fosse has been coming here since 2000 and spends about a month each year working inside. Although he also works at caves throughout Europe, studying cave bears and other extinct fauna, Chauvet is something special.

"Also, there are so many beautiful, well-preserved paintings. It is an exceptional site . . . You cannot believe that the paintings and bones are thirty thousand years old. The cave was closed maybe fifteen thousand years ago [the entrance collapsed at the end of the last Ice Age]. And because it was closed very quickly, all of these things are well preserved. We have flints and charcoals—things we almost never find in caves. You can see the footprints of bears in the mud."

The footprints were made by cave bears. Unlike brown bears, which only occasionally shelter at the entrance of caves in winter, cave bears ranged into the deepest recesses of caves—over half a mile from the entrance. "There is evidence cave bears used caves not only in winter, but throughout much of the year," Fosse says. "And we think maybe cave bears lived in small groups—between five and ten individuals—in different parts of the cave. But we can't prove it."

I register my surprise. If true, wouldn't this mark a behavior not found in living bears?

"Yes. When we search for information in other parts of the world, we do not see the same thing as we see with the cave bear. We think they were more social creatures than extant bears. But that's not so easy to prove. We work only with bones—that's why we have to be very cautious."

But much can be told from bones. The cave bear (*Ursus spelaeus*) appeared around 150,000 years ago and died out during the last Ice Age, about 10,000 years ago. While closely related to the brown bear (*Ursus arctos*), the cave bear was a distinct species that was once abundant throughout Western Europe. Their bones give us a picture of their approximate size: They were on average about 30 percent larger than European brown bears, weighing around a thousand pounds. When analyzing cave bear teeth, Fosse says it is easy to see that their diet was almost entirely vegetarian. Cave bear bones were also found purposefully stuck into crevices in cave walls and the soft ground of the floor. They were put there by humans. This practice—found in other Upper Paleolithic decorated caves throughout the region—was a long-held custom. It continued over at least a period of 14,000 years.

In addition to the bones, Fosse spends much of his time analyzing the scratches made by cave bears. He has two hypotheses as to why cave bears would mark the walls. First, as with living bears, they could be territorial marks to indicate that a specific area was occupied. Second, it could be the bears were simply sharpening their claws.

It was once thought that humans hunted cave bears to extinction. Evidence, it seemed, could be found in the thousands of bear bones discovered in caves where people must have butchered and consumed them. Looking more closely, modern scientists have noticed that there are precious few cut marks on any cave bear bones, indicating that people had eaten them. Fosse says that perhaps prehistoric people occasionally killed cave bears, but it was "very, very uncommon."

Cave bears and humans did not occupy Chauvet Cave at the same time. So far, the oldest radiocarbon date obtained from a cave bear bone at Chauvet is about 37,000 years old, which is some 5,000 or 6,000 years before the first human occupation. Cave bears predated human presence in the cave, reoccupied it between the two periods of human activity (30,000–32,000 BP [before the present] and 20,000–27,000 BP), and again after the humans were gone.

Why is Fosse attracted to the study of extinct species? "Because these species lived with prehistoric humans, in the same context, because predators and carnivores are fascinating, and because we believe that predators played a very important role in human evolution."

It is believed that large mammals shaped human development through competition for food, and by encouraging us to cooperate for protection and hunting. In the case of bears, we also know that from the earliest times they were venerated as objects of worship. In the first two decades of the twentieth century, archeologist Dr. Emil Bächler excavated several caves in the Alps. In two of the caves he discovered remains judged to belong to the Riss-Würm

Interglacial Stage, no later than 75,000 years old. What he found was astonishing: flints, charcoals, benches, worktables, flagstone flooring, and "altars" apparently used for rituals. These, the oldest known altars in the world, had carefully arranged bear skulls and stones. Some of the skulls had longer cave bear bones placed below the snout and through empty eye sockets. They date to the time of the Neanderthals (*Homo neanderthalensis*).

Across various cultures and epochs, bears have been associated with rebirth and renewal, power and virility, kinship and healing. In regions where bears hibernate, they were seen as possessing a mastery over life and death. They were revered for their fierce maternal devotion. In some Western cultures, bears gave rise to the concept of virgin birth, since bear cubs are born during hibernation, giving the appearance of immaculate conception. Much later, in the Middle Ages, the she-bear was adopted as a mascot by the Catholic Church and compared to the Virgin Mary. Two-thousand-year-old terra-cotta figurines of half-bear, half-human Madonnas have been found in Europe, and the Greek god Artemis was believed to have been nursed by a bear as an infant. Calisto and her son Arcas (both of whom had been transformed into bears) were hurled by Zeus into the night sky for their own protection. They became Ursa Major and Ursa Minor. Remarkably, North America's Algonquin, Iroquois, Illinois, and Narragansett peoples also associated the constellation Ursa Major with a gigantic bear. And then there are the well-documented bear rites and rituals across Mesoamerican culture. But these are all relatively recent examples of bear cults and reverence among modern humans (*Homo sapiens*). In the revealed history of our relationship to bears, Chauvet Cave appears in the opening lines.

Deep inside Chauvet Cave is a relatively small room called the Skull Chamber, where a single cave bear skull rests on a large block of stone that had fallen from the ceiling. That single, elevated skull is accompanied by fifty-two other cave bear skulls on the floor. From the moment of its discovery, it has been a focal point of speculation. Some have said that it was proof of a bear cult. The photograph of this lone skull was among the most captivating images I saw in the *National Geographic* article that introduced me to Chauvet Cave. With its combination of bear imagery, scratch marks, skeletons, and a skull on a stone "altar," Chauvet Cave seemed to me the natural starting point of any meditation on the relationship between humans and bears. Fosse, however, is eager to keep speculation in check.

"It's not so easy to answer this question [of the bear cult] for several reasons," he says. "First, because the international scientific community now waits for the results of the Chauvet investigations to prove that in other caves there is symbolism related to the cave bear. Second, because up to now, we don't have any proof that prehistoric people came into the cave and put not only this skull on the stone, but the other fifty-two skulls in [what appear to be] circles around the stone."

What this proves, Fosse says, is only that there are bear skulls in the Skull Chamber—nothing more. They could have been placed there by prehistoric humans, or not. It is clear that water flowed through the caves at several different periods of history, and perhaps the skulls floated into their present position. To understand the hydrodynamics in the cave, the Chauvet team works with all the available geological, paleontological, and archaeological data. Only after all that scientific work has been completed can it be said—with any degree of probability—that the skulls were placed there by humans.

Fifty years ago, when paleontologists discovered cave bear skulls in some remote corner of a cave, they would automatically say it was evidence of a cult. In Chauvet Cave, they've found a total of 190 skulls—and 53 of them are located in one, central room. It's the first time so many cave bear skulls have been found in so small a space. "Maybe in a few years we can have a better idea," he says. "But the explanation is not only important for us, it is heavily anticipated by the scientific community. We can't rush it. It would be a pity for us."

I deeply respect his discipline and self-restraint when it comes to avoiding speculation, but isn't it also important to honor the human need to dream and wonder?

Even his dreams are rooted in science. Because Fosse spends so many hours in caves bending over the bones of this extinct species, he admits that his greatest fantasy would be to travel back in time and observe a living, breathing cave bear to test his hypotheses. The idea clearly captivates him. Were they as large as he thinks? Is he right about cave bear behavior?

When confronted with the fact that there are, perhaps, fifteen wild brown bears (*Ursus arctos*) still alive in France, Fosse is at best ambivalent. He shrugs and says that while the brown bear may be going extinct in Western Europe, it won't disappear throughout its entire range. Ultimately, he says, their fate is a "political decision."

"Of course they slowly disappear because people kill them—because of tradition and because they kill sheep. So we cannot say that we have to save the brown bear. I think it would be a mistake to reintroduce brown bears in the Pyrenees if we don't help shepherds . . . I spend a lot of time in the mountains. We have to help not only the natural background—mammals and birds—but also the people who live there."

On the slope above the parking lot and field office, the base has permanent facilities, meeting rooms, a dining room, and college-style dormitories. In the absolute darkness of my room, I try to fall asleep but my mind wanders the cave. What kind of courage must it have taken for prehistoric people to enter such a forbidding place to draw the beasts that prowled their world and imagination? That they could render their experience into a visual language their contemporaries could understand is astonishing in and of itself—but they were able to communicate to their descendants across a span of 35,000 years. As someone who works in a relatively young and ever-shifting language, the feat seems to me a miracle of the greatest magnitude. I wonder, Am I ready? Have I earned the right to finally stand before these images and "read" their ancient stories?

As THE MORNING shift leaves for the cave, I sit down with Dr. Jean Clottes, founding director of the team of experts who've been studying Chauvet Cave since 1998. Although he retired as director at the end of 2001, he remains an active member of the team. Clottes is a man of forceful intelligence. At seventy-one years of age, he is still tall and physically imposing; his long legs stretch out in front of him and his gestures abound with energy. I tell him that it was the article I saw in *National Geographic* that sparked my obsession. He smiles and reminds me that he wrote the article himself. He was not interested in having some outsider come and write about Chauvet Cave.

Titles held during Clottes's long career include director of prehistoric antiquities for Midi-Pyrénées, general inspector for archaeology at the French Ministry of Culture, scientific advisor for prehistoric rock art at the same ministry, president of the International Committee on Rock Art, president of the French Prehistoric Society, and editor of the *International Newsletter on Rock Art* (distributed in over one hundred countries). He has published over 350 scientific articles, and has written or edited twenty-one books—including two on Chauvet Cave. He is curious about which other team members I've met so far, and if I'm learning what I need to know. If I haven't already, I will soon discover that there are friendly disagreements among his colleagues, he explains. It is this dynamic that makes the project successful.

When Clottes was first called to investigate Chauvet Cave, his initial report speculated that the age of the paintings was between 20,000 and 22,000 years. Then the radiocarbon dates began returning from the lab.

"The first time I heard about it was on the telephone in the spring of 1995, and I was astounded," he says. "I couldn't even imagine that it could be that old. I was like everyone else. I was functioning within the same paradigm—the evolution of art . . . When I got that information, my first reaction was one of incredulity. But now we have around forty-five radiocarbon dates taken from Chauvet Cave—more than any cave in the world."

Although Clottes considers Lascaux Cave the "acme" of cave art, he calls Chauvet the "discovery of the century."

"Chauvet has fantastic cave art from the point of view of aesthetics. And with dates from thirty to thirty-two thousand years, Chauvet is much older than Lascaux—at least twelve thousand years. Chauvet shows us that the evolution of art is different than what specialists had thought for over a century. Ever since cave art was acknowledged in 1902, the paradigm was that art began thirty or thirty-five thousand years ago with very crude beginnings. With Chauvet, we see that we have something outstanding right from the start, very close to the time the first *Homo sapiens* arrived in Europe. Chauvet is very, very important because it changed our conception of the evolution of art for the whole of humankind."

There are, for example, very few representations of rhinoceros in Paleolithic art. Before the discovery of Chauvet Cave, there were less than twenty. Chauvet has sixty-five, including two individuals facing each other. There is a dynamic tension between the two, possibly representing two males fighting. "So this is probably a season for rutting or it represents sex or confrontation or something else," Clottes says. "We have no way of knowing the ideas behind this, but it is unique in Paleolithic art.

"What is striking are the aesthetics that come across the ages. It's the impression you find with any work of art that is very potent—even if you don't know about the cultural surroundings and the meaning it had for the artist. You can be very impressed with some church paintings of the sixteenth century without knowing anything about Roman Catholicism . . . The paintings [inside the cave] are very impressive. You've got lions two and a half meters [eight feet] long—and that's really a powerful image.

You can feel emotion seeing some aboriginal rock art in the depths of the Kimberly—something which I know—but Chauvet touches us maybe a bit more because it is so realistic. It is naturalistic. When you see the Chauvet lions you say, okay, those are lions and these are mammoths. So you can relate to them more easily, despite the immensity of time."

Human images in the cave are confined to handprints and stencils, and female pubic triangles. Overwhelmingly, it is the large, dangerous, nonhunted mammals—including cave bears—that captured the artists' imagination.

"My paleontologist friends Philippe Fosse and Michel Philippe say that in their opinion, Chauvet is as important for the study of cave bears as it is for cave art . . . We have bear beds, their scrapings on the walls, footprints, and bones that have been undisturbed. And also humans have sometimes tampered with some of those cave bear remains. We have cave bear paintings on the walls—so we've got a cave about cave bears. Many paintings are *on top* of the cave bear scratches; others have been defaced by the cave bears because they are scratched over. You have it all. This is the only cave in the world like that."

Some people have even wondered if the artists were inspired by the bears that stood on their hind legs to reach up and leave their marks high up on the walls—up to twelve feet off the floor. Some of the paintings are at this height, covering the earlier ursine scratches.

Ten years on, Clottes remains captivated by the cave bear skull on the stone block and the arrangement of skulls in the Skull Chamber. He was the one who carefully removed tiny samples from underneath that skull by reaching through the eye socket with a pair of tweezers. Radiocarbon dates confirmed that someone made a fire on that block between 30,000 and 31,000 years ago. Then later—"maybe five minutes, maybe five thousand years"—the cave bear skull was placed on top.

While he admits that it is quite possible that some of the skulls floated into position, or were inadvertently knocked around by bears or careless people passing by, Clottes sees the hand of human intent. He also acknowledges that this is a point of disagreement among his colleagues.

"Personally, I think that very probably some of the bears died there—but the proportion is too big. Because in that particular place, we've got one-quarter of all the bears in the entire cave. It is a lot. And it is a very restrictive place. Why should all the cave bears die in the same spot? Personally, I don't believe it. The skull deposited on the stone, and the one marked with black [charcoal] lines, show definitely that people tampered with the bones. We have definite proof of that . . . So, as a hypothesis, I think that very probably quite a few of those cave bear skulls were brought there by people from other parts of the cave."

Clottes sits back and folds his hands in his lap.

"Everyone agrees on one thing—and it is rare that we all agree on something. When people went into a deep cave, they did it within the framework of a religion. They did it for one simple reason—because they didn't live inside the deep caves. All archeologists know that. They went into those caves, made drawings and had ceremonies in the course of a religion. Where people disagree is what kind of religion it was and what kind of practices they had. Most specialists just don't want to be bothered with that. That is to say, 'Well, we'll never know. So let's date it and study it to see the relations between one region and another, et cetera, and leave the problem of religion alone.'

"Generally, people say that they represented their myths. Of course they represented their myths! It's obvious if you go to a church. The myths, the religious stories are there in the stained glass, paintings, and sculptures. Because you cannot function otherwise. This is absolutely obvious. So by saying that, in my opinion, you're saying nothing. It's a way of pushing the problem away—of not addressing it . . . Putting the myths on the wall of a church where people go repeatedly really has a purpose, because it strengthens the cohesion of the people by reminding them of those myths. But inside the cave, where very few people go, you've got to find something else. That's where the shamanic explanation comes in.

"I argue that people thought the caves represented the supernatural, that people went into the caves deliberately thinking they were entering the supernatural world. Very few people went there, and we know this from the archeology . . . I think they went into the cave to get in touch with the spirits that lived there because they believed they were going to the world of the supernatural. And if so, they were taking a big risk, right? The paintings were a means for them to tap that power. And, of course, the paintings were in the scope of their myths. They would tell stories there. Probably very complex stories. No stories are simple, ever."

ANOTHER DAY, another feast. It begins with cheese, salami, and aperitifs made from anise and pear, plus cherries preserved in liquor. The conversation centers on current work in the cave, greetings to new members joining the team, and farewells to those preparing to leave. Because they want to avoid the mistakes made at Lascaux—where the breath of thousands of curious sightseers began to destroy the paintings—the number of people allowed inside Chauvet Cave at any one time is kept to an absolute minimum. There are two short seasons for scientific fieldwork inside the cave (spring and fall), and the team consists of about sixty people who work in shifts. Tonight, about a dozen or so are seated around the large, family-style table.

Next to me is the youngest member of the team, twenty-seven year-old Julien Monney. A student of prehistorical anthropology, he has a ponytail, a Vandyke, and a little dirt under his nails from crawling around inside the cave only a few hours ago. Because research doesn't pay the bills, after his work at Chauvet Cave, he will

return to his home in Geneva and his second great passion—
teaching unicycle stunt riding. His dark eyes grow large as he casts
his mind back to the time he first entered Chauvet Cave, which was
only two weeks ago. He relives the experience for me over mustard
chicken and local white asparagus smothered in Lyonnaise sauce.

"The first time I entered the cave, I had no questions," Monney
says. "The second time, I had some questions. The third time, I
had many questions . . ." Seeing the art in situ, as it was created, is
an overwhelming experience that affected him on philosophical,
spiritual, and emotional levels. For him, Chauvet is absolutely
unique. "I've never been at an archeology site where they don't
play music while they work," he says. "It's quiet inside the cave
because it is a sacred site. You feel it when you enter. Some people, when asked if they want to enter again, say no because it is
too overwhelming . . . For the first five years, the scientists didn't
want to talk about interpretations of what they saw—only facts.
That's why nobody dares to write about it. It is too dangerous."

From the start, the study of Chauvet Cave has been a multidis-
ciplinary effort, he explains, a collaboration among archeologists,
ethnologists, geologists, paleontologists, and artists. Occasionally, they bring in amateurs because "They often find things the
professionals don't." However, the waiting list of supremely qualified researchers wanting to enter the cave is long. He can't believe his luck at having been chosen to work on such an important
and exclusive project. "We're not doing archeology on garbage,"
he informs me. "We're doing archeology on the human mind.
This is the beauty of Chauvet Cave."

When I ask about the cave bears, the placement of the skulls in
the Skull Chamber and the controversy surrounding them, Monney nods. "Sometimes we don't agree about it. Some people have
other points of view about the cave. When you enter Chauvet
Cave, you will have your own point of view."

My pulse quickens. This is only the second time the subject of
my entry into the cave has been directly addressed. A few days

ago, Dr. Fosse said I would learn more if I accompanied him into the cave while he works. However, not being the director, permission wasn't his to give.

Six months ago, when I first spoke to Dr. Jean Clottes, I never directly asked if I would be able to enter the cave. I had two strategies here. First, I didn't want to hear the answer if it were no. Second, I was sure that if I traveled all this way they couldn't possibly refuse a writer so fascinated with their work. If all else failed, I would charm them. Since my arrival, I've acted *as if*—as if it is only natural that I will be invited into the cave, as if an invitation to enter the cave is imminent, as if my entry into the cave is a foregone conclusion.

As dessert is served (quince terrine and fresh strawberries with cream), I'm introduced to another guest at tonight's dinner, a man in his early forties who I'm told is a well-regarded documentary filmmaker. After some small talk, I discover that he has been preparing to make a film about Chauvet Cave for a while now— five years to be precise. He says in all that time he's been allowed inside the cave only once, very briefly, and without a camera. He's curious about what I'm doing here. After a vague explanation, I change the subject and quietly hope my admittance to the cave won't be delayed another day—let alone half a decade.

IN THE HOPEFUL LIGHT of a new day, I seek the blessing of Dr. Jean-Michel Geneste, a polymath in the truest sense of the word. A doctor of both medicine and geology, he has extensively studied psychology, psychiatry, ethnology, and cultural anthropology. At fifty-seven years of age, Geneste is a slimmer, more handsome version of Albert Einstein with brown eyes, long gray hair, and salt and pepper moustache. He has replaced Dr. Jean Clottes as the director of Chauvet Cave's research team. In addition, he is also the director of conservation at Lascaux Cave.

"We know from modern life that humans produce pictures for producing emotions," Geneste says in a soft tenor voice. "And that

appeared immediately at the beginning of the culture." He under-
scores the fact that the artists almost exclusively chose to repre-
sent the large mammals populating their world—both herbivores
and predators. "Because they are only a very small part of the living world, it's clear that they are a codified syntax of symbols.

"One of the most beautiful things we can observe in the cave is
the progression and organization. You progress in a symbolic system. At the beginning we have only separate panels and separate
paintings. The more we progress, the more we have connections
of different species and animals. And at the end, you are in the
front of something like sixty animals on the same panel. You look
at them, but they look at you—and that's very strong . . ."

The strength of the images comes not only from their lifelike
quality, Geneste says, but also from the narrative structure.

"The more I look at it, for me it's the association of the lions—
the eyes of the lions," he says. "The lions are moving from the
right to the left. Opposite that, you have a herd of herbivores.
This is what I can call a narrative structure because you have the
lions moving against the herbivores. You also have the links
between the horses—which is well-known—and this narrative
structure is reinforced by the faces of the animals.

"Some of the herbivores have eyes," Geneste explains, "but it's
only a dot. For the lions, the eyes are very detailed with the white
part of the eye and the black dot in the center. And on all of
them, looking at the profile, they have two eyes on the same part
of the face. That's very significant. The representation of the face
of the lions is very well detailed, and for me, it is an anthropo-
morphic association between the lion and the human and it is
impossible that you don't see that in the cave. The lions are looking at you. It's very strong."

And what of the bears?

"All the bears of the cave are without eyes," Geneste says.
"Why? I have no explanation, no evidence. I have too much
guess, and for that reason I have no guess . . . It's a difficult job to

coordinate all the research in the different fields. It's a lot of work and we are very busy."

He is too careful to get caught up in what would amount to speculation—yet another reason I could never be a scientist.

Europe's lions, mammoths, rhinoceros, and cave bears are long gone. When asked about his opinion of the looming extinction of brown bears in France, Geneste is remarkably succinct. "It is not the first time and it will not be the last," he says. "It is one second in the evolution of the planet, and also the evolution of man's behavior on earth. No more."

It seems these men are chiefly interested in bears and other mammals as they relate to human culture. Their value is seen in the supporting role they have played in our story. During my time here, I have come to confront a question about my journey as well. Am I fascinated by bears for their own sake? Or only for what they can do, have done, or might have meant to us? Once, bears were viewed as being closely related to humans, as intermediaries between men and the gods, and as gods in their own right. Will their final role—and that of other large wild animals—consist of serving as a nostalgic reminder of a part of ourselves we no longer understand?

Geneste asks if there is anything more he can do to help me gather the information I need for my story, anything at all. With that, I realize I have arrived at one of life's decisive moments— where hope, opportunity, and fortune collide.

"Thank you, Dr. Geneste. Actually, there is only one more thing . . ."

THE UNMARKED TRAIL to Chauvet Cave begins at the edge of a vineyard. It's a warm spring day and the coaxing sun has the new leaves unfurling in a deep, emerald green. I walk through the manicured rows past the final vine, and then into the shade of the forest. The way is neither well-traveled nor obvious but I have a hand-drawn map, courtesy of Julien Monney.

The path leads through the shade and up the limestone cliff. At one point, it breaks out into an exposed, narrow trail along a precipitous rock wall that affords an excellent view over the valley. In the ancient past, the Ardèche River would flow here in times of flood. Other than that, the geography of the area is much the same as it was in the Upper Paleolithic. The path leads back into the trees and it isn't long until I'm at the modern entrance of the cave.

I think of the people preparing to descend into the netherworld 35,000 years ago. What did they imagine was inside? Did they come armed with more than flickering torches? The people who entered Chauvet Cave possessed power—of this I am certain. They braved known and unknown beasts to enter the bowels of the earth and immortalize their visions. Who was allowed to accompany them to see the images they had created? Some believe that the various chambers were used for specialized practices, perhaps by people at different levels of initiation, as seen in religious practices today. If so, was the Skull Chamber a *sanctum sanctorum*? What religious practices, if any, took place around the fire atop that block of stone? Under what circumstances was a young initiate allowed access to this supernatural world? So far, the only human footprints discovered in the cave belong to a preadolescent child—they lead toward the Skull Chamber.

The modern entrance to Chauvet Cave consists of wooden stairs leading up to a heavily fortified metal door framed with stone and mortar. Remotely controlled cameras are trained on the shaded passage. On the right is a tastefully designed plaque honoring the cave's discoverers next to an electronic keypad, whose combination remains a mystery to me.

Admission to the wonders of the cave will always be reserved for a precious, chosen few, and I suppose that's the way it should be. But as with life's other great mysteries, I find myself left outside, with only the stories and beliefs of others—and the burden of imagination.

I reach out and touch the smooth, cool door, then turn back the way I came.

8

CURE FOR
THE MOUNTAIN SICKNESS
Colorado Plateau,
United States of America

ALTHOUGH HE HAS been here countless times, conservation officer Eddie Benally seems uneasy sitting down for lunch at the Diné Restaurant in Window Rock, Arizona—capital of the Navajo Nation. The problem is that I've unwittingly taken his preferred seat (the booth) and have left him sitting in the chair across the table with his back exposed to the middle of the room. When I ask what's wrong, he explains that as an armed and uniformed member of the Navajo Fish and Wildlife Department, he prefers to keep his back to the wall so he can survey the citizens. I offer to switch seats but he waves me off. Instead, he sits stiffly across from me in his pressed gray uniform, white cowboy hat, and dark sunglasses, forever glancing over his shoulder.

The Diné Restaurant, whose name means "the people," is filled with Navajos of mostly middle age. Benally introduces me to coworkers and friends, and discretely points out people suspected of wildlife violations. It isn't long until he has surveyed and assessed every person in the large dining room.

I order the Navajo taco, which consists of ground beef, beans, cheese, lettuce, and salsa on a large piece of flat Navajo fry bread.

It is the biggest single "taco" I have ever encountered, more closely resembling a pizza with salad on top. I only get a few bites before Benally asks for a detailed recounting of the bear experiences I've had over the past five years. He shakes his head often, particularly at the stories of wildlife protection challenges in the Kingdom of Cambodia.

Soon it's my turn to eat and Benally, forty-six, tells me about his career in law enforcement, which includes a stint as a narcotics officer and a member of the tribal police. When he saw an opportunity to move from being a tribal cop to a "fish cop," he jumped at the chance. His latest career allows him to spend a great deal of time out on the land and provides the occasional opportunity to indulge his passion for fly-fishing.

Like the other three officers in the Navajo Nation's Fish and Wildlife Department, Benally clocks most of his hours working to stop the poaching of eagles and the illegal trade in their feathers, which are highly prized for use in Native American dances and ceremonies across the western United States.

"The feathers are used for powwows," he says. "The immature golden eagle between one and five years old is the premium bird. They have white feathers with a black tip. After it matures, the tail feathers darken and turn brown. Prime feathers from an immature golden eagle sell for a thousand to fifteen hundred dollars per set."

Eagle feathers seized as evidence (or collected as roadkill) are sent to the U.S. Fish and Wildlife repository in Denver, Colorado. From there they are distributed to Native Americans. In order for a Native American to legally possess and use eagle feathers, it must be in the context of religious practice. But a powwow is not a religious ceremony, Benally says. It's a social event. "In Navajo culture, it used to be that when you did something honorable, they would give you an eagle feather. In the old days, they used to build a little rock shelter with a hole at the top where they would put a rabbit. Then an eagle would come and the Navajo hiding inside would pull out a single feather from the living eagle. It was never meant to kill the bird . . . Today the feathers are a sign of wealth."

Unlike eagles, American black bears are relatively safe from poaching in Navajo territory, Benally explains. He has heard of bears being killed for their gallbladders in other jurisdictions, but doesn't think it happens here. The Navajo Nation is confident enough in the vitality of its bear population (currently about three hundred) to allow a fall hunt. Licenses cost $20 for Navajo seniors and veterans, $40 for adult Navajos, and $490 for non-Navajo hunters. All revenue from hunting licenses goes toward funding the Fish and Wildlife Department. Last year, fifteen licenses were issued, but only eight bears were killed—all by non-Navajo hunters. Among Navajo people, the taboos regarding bears—particularly the killing of bears—are still strong, he says. This helps preserve the local population.

"Taboos . . ."

It is a commonly held belief that if you kill a bear, you will go crazy, Benally explains. The mental illness will surface later in life. This also happens if someone makes fun of or laughs at a bear. There is also danger in crossing bear tracks or touching anything a bear has touched, touching a bear itself, or breathing the same air. If a bear eats fruit out of someone's fruit tree, they will cut it down or burn it. If a hogan (a traditional Navajo eight-sided house) or summer cabin is broken into by a bear, then it must be ceremonially cleansed before people can use it again. It is forbidden to touch bear droppings or eat their meat.

"We don't have much to do with bears," Benally says. "The Navajo name for the bear is *shush*, which in English means to be quiet. He is known as a protector. But you never talk about him. He hears you all the way up in the mountains.

"One time I had to shoot a bear in the line of duty. The bear had killed forty-two sheep and the shepherds were too afraid to even touch the dead sheep because the bear had killed them. After I put the bear down, I went and got a bear song sung on me by a medicine man. I had to. I'm a modern guy, but when my mom heard I had shot a bear, she about had a cow. She about had two cows. She said, 'Get it done right away. Don't let any time go by.' He's that powerful."

I chase the last of the green salsa around my plate with a piece of the sweet, oily fry bread. Benally and I have been corresponding about my interest in Navajo bear stories for some time now. This is his first mention of any taboo. "If people won't talk about bears," I ask, "how will I learn anything?"

He wipes his mouth and leans back in his chair. "I was wondering about that. I'd say it looks like you've got your work cut out for you."

AMERICAN BLACK BEARS (*Ursus americanus*) are endemic to North America and once ranged throughout most forested regions of the continent. Today, they are currently found in northern Mexico, forty U.S. states, and every province and territory of Canada (except Prince Edward Island). Although black bears have disappeared from significant parts of their historic range, biologists estimate that about 600,000 black bears roam the continent. They are, by far, the world's most numerous bear species. While some local populations are at risk, overall their numbers are stable or growing in most of their current range and there are no major threats to their long-term survival.

Black bears are omnivorous and feed on berries, nuts, roots, grasses, and other vegetation in season. They also can be effective predators of deer, moose, and spawning salmon. Black bears are highly adaptable to most North American forests, from moist to arid environments, and from sea level to over 6,500 feet. Aside from mating and the rearing of young, black bears spend most of their time alone. In areas where brown bears (*Ursus arctos*) occur, black bears shun open areas to avoid confrontations with this larger species.

Part of their success is due to their superior adaptability to changing conditions and their tolerance of human presence. Black bears are commonly found living on the edge of towns and cities. Unprovoked, predatory attacks on humans by black bears are exceedingly rare but highly sensationalized in the media. During the entire twentieth century, only 51 people were killed by black bears. For each person killed by a black bear, approximately 45 were killed by dogs, 120 died from bee stings, 249 were killed by lightning, and 60,000 were victims of homicide.

Because brown bears have long since been eradicated from almost all of the contiguous United States, black bears are the only bears that most Americans ever encounter. Given their historical distribution, virtually all Native American cultures were in contact with this bear and many established elaborate rituals and belief systems in which the black bear played a central role.

The Navajo Nation, which covers over 27,000 square miles of the Colorado Plateau, is the largest Native American jurisdiction in the country. Sprawling across the northeast corner of Arizona, northwest New Mexico, and north into Utah as far as the San Juan River, it is larger than ten of the fifty United States. Encompassing some of the continent's most spectacular scenery, the Navajo Nation includes the Painted Desert and Monument Valley—landscapes made famous in John Ford Westerns, countless television shows, commercials, and Warner Bros. cartoons featuring the Roadrunner and Wile E. Coyote. It is a land of stark, elevating beauty. Within its boundaries are some of the most important cultural sites in the western hemisphere, including Canyon de Chelly National Monument with its well-preserved ruins of the ancient Anasazi culture, and Chaco Culture National Historic Park, a UNESCO World Heritage Site that was a major center of ancestral Puebloan culture. One of the longest continuously inhabited landscapes in North America, it is currently home to well over a quarter-million Navajo.

EDDIE BENALLY WANTS to show me around, so we climb into his cluttered Navajo Fish and Wildlife "unit," a mud-splattered four-by-four pickup truck, and turn east on Highway 264. Window Rock (pop. 3,059) consists of a few cross streets at the edge of a broad plain. Beyond its dramatic backdrop of sandstone walls, past its strip mall and outdoor market, the land spreads out in a rolling expanse of juniper and sage.

An hour later, we arrive at the Hubble Trading Post, purportedly the oldest "continuously operated" trading post in the United States (since 1876). The pink sandstone building has the look of a Wild West jail. It still sells groceries and dry goods along with souvenirs and is, according to Benally, a good place to meet the locals.

Inside is a pair of wizened Navajo grandmothers. They weave traditional blankets on a wooden loom in front of a couple of captivated tourists, but seem present mostly for the benefit of each other's company. They wear their gray hair braided, and each sports a turquoise and silver squash-blossom necklace and matching earrings. Despite Benally's respectful entreaties in Navajo, neither has anything to say about bears. After another concerted but ultimately fruitless effort, he shrugs his wide shoulders. I decide to make myself small while he turns his attention to a stern-looking Navajo woman behind the antique wooden counter.

I pick out the words *shush* and *Canada* from their Navajo conversation as I peruse the ceramics for sale. I notice a few bear figurines and a rather inelegant mug with a black bear hugging the outer rim. When the conversation comes to an end, I am politely informed by the woman that Navajo people don't like to talk about bears; particularly older, traditional people—and most especially women. Bears can hear when you talk about them and it is best not to discuss them at all. This is nothing against me personally—it's just the Navajo way. Perhaps I would have better luck down the road with the Pueblo or Zuni, who may be more loose-lipped about their bears.

I gesture to the bear mug and figurines for sale. Why is it okay to make likenesses of bears but not talk about them?

Reluctantly, she admits that these items were in fact made by a Navajo woman. This, I'm told, is yet another taboo. These items really shouldn't be here, she says. In fact, the woman who made them has no business making bear images at all and will be informed of the fact the next time she shows her face around the trading post.

As we climb back into the Fish and Wildlife unit, I get that sinking feeling. I have left this journey for last because it seemed so easy to reach, so ultimately *available* compared to Asia or South America. Consequently, I let some of the planning slide. The result is that—out of North America's vast black bear range—I have come to a place where people won't talk about them. Now what?

The sun slips toward the horizon as we drive east to Window Rock. At first, Benally has little to say. Then he admits that this first foray didn't go as planned. Although he never really considered the challenge of helping me collect Navajo bear stories, he is now fully committed to the task. He is proud of his heritage and, as a conservation officer and outdoorsman, believes that the stories deserve to be told—regardless of taboos. While elders hold tight to the culture, the younger generations don't have a clue what they're losing, he says. The beliefs surrounding bears are a good example. The reason Navajo elders are reluctant to speak of them is out of respect. Unfortunately, this also means that too few young people learn the stories. When young people see a bear, they immediately react out of fear.

People are afraid—not of the immediate physical damage bears can cause, but of the unseen supernatural trauma they are capable of inflicting. When they call to report a bear sighting, Benally tells them that bears are protectors of the Navajo people, and that this one is probably just passing through. In fact, he keeps the tip of a bear claw in his medicine pouch along with herbs collected from the four mountains that are sacred to the Navajo people (Mt. Blanca in the east, Mt. Taylor in the south, San Francisco Peaks in the west, and Mt. Hesperus in the north). He wears it every day for protection from evil.

"What kind of evil?"

Benally pauses, gazing down the broken yellow line.

"Sometimes, we go out on a bear call, and it turns out to be a skinwalker," he says. "This happened to me I don't know how many times."

"Skinwalker?"

"*Yeenaal dlooshii*. Half-man, half-wolf."

I let the deep hum of the eight cylinders and the whine of the poorly aligned tires beg the question for me.

"People say that there is such a thing," he says finally. "I haven't seen one, but it has had an effect on me several times. When I was with the tribal police, one night I had a call. Something was making weird noises up on someone's roof. When I got there, I saw the shadow of it jump off the house and run. I saw the image of it. As soon as I turned my spotlight on it, it was off. Maybe fifteen dogs were chasing it.

"I was following it in my Navajo police unit. I heard a yelp, then I came across a dead dog. As soon as I got my lights on it, my whole truck shut down. Everything. Engine, lights, electrical. I was talking to dispatch, and it just shut down. My heart was beating pretty fast. You want to find out what's going on, but what are you going to do if you catch him?"

An excellent question.

"The dogs were barking and crying as they were pursuing it. Another sixty yards away was another dead dog. Then it took off into the trees and I couldn't follow it. Five minutes later, the truck starts back up. Right then I heard dispatch asking, 'What's going on?' They had sent another unit toward me."

"Could it have been a bear, or a wolf?"

"Oh no. It's half-man, half-wolf. I'm sure. It's in our culture."

The western sky in the sideview mirror has that luminous, abalone pink that quickly gives way to purple, then to black. The only other lights come from passing vehicles and the odd house nestled in the bush. Benally does not remove his sunglasses. I stare straight ahead, wondering where and how to proceed.

"I'm not the only one," he continues. "Other officers have run across it."

"Why was it up on that roof?"

"Maybe he didn't like that family for some reason. These people have something against someone, or they are jealous. The skinwalker's purpose in life is to bring harm to other people. In order to become a skinwalker, you have to give up a family member or a relative. You have to basically wish them bad enough that they die. That will turn you into a skinwalker. Then you live as a normal person most of the time, but you can transform into a skinwalker."

If there was ever any hesitation, any reason at all to hold these secrets within the confines of the community, Benally has long since left it behind.

"When I'm on the eagle watch with Fish and Wildlife, I camp out for four days and three nights. It might be a meeting place for skinwalkers. There's a network of them . . . I usually sleep in the bed of my truck. When I camp out there, I always have a dog with me. She's my eyes and ears. If it's anybody else—from gang-bangers to someone else causing trouble—she will bark and growl. But if it's a skinwalker, she races off.

"Once, they started rocking the truck and the dog was gone," he says. "It woke me up. When I looked out, I didn't see anything other than something going up the side of the hill."

I nod my head knowingly, like I hear this stuff all the time.

"A skinwalker is a very powerful person. He is the evil of all evil on the Navajo Nation. If he wants to harm you, he'll do it. He doesn't like me chasing him. He can make me suffocate, or stop my heart. Just like that," he says, with the snap of his fingers. "He does it because I cross his path when he's on his way to do evil to someone else. I just happen to be there."

I am no expert on Native American culture, but I do know from personal experience with native people—from the Aleutian Islands and the Yukon to the coast of British Columbia—that humor and teasing are alive and well in those indigenous cultures. Especially when outsiders are involved.

"What does it look like?"

"Kind of moving on all fours," he says. "Half hunched over. It's hard to see because it's always at night . . . I can give you another example. You know about the Mormon church? They're intense. They believe what they say. These guys come on the Navajo Nation. When I was a kid, that's how they recruited me to live with the white people in Utah. They convinced my mom to let me go." For many years, Benally lived with a Mormon family while attending school, but he is no longer a practicing Mormon. He still speaks his native language and holds his traditional beliefs.

A few years ago, a couple of young Mormon missionaries were trying to recruit another family on the Navajo Nation. They had been visiting the family's home two or three times a week and were "pretty intense." One day, an older member of the family announced that they had had enough and told the missionaries not to come around anymore. Aflush with the conviction that God was on their side, the missionaries returned that same night.

"This really pissed off that Navajo guy. He told them not to come back ever again. They finally left, but by that time it was dark. They were saying, 'Hey we made some progress. We're going to get someone in the church.' They were driving down the highway at about sixty-five miles an hour and this is what they heard." Benally raps his knuckles on the driver's side window. "They looked over and saw a skinwalker running alongside the truck. They sped up to eighty miles an hour and still they heard the knocking on the window. That kid said he saw the image of a person. He said the eyes of the thing were something he never wants to see again." The missionaries hightailed it back to Utah, never to return.

This has been truly fascinating, but the night is closing in and I'm feeling the need for a stiff shot of rationality. "Is it possible that when people think they see a skinwalker that they are seeing a big dog, a wolf, or even a bear?"

"Nope."

"You're sure?"

"Oh, I'm sure. It's a feeling you get. You know it's something evil right there. You don't get that with a bear. When I felt that skinwalker rocking my truck that night, I just had a feeling of something evil. You'll know the difference."

As luck would have it, I'll have a chance to test my powers of paranormal observation tonight. Instead of checking into the comfortable hotel back in Window Rock, I have already committed to camping out. I had hoped to not only save money, but to get the best chance of seeing a bear at dawn.

On the way to pick up my rental car, Benally tells me that tomorrow he will make a concerted effort to find the medicine man, the same one who sang the bear song on him. Now that he has had a chance to consider all the contact I've had with bears over the past five years—touching them, breathing their breath, looking in their eyes—he has become concerned for me. Those bears might not be aware of my good intentions. It never hurts to be sure.

I drive alone along a dark dirt road to a secluded clearing framed by ponderosa pines. Benally recommends this as a safe spot for camping. I clear pinecones and set up my tent in a flashlight beam, trying not to think about bears, wolves, gangbangers, or skinwalkers. Miraculously, I drift off for a few hours—but an ill wind gathers. The gusts come in bunches, shoving and shaking my tent, portending all kinds of unimaginable danger. I check outside now and then, but see only stars. The gusts continue into the small hours of the morning, which are too cold for sleeping.

I think of hopping in my little Hyundai and driving back to town and a warm, dead-bolted room. But I can't. I force myself to wait out the night. I stay because I am still engaged in a lifelong struggle to come to terms with my own collection of fears and beliefs. I recognize this night for the test it is. So I lie there shivering on the forest floor until I'm reasonably convinced of morning's first light. Then I throw everything in the trunk and race back to Window Rock and the pedestrian comforts of breakfast at Denny's.

TWO DAYS LATER, I step out of a Department of Natural Resources vehicle at an abandoned hunters' camp in Utah's La Sal Mountains, one hundred miles north of the Navajo Nation. A trailer and two late-model pickup trucks are parked in the quaking aspen; an empty case of Bud Light has been tossed in the grass. Here, at the center of the Colorado Plateau, it is the dying days of this year's spring black bear hunt.

Sergeant Investigator Edward Meyers is my guide. A professional acquaintance of Eddie Benally, Meyers is a lean, no-nonsense, thirty-five-year-old who wears a bulletproof vest under his uniform and a blond, Fu Manchu moustache. He says that, around these parts, only two types of people wear moustaches: men in uniform and men attracted to same. Meyers makes it clear that he's of the former persuasion. He also lets it be known that, in addition to being a hunter, he is a "card-carrying Republican and lifetime member of the NRA [National Rifle Association]." I like him just the same.

Meyers jots down vehicle registrations and runs them by

dispatch. When word comes back, he explains that the owner of one of these trucks has been busted for wildlife violations in neighboring Colorado. The man was hunting bears with hounds and was convicted of harassing wildlife. Bears can be hunted legally in twenty-seven states. Of those, seventeen allow bears to be hunted with hounds and nine allow the use of bait. Only six states allow bears to be hunted in springtime. Utah allows it all. Regardless of the permissiveness of the state he's currently in, this man has a wildlife conviction in Colorado; therefore, he has lost his hunting privileges throughout the twenty-two member states of the Interstate Wildlife Violators Compact. Meyers is curious to see what he's up to.

The distant grinding of gears can be heard and we return to wait in the truck.

Meyers has a bachelor's degree in zoology with a minor in law enforcement. He has been patrolling these mountains for nine years. During the bear hunt, he looks for infractions and tags bears that have been "harvested." Every harvested bear must be inspected by a conservation resource officer like himself. The information is collected and compiled by the state.

I ask about the use of the word *harvest* as a replacement for *shoot* or *kill*. Of course, *harvest* has always been associated with the season, act, or process of gathering a crop, a *crop* being cultivated plants such as grain, vegetables, or fruit. Its Old English root wood, *hærfest*, is related to similar words in Old Frisian, Old Saxon, Middle Low German, and Middle Dutch. It was well-established in the language by the Middle Ages and has been used in the same way ever since. But they say language is constantly changing. When was this venerable agricultural word reassigned as hunting newspeak?

"It's not a directive or anything," Meyers says. "I think it's just the lingo of management and biology. I don't know that it's a conscious effort. I see the value of softening words when talking to certain groups of people, and there has been some encouragement of that by the hunting organizations . . . But I don't object to calling it killing. People need to realize that's what it is."

Meyers knows what I'm getting at and readily concedes that hunting bears with hounds is a contentious issue. However, people are misinformed if they think it is somehow unfair or easy.

"I can tell you from experience that is certainly not my impression," he says. "But sometimes it is really easy when you see the bear cross the road, let the dogs go, and in twenty minutes they have the bear up a tree. And shooting a bear out of a tree—there's really nothing to it. The biggest challenge of the hunt is to get those dogs to do what they are trained to do. Basically, you accomplish that by getting the bear. Killing the bear is secondary. A lot of the time you don't accomplish anything. You just lose your dogs and spend the rest of the day trying to find them."

Still, Meyers admits that most of the hunters he encounters have a low regard for bears and "don't have a fraction of the respect the Navajos do." Most don't eat the meat of the bears they kill, he says. The goal is catching a bear. "It's different than hunting a deer where you're just getting something to eat. It's the idea of bringing home a predator. It's a different feeling."

I am interested in understanding that feeling. For months I tried to get representatives of hunting organizations to allow me to accompany them on a bear hunt—to no avail. I can't say I blame them. Many claim to have been "burned" by the media before. Ed Meyers, who hunts a variety of mammals and birds with bow or black powder muzzle-loading rifle, has himself been on two bear hunts, albeit both unsuccessful. The invitation to ride along with him now seems infinitely better.

Meyers has highly developed people skills and a genuine interest in wildlife and the outdoors. He also understands the attraction of hunting with dogs. His own hunting dogs are currently in the back of the truck enjoying the mountain air: a German wirehaired pointer and a chocolate lab. This all adds to the natural rapport he has with the men out on the mountain today. What they don't know is that his favorite form of hunting actually involves catching hunters.

"We use deer, turkey, elk, and grouse decoys," he says. "They are working on a bear decoy right now. We use these simulators where we have a problem with guys shooting from the road or shooting after hours. We put it out and hide in a blind with a video camera. It gets pretty exciting. There isn't anything that is more fun." Some people are so convinced by the decoy, that when Meyers jumps out to arrest them, they say, "Wait a minute, I'm about to shoot an elk."

Finally, a truck pulls into camp carrying a man, a boy, and a load of barking hounds in a custom-built "dog box" on back. The dogs—Walkers with a little Red Bone mixed in—bear a resemblance to English foxhounds with their thin tails and floppy ears. These specimens, like virtually all the dogs on the mountain, are wearing expensive radio collars with foot-long antennas. The man leers at us through half-closed lids. He cuts the engine, then gives a perfunctory wave. Meyers steps out and starts the small talk.

The man, in his late forties, has a pronounced scar across one cheek and what appears to be prison tattoos on his hand. Even to the untrained eye he looks like trouble, or at least has been in trouble's general vicinity. He tells the adolescent boy to show his pursuit permit. The kid exudes a twitchy, jacked-up vibe like he's ready to bolt. He produces the required paperwork.

In the La Sal Mountains, a pursuit permit allows the holder to loose his hounds on a bear at any time from April 9 to June 1, and from November 1 to 26. The pursuit permit does not allow for the harvest of a bear. In order to do that, a hunter must have a specific "bear" permit. The boy has a pursuit permit. This is how the father gets around the suspension, by saying he's just along for the ride. Legally, the man can't let his dogs loose on a bear: His son has to do it. But in order to arrest him, someone would have to catch him in the act. Meyers settles for searching their truck for weapons, which are not allowed on simple pursuit.

During the shakedown, a smug grin curls across the man's face. Meyers, ever the gentlemen, hands back the boy's permit and wishes them well.

From the cab of Meyers's truck, we watch father and son carry on with their family outing.

"Did you get a feeling off him?" Meyers asks.

"You tell me."

He pauses, choosing his words carefully. "It definitely seems that there are more bad-ass guys among the bear hunters. For whatever reason, they don't respect the rules or want an edge. I don't know what it is. There seems to be a lot of that type in the houndsmen ranks."

Meyers explains that in this part of the world, it is a common sentiment to ignore laws. It's part of the culture. However, he believes that 95 percent of the people using these mountains are doing so legitimately. Of the remainder, 3 percent are making an honest mistake and 2 percent are trying to get away with something. "Those are the guys you want to catch."

We ease back onto the paved mountain road. Utah's second-highest range, the La Sal Mountains soar above the surrounding red rock canyons with six peaks that reach over twelve thousand feet. The slopes are covered with fir, pine, and aspen. A glance back toward the valley affords a view all the way to the sandstone phenomenon known as Castle Rock. From top to bottom, the palette changes from white and gray-green to brown and rust.

Hound Talk, Level I: Ed Meyers, Instructor. When hounds are set on a bear, it is called a race, not a hunt. A wreck is what happens when a pack of hounds get all fouled up and lose the scent. The owners can tell what's going on with their dogs by the tone and variety of their barks. A booger bark, for instance, is what a hound does when it has a bear bayed, or cornered. It's a kind of wavering, frightened bark. The houndsmen communicate with each other via marine-band radios and have handles, or nicknames, for each other. They even have code names for Meyers, the "fish cop" on duty. They tell each other that the "man" is on the hill, or that the "fireman" has been spotted on the road. This allows everyone to govern themselves accordingly. It doesn't take an Enigma machine to break the code.

As we continue our patrol, Meyers spots a wild-looking character by an old pickup truck on the soft shoulder. He quickly pulls over behind. It's not that he suspects this man of being in violation of the law, he just wants to make sure I get a chance to meet a legend.

Grizz Baker is the genuine article. An aging mountain of a man with a shock of gray hair and a feral beard, he wears camouflage pants held up by rainbow suspenders and a bright red shirt stretched across a remarkably distended belly. His hand is stained with engine grease and is easily twice as thick as mine—which he shakes reluctantly. While it is clear that Grizz Baker is not happy to see Sergeant Investigator Meyers, it is also made plain that his presence will not in any way alter the course of events.

Baker has been running dogs for about thirty-five years, mostly a breed called Plotts. At the moment, he doesn't own any dogs and is just helping train some for a friend. I see a couple of wet noses poking out of the tattered plywood dog box on the back of his old truck. So far, he is one of the only houndsmen we have seen who is not equipped with the custom steel box on the back of an expensive, late model rig. He listens for both the far-off bark of hounds and the intermittent squawk of the radio. I ask what he likes about chasing bears.

"I'm *chasing* hounds," he declares. "Most guys go to chase the bear, but they don't catch the bear. There is a world of difference . . . Hear the dogs on the side of the mountain? That's all there is, isn't it? Killing? What the heck's that? I haven't yet [on this trip]. Don't say I won't. We killed four bears last trip . . . People did . . . It's a lot of work."

Baker lumbers over to the hood of the truck and grabs his radio telemetry antenna. He listens for the beep he hopes will tell him where the dogs really are. "I hunt in all my spare time," he says. "Took all my vacation and spent it with the dogs. I get up at three-thirty or four in the morning. I go out every day."

So we all share common ground: a love of dogs and the great outdoors. But why harass the bears?

His eyes narrow and shift in my direction. "You have to have something for the dogs to *do*. And you're not harassing the bears anyway. Anyone with enough brains to come out here would see that the bear is harassing you more than you're harassing that guy. Where does the bear go? Up a tree. He goes to sleep. Nine times out of ten he goes to sleep up there. He doesn't even know you're around."

A couple of Baker's friends arrive, including a bricklayer from Provo. He has a white goatee, thick prescription sunglasses, and a beer belly to rival Baker's. He likes to hunt bear for the "adrenalin," but has no idea how many he has killed in his lifetime. "I'd like to watch them tear a bear up," he says of his dogs. "I'd like to see them kill a bear before we get there but it don't happen. The bear usually wins. You get dogs hurt pretty good sometimes."

"I don't know why they're building so many jails," Baker opines. "I don't know why anyone wants to stop us. They took the mountains away from people and kept the kids in town. If you keep the kids in town, they're going to get in jail. [If they're hunting] they'll be gone and they won't be in town getting into trouble. That's how I raised my kids, all girls."

Despite pointing his antenna to the four cardinal directions, Baker is not having much luck getting a signal. At this point, I'm sure he has me pegged as a big city liberal or some other style of pussy. Still, he's willing to indulge—until I ask the following question.

"Most people don't have any trouble with hunting. What do you say to people who believe it's wrong to kill animals for fun and then throw away the meat?"

"I say why do you hate your grandkids?"

"Why . . . do . . . I . . ."

"Your grandkids might like it. If you take it away from them, they won't get a chance to like it or not. We hate our kids to hell. Look at the things we're doing to them. We're taking everything away from them. The goddamn government makes these stupid parks and ruins the ground [until] there's nothing left."

Sergeant Inspector Meyers dons his sunglasses and gazes off into the mountains.

"I think the first thing every school should have is a shooting range," Baker continues. "And I don't think schoolteachers should teach it. I think a decent hunter should have a class in shooting and let them know what the hell a gun will do. These idiots in [Littleton,] Colorado, they didn't know nothing about guns. Or they wouldn't have shot four hundred shells and killed three people. They would have shot four hundred shells and killed four hundred people if they had known anything about it . . .*

"If you don't teach your kids something," he concludes, "they are going to go out and try it sometime. They're not going to be good. If they knew about hunting and guns, they probably wouldn't have done it. A little education don't hurt. But you don't want schoolteachers teaching it or they won't learn nothing."

Some logic is irrefutable. "But wasting meat . . ."

"A lot of bear meat is ate! The hunters who don't use the meat are not the good hunters. We eat some bear meat. And I use the grease on my shoes. Use a big bunch of it. It waterproofs my boots. One-third lamb tallow and two-thirds bear. The best you can get. Then when you go to town, all the dogs either want to come over and see you or all of them run. My dogs lick the boots. And I feed them the bear meat. A lot of the times

---

*On April 20, 1999, two teenage assailants killed thirteen people and wounded twenty-one others before taking their own lives in the massacre at Columbine High School in Littleton, Colorado. Evidence shows that the attackers had more than a passing knowledge of how to effectively use firearms, including assault weapons.

you can't get it out of where you shot it. It just isn't worth going back for. You take out the back straps or the butterfly steaks if you can.

"[People say it's wrong] because they have never been here," he says, by way of summation. "You ask them how many times they have been out here. They have never been on a bear hunt, or a lion hunt. Never been with the hounds. They just watch the six o'clock news. Then some guy on the six o'clock news says, 'Hey, this is what I want you to do'—and TurnerVision's got 'em."

We take our leave of Grizz Baker and continue the patrol in silence. We pass more hounds, houndsmen, and numerous groups of serious road cyclists who favor these mountains for the scenic and challenging ride. It all culminates in the disorienting impression that they are holding the Tour de France in the Ozarks.

UTAH IS HOME to an estimated three thousand black bears. In 2000, after a seven-year hiatus, the state reinstated a spring bear hunt on a five-year trial basis to see if the "resource" could support a second hunting season. This is the last year of the trial. In all of 2004, 104 bears were killed by hunters, 39 were shot as nuisances, and 11 died in road accidents.

State wildlife managers hope to maintain a healthy, sustainable black bear population while avoiding an increase of nuisance bears and livestock depredation. However, Utah also allows bear baiting, which involves attracting bears to food stations where hunters wait in blinds for a shot at point-blank range. Critics (and some wildlife managers) claim that, aside from perverting any claim to the concept of fair chase, baiting might even encourage bears to develop a taste for human foods and thus become "nuisance" bears. Others maintain that bears, being omnivorous, are attracted to any source of food. Bait stations, they point out, are located well away from populated areas.

Many people object to bear hunting on ethical grounds, arguing that killing solely for amusement is morally indefensible.

Those specifically opposed to the spring bear hunt believe hunting bears at this time of year is repugnant because that's when they are at their most vulnerable—weakened by hibernation and, in the case of females, nursing young. Although adult males are the target, females are killed during the spring bear hunt and the death of a nursing sow results in the death of her cubs. Cubs also die after being separated from their mothers by hounds. However, some people see this hunt as a "right."

Ed Meyers and I roll into the hunting camp of a convicted poacher and his friend with a pending court date. Meyers was the arresting officer on the latter charge. There are three trailers, a half-dozen trucks, and numerous loose hounds. Although it is midday, the poacher must be summoned from his trailer. He presents in stocking feet, bloodshot eyes, and an air of contempt. Meyers inspects permits and gives their camp the once-over. Everything seems to check out, this time. We keep our eyes on them as we return to the truck.

Meyers doesn't want me getting a skewed opinion. Not all hunters are outlaws, he says as we drive away. He is keen to show me that bear hunting can also be a family affair. I decide not to remind him that the camp we just visited was made up of at least two families. There were several children playing with the fire while the poacher was in his trailer, sleeping off the effects of a bottle of Seagram's I noticed abandoned on the barbecue.

As we entertain thoughts of calling it a day, it is announced over the radio that someone has "taken" a bear. Meyers makes contact with the hunter and suggests a rendezvous for tagging it. We turn the truck around.

"It's Jimmy Dade," Meyers announces, referring to one of the top houndsmen in the area and a professional hunting guide. The Dade clan is infamous in these parts. The now-deceased patriarch was also a professional guide who was twice convicted of poaching mountain lions (Wanton Destruction of Protected Wildlife). In one case, his client wasn't having any luck, so he roped a mountain lion, put it in a vehicle, and drove to the general vicin-ity of the hapless hunter. He released the cat, hounds were let loose, and it was treed so the client could shoot it. In addition to staging this "canned" hunt, he was also convicted of allowing a client to shoot a mountain lion on his own hunting tag.

"It was a big federal case," Meyers says. "He was convicted of felonies, lost his hunting privileges for eight years, and was or-dered not to be around guiding for three years. But that was years ago. As far as I can tell, Jimmy is clean."

We meet at a picnic spot where there is plenty of open grass and sunshine. A family is parked in a new white pickup truck with a bearskin neatly rolled in back. As soon as we cut the en-gine, Tammi Dade—twenty-year-old mother of three—comes bounding out of the passenger door, beaming. This is her second bear, and her enthusiasm is hard to contain. She introduces herself and her kids with genuine warmth, friendliness, and pride.

I explain that I am writing a book about bears and would like to hear her story. Tammi Dade explains that she hunts "everything," including mountain lion, deer, elk, turkey, and antelope. But there's nothing quite like bagging a bear. Her first was in 1997. "It's the biggest high you could ever give yourself," she says. "I love working with the dogs and I love these mountains. We bring all our family over here."

The men take the skin off the top of the kennel. It has been filled with snow, then rolled tight to help keep it cool for the ride to town. The fur is a beautiful milk chocolate. Most *Ursus ameri-canus* have black fur with a brown muzzle, although their color can range from white (British Columbia's Kermode bear) and blue-gray (Alaska's glacier bear), to the brown and cinnamon variations commonly found in the West. A shiny white testicle has been removed from the scrotum and nestled in the fur of this specimen, like an egg in a furry nest. Hunters are not supposed to kill cubs, or females with cubs, and are required to prove the sex of any bear they kill.

Meyers grabs hold of the snout and opens it to get a look at the teeth. Black bears can live up to twenty-five years in the wild. He estimates this one to be about five or six years old, although it is difficult to tell. He removes one of the bear's premolars with a pair of pliers and drops it into a small envelope. This, along with a fur sample, will be sent back to the lab in Salt Lake.

As the men continue their work, Tammi Dade recounts the hunt. The hunting party arose at half past five and loaded the dogs in the trucks. They were on the road only a short while before spying bear tracks. The dogs were set loose, picked up the scent, and chased the bear over the mountain. It lasted about three or four hours. "It was a pretty good chase," Dade says. "We got him set up on a tree and got all the dogs tied back. We took some pictures. I hit it where I was supposed to on the first shot. Right through the shoulder and lungs." She says it took four men only half an hour to skin it. "A skinned bear looks like a person," she says. "It's a little weird. I told Jimmy, 'I think he's got longer legs than I do.'"

Dade says she enjoys a wide variety of game meat, especially elk. When I ask if she'll eat the meat of the bear she's just killed, her expression sours.

"No. I don't think so . . . If you've ever seen a carcass, you'd know why. The fat. It looks greasy and stringy. Bears and lions eat meat and I don't want to eat anything that eats meat. It's just weird to me."

What did they do with the meat?

"Left it. The crows and other bears will eat it . . . Should I show you the part I keep?"

I glance over at the bear skin and testicle, wondering what I've missed.

"My drink stirrer," she says, giggling.

Then it dawns on me. She is speaking of the bear's penis bone, its baculum. This will become her swizzle stick.

"I have them from bear and porcupine," she says. "I clean it and boil it and have it on a little chain. And I'll keep the hide. I want to full mount it. When we get the trophy room done, I want to have it by the fireplace."

The hide is stretched out on the grass. It measures seventy-nine inches from snout to tail. Although it's too late to weigh this bear, adult male black bears typically weigh between 130 and 660 pounds. Males are 20 to 60 percent larger than females. Meyers tags the limp skin of this specimen with a strip of orange plastic. Suggestive of recent, vigorous life, it is now utterly deflated—like an abandoned wetsuit or a used prophylactic. Only the bear's head holds its former shape, eyes shut tight.

A couple of anemic-looking Yorkshire terriers appear and begin vying for Dade's attention. She scoops up the smaller one and holds it up to the bear's snout.

"Some people say you should only kill animals you are going to eat," I say. "What would you say to that?"

She puts the lap dog down.

"I would say if you don't control the population of these bears, you will not have any bears left.* You can talk to anybody, and anyone who has been out and studied this will tell you the true conservatives are the hunters. We're the ones who put the money back into the wilderness and the studies making sure we have the animals to harvest them.† Obviously, we want to keep them here. We enjoy doing this. It's our livelihood. We are not going to do anything to jeopardize it. In California, they don't hunt lions anymore and there's no deer. The deer population is gone and

---

* "There is no truth in this statement—no research to back this up."—Kevin Bunnell, mammals coordinator, Utah Division of Wildlife Resources.
† Most of the revenue that supports the Utah Division of Wildlife Resources is generated by the sale of hunting and fishing licenses and permits. This raises the question: To whom is the department truly responsible—society at large or the hunters who pay the bills?

they kill lions left and right on the highways. They are eating people's dogs, cats, kids. It's ridiculous."*

We manage to steer the conversation back to neutral territory. The bear skin is rolled back up and lashed to the top of the dog box. As the family pulls away, I watch the pack of flaring nostrils poking out the back of the truck, savoring the sweet smell of success.

———

EDDIE BENALLY is a busy man, yet he takes the morning off to drive me to a place called Crystal and the home of Albert Sagina, the Navajo medicine man he consulted after killing a bear. Sagina hasn't been answering his phone, so Benally reckons it's time to go out and see if we can track him down.

We arrive at a small housing estate in a vast field of sage. The humble tract houses are finished in pink sandstone stucco and look like a chunk of suburbia sprung fully formed in the middle of nowhere. Sagina isn't home, but his truck is in the driveway. Benally knocks for a good long while, then takes a gander through the windows. Either he has a close relationship with this medicine man, or he can't shake the habits of a tribal cop. Finally, we climb back into his unit and drive away.

On the trip back to Window Rock, Benally explains that the decision whether or not to have a bear song sung on me is a personal one. Some medicine men might suggest it, others might not. Because I haven't killed a bear, perhaps a smoke will be good

---

* In 2002, an estimated 33,311 deer were killed by hunters in California. "We have no information indicating that mountain lions are a major factor regulating deer numbers in California," says Doug Updike, senior wildlife biologist with California's Department of Fish and Game. "Habitat regulates deer numbers. In fact, if mountain lion numbers were cut in half, that would have no effect on deer numbers." Mountain lion attacks on humans are rare. Only fifteen verified attacks have occurred in California since 1890. Of those, six were fatal. "It's astonishing that we don't have more. It is clear that mountain lions are not interested in eating people. We would have hundreds of dead people if that were the case."

enough. He says it's like making any major medical decision: Educate yourself and seek a second and third opinion. In the meantime, he says he knows where to track down Sagina's daughter. While he does, I might want to stop by the sports arena where the Navajo Nation's entire Natural Resources Department has assembled for its annual convention. Over a hundred people have gathered inside the dim concrete arena to take stock of the department's accomplishments over the past year and forecast the challenges ahead.

At the first coffee break, I meet Larry Joe, another Navajo fish cop. Joe is solidly built but possessed of a gentle disposition. Like Benally, he exudes a confidence that saves him the trouble of having to pull out the handcuffs or Glock .357 affixed to his duty belt. He seems grateful for any excuse not to go back to the bleachers for more sleep-inducing PowerPoint presentations and bureaucratic blah, blah, blah.

Joe asks me to repeat all the places I've been looking for bears around the world and listens carefully to the descriptions of bear encounters. He doesn't seem impressed, exactly. Concerned would be closer to the mark. Like his fellow officer Benally, he is one of the few people who have direct contact with bears in the Navajo Nation.

"They know when people are afraid," Joe explains. "They sense it. And if you are lost, they would know it too. They try to lead the way back to where you need to go, off the mountain or back to the trail. They say the bear is mostly the symbol of protection."

Back in the old days, he says, Navajo were captured and taken to Mexico as slaves. When they escaped, they would get lost in the border country. They would chant and pray for help and the bear would appear. By leaving tracks for the people to follow, it led them out of the wilderness. Traditionally, Navajo medicine men were interested in obtaining bear parts for their ceremonies, particularly the bear paw. But in order to be able to kill a bear, a man had to be an ordained "bear priest," a position he believes is extinct among his people. In the past, people's respect for the bear was complete. But times are changing. Now a few Navajo have even applied for permits to hunt them.

In his work with Fish and Wildlife, Joe has handled plenty of bears, although he's never had to kill one. After he's had contact with a bear, the next time he comes across bear tracks, he prays and explains to the bear what he was doing and why he had to do it.

"You use corn pollen, or white cornmeal," he explains. "I put that in his track. But you would get sick because you are not ordained to do this. I can do it. But I wouldn't even say it in front of young kids."

I appreciate his sharing this much with me. In exchange, I tell him of the dream that started it all—the dream where I found a bear sitting on the log in the forest. Partly human, the bear was wearing pants and glasses and was trying to sound out the words of an open book. In the dream, I sat down next to the bear and began to teach it how to read.

Joe's eyes grow large. "If a bear comes to you in your dream, you have to go out and make an offering to him right away. He is your guardian angel. For me, it is the wolf. I dreamed about the wolf, and that means he is coming around to tell me something. When the medicine man ordained me for the Wolf Protection Way, I dreamed about it that night and the wolf came to me. He was talking to me in Navajo and English. He showed me a lot of stuff. Just before he left he said, 'I will always be with you.' And when I woke up, I saw wolf tracks. I can always find some sign or image of him inside a building or out on the land. He is around all the time. He is my guardian angel.

"The bear is your guardian angel," Joe continues. "He came to you in your dream. I have never dreamed about a bear. The bear is you. He's guiding you, making tracks for you, and if you follow the tracks he will show you what to eat and what not to eat. And then you eat it. So that way, you collect all these bears stories while you are following his tracks. You are learning from him, but you are learning the basic stuff. To learn the harder stuff, you have to be ordained a bear priest."

Although the prospect is tantalizing, I already know I am not cut out for the religious life. What if I decide not to pray to the bear?

"Because you have seen the power there, you have to undo it or you will go crazy like a mentally retarded person. You do the smoke and the prayers, backtracking along the way. Whoever has seen you doing it, they will have to do it too. They will go crazy later on if they don't.

"I know a medicine man up in Red Mesa," he says, pulling out a pen. "He does the ceremony. One time, people took photos of a trained bear at a circus. They didn't even touch it and still the medicine man had a hard time undoing that. The kid didn't believe it at the time. It got to him when he was old. Psychological problems."

Joe pulls out his business card and writes the name of the medicine man on the back, a good medicine man he's had dealings with in the past. He doesn't know the phone number, but he gives me a detailed description of where to find his trailer. I will need to bring two things: a blanket I don't mind losing, and a gun. These will be used in the ceremony.

That night, the wind howls and I have no intention of pitching a tent. I drive for a long while, pondering all I have learned, until I find myself on the outskirts of Gallup, New Mexico. I eat alone in a Mexican restaurant, then find a cheap motel by the railroad tracks along the now "historic" Route 66. It's on a long, forlorn strip of similarly aging motels all in a race to the bottom of what can be charged to let a single room ($17.99). If ever there was one, this is a monument to the transitory nature of America's Western culture.

Inside my green shag and cinderblock room, I stretch out on the sagging mattress and listen to the passing trains. I obsess about a cleansing ceremony that involves a gun and an old blanket. I let my mind run wild.

LONG AGO, when people could still communicate with the animals, there was a family of six brothers and one sister. The brothers were excellent hunters and their hogan was filled with well-tanned hides. The sister had two sharp awls for making moccasins for her brothers. She also made their clothes, which she decorated with porcupine quills. Her exceptional skills had many a young man wanting to marry the maiden, but she had high standards. She said she would only marry the one who could steal a giant's quiver.

Word of the maiden's challenge spread and eventually reached Coyote's ears. An accomplished trickster, he promised to teach the giant the magic for growing strong limbs and muscles. In a sweat lodge ceremony, Coyote convinced the giant that the only way to learn the magic would be for him to cut off his own leg so it could be grown back bigger and stronger. Coyote pretended to chop off his own limb (a cleverly substituted deer leg), and then convinced the giant to proceed with the self-amputation. As the giant tried to regrow his leg, Coyote ran out of the sweat lodge, stole his quiver, and ran straight to the home of the maiden. She had no choice but to honor her own standard and agreed to be his wife. They immediately consummated the union while her brothers were away hunting.

When her brothers returned, they were not pleased to discover their new obnoxious and annoying brother-in-law. They took him on a hunting expedition where they planned to test him. Coyote was given the first kill, which was a large mountain sheep. On the journey home to present the meat to his wife, Coyote passed a village of spider people. He immediately began to boast about his trophies—a beautiful human wife and ample game. The spiders would not tolerate Coyote's rudeness, so they caught him in their web. When the brothers returned home, their sister asked, "What have you done with my husband?" But they did not know what had become of Coyote. She vowed to kill whoever had harmed him.

The maiden went looking for Coyote but could not find him. She returned and told the brothers to go and search. After sending each in a different direction, she decided to follow them. When she went east, she put her awls into her mouth. These became sharp, canine teeth. When she ventured south, her nails grew into claws. When she traveled west, her ears and nose grew large, and when she went north, she grew fur. Thus transformed into an angry bear, the maiden hunted down her brothers and ate them one by one. Only the youngest escaped. His name was Reared in the Mountain.

Reared in the Mountain fled north to the land of the Ute people, who gave him sanctuary for a time. Eventually, he was forced to leave. On his way home, he encountered a cave with a white bear at the entrance. The bear wanted to see whose tobacco was stronger. They smoked the young man's tobacco and the bear passed out. Reared in the Mountain revived the bear by rubbing tobacco ashes into its skin. He repeated this experience with a blue bear and a yellow bear. After reviving the black bear, he was welcomed and given protection in the cave.

When the maiden heard that her brother was coming home, she reverted to human form and greeted him with tears and tales of how much she missed him. He was suspicious of her and when her true intention was revealed, he narrowly escaped.

As the maiden searched for her brother, she discovered Coyote trapped inside the spider's web. She freed him and let out all her pent-up rage and sexual energy. She was consumed with lust. There was an orgy with the Coyote, skunks, and other creatures. Young men were lured to the site of her sexual power and lost their lives. When she finally had her fill, the bear maiden resumed the hunt for her brother.

Reared in the Mountain was ready. He shot an arrow through the bear maiden's chest but she did not die because she had removed her heart and given it to the chipmunk for safekeeping. But the wind whispered its location into her brother's ear. She cried out, "No, brother! You are my heart!" Unmoved by her ploy, he found the still-beating heart in some oak leaves and shot it with an arrow. Blood spilled from his sister's mouth. Reared in the Mountain cried over her dead body and said, "You are my sister and will always be here to help the people." Then he cut off her head and threw it up on the mountain. He butchered her body and threw the pieces to the four directions. These were transformed into the food and medicine the Navajos still use today.

Because of all the contact he had with bears, Reared in the Mountain became sick. First his feet were affected, then his blood, intestines, sexual organs, and finally his mind. And so he appealed to the bears for their help. They held a ceremony, sang over him, and he was cured. Reared in the Mountain was given the ceremony to pass on to others in need.

DURING THE TIME it took to tell this tale, Steven Begay has let his steak go cold. As soon as it arrived at our booth at the Denny's near Window Rock, he cut the meat into bite-sized chunks, set his knife and fork aside, and then spoke without a break. My plate is nearly clean.

Below his baseball cap, Begay, twenty-nine, wears bright turquoise earrings dangling from both ears. Unlike the other Navajos I have met, he does not shy away from direct eye contact, which is considered impolite among his people. He is confident and assured when speaking of Navajo culture, which he says is built on the natural world's duality: light and dark, good and evil. He confirms that the reason Navajo people are reluctant to speak about bears is because they can hear us speaking about them. Therefore, it is important to be respectful. As assistant director of the Navajo Nation's Historic Preservation Department, he says he can talk all day about the role bears play in Navajo tradition.

"Formerly, you always greeted someone with a kinship term rather than their given name. The bear is the same way. When you see a bear you don't say *bear* or *shush*. That will offend it and it will attack you. You call them *shitsóí*, my [maternal] grandchild. That's the kinship term for the bear, a term of endearment. When you see a bear, you always stand on top of a rock because that tells the bear that you honor and recognize its importance.

"The bear is very powerful and is a protector of the people. Just like lightning, the animals under the plants, snakes, and the wind. Those are the beings we rely on for protection. The bear is very powerful in the sense that it kills at the same time it protects. If you hurt or kill a bear, then you have to remake that being, and appease it. We take 'life feathers' [eagle's down] and put it in the left hand of the bear. We believe that bears are left-handed."

A fellow southpaw. I don't believe in signs, but I revel in even small coincidences.

Begay explains that any contact with bears can cause the "mountain sickness" and the ceremony to cure it is called *dziłk'ijí*, which ethnographers translate as the Mountain Way ceremony. The same ceremony used to cure Reared in the Mountain, it has survived into the twenty-first century.

The first medicine men had to learn about the plants from the "mountain people," the bears. They did not offer their knowledge; humans had to appease them with offerings in exchange for their magic and medicine. The Mountain Way ceremony consists of making offerings to the bear and a recounting of the Changing Bear Maiden story.

"The bear figures into almost all our ceremonies," Begay explains. "If we have to tear things up for a ceremony, like yucca, we use the bear claw—not a hand or knife. When ritual paraphernalia were constructed, certain things had to come out of the bear's den while the bear was still inside. And certain things had to be given directly to you by a bear. The old singers could spread a buckskin down in the forest and sing a bear over to them. The bear would come to them and they would request what they needed."

When Begay finally takes a few bites of his food, a young mother passes our table with an infant tied to a traditional Navajo cradleboard.

"Like us, bears love children," Begay says. "A female bear will take a child to raise as her own."

I ask if this is another story from the olden days. He shakes his head.

"There is a guy in my community that was taken by a bear when he was three or four years old. He still remembers."

The boy was playing outside when a female bear approached. She sat down beside him and played with him as a dog will play with a child. She let him sit on her back. Eventually, the bear got up and walked away, looking back over her shoulder from time to time to urge the child to follow. Usually, when this happens, the bear already has cubs and just adds the human to her litter. She digs up roots and feeds him, letting the child nurse along with her cubs. More often than not, the child ends up calling the bear its mother. This bear, however, had no cubs of her own. The boy followed her all day until finally the sun was going down. She brushed dry grass and pine needles into a circle and then lay down to make them warm. The bear got up, nudged the boy into the nest, and then lay down to sleep beside him. She kept him warm through the night.

Naturally, the boy's family wanted him back so a ceremony was held and specially appointed men ("cornmeal messengers") were sent out to find him. Begay's grandfather sang on three occasions when a child was taken by bears, including this one.

The next day, the boy awoke and the bear was still with him. They went off together and the bear showed the boy what foods were good to eat. When they came to a thicket of chokecherries, she grabbed branches and pulled them down so the boy could eat. Eventually, he had his fill and wanted to go home. He walked away from the bear and the messengers found him. That boy now has children of his own.

"Are you a medicine man?"

"In Navajo, we are not supposed to say we are."

"But you are a singer of the songs."

"It is common knowledge who the singers are . . . I am just a young singer."

"So what can you tell me about skinwalkers?"

Begay pauses for a moment, then lowers his voice. "We are very careful about this kind of knowledge. In order to take part in this dark side, you have to sacrifice a member of your family. It has to be your child or a sibling. Someone who has your direct blood. You don't physically kill them yourself, but they will die and their death will be your payment to get that knowledge."

Suddenly, the clatter of cutlery and the murmur of distant conversations intrude. There is something incongruous about learning such things in this generic link in a restaurant chain. I feel a twinge of guilt for having doubted the sincerity of Eddie Benally's stories. I decide it is time to share a few of my own, stories of bear myth, medicine, and encounters I've had over the past five years. In the end, I ask if—as a non-Navajo—I am susceptible to the mountain sickness.

"In the Changing Bear Maiden story, we don't say that the family was Navajo. We just say that it happened a long time ago." Begay holds up his hand and extends his fingers. "We are all five-fingered people, the holy people. My grandfather and uncles always said that when we are taught these things, they are for the people, the children, and whoever comes to you wanting your help and the medicine of our ancestors. It is our responsibility to help them.

"Just being in the presence and power of the bear—almost communicating with it—is too powerful for humans. When you communicate with the things of power, even though they don't mean to harm you, they will effect you one day. It surfaces in epilepsy in its harshest form."

I propose that there can be a difference between respecting the power of myths and believing them to be literally true.

"As a singer of a ceremony, I am supposed to believe it in my heart," Begay says. "And when I'm part of the ceremony, when I'm part of the rituals, it does come from my heart and I believe wholly in it. But when I bring myself out into society, I have to take two looks . . .

"I would say, be careful as you put this book together. There is a kind of blessing or offering that can be done and it's up to you to choose to have those things done on your behalf. But I would urge you to do that. I've seen people who couldn't walk anymore because they walked in the trail of a bear. They had a ceremony and now they can walk fine . . . From the limited time I have been doing the ceremonies, some things you just can't explain."

"Why are you telling me these things?"

"Because you asked," Begay says. "We are the last of the Mountain Way singers. I am one of three singers who perform the full ceremony. The man I got the knowledge from said, 'It is going to be your job to ensure that you pass it on in whatever form you can.'"

"Now that I have the story, what is my responsibility?"

"Make sure it is told respectfully and acknowledged as pure Navajo. And have it available to the people. Give it back to a Navajo somehow."

WHEN I CHECK IN with Eddie Benally, he is convinced that the reason we haven't been able to find Albert Sagina is because he is up at his mountain home. Therefore, he takes yet another afternoon off to drive me up Fuzzy Mountain. He tried for the better part of a week to get in touch with the medicine man, but no one returns his calls. I ask if it's any trouble, if he really should be doing something else, but he says it's a slow time of year.

Besides, he believes this meeting is important for my well-being and he feels responsible for me.

We travel along muddy trenches that in a few dry weeks will pass as roads. They lead up into soaring, pine-covered slopes and rapidly greening meadows. Along the way, I tell Benally about what I've learned, including the story of the boy abducted by a bear.

"I was taken by a bear when I was a boy," Benally says, without missing a beat. "We were up in the mountains. I was just a tater [about three years old]. I was sitting there while my parents were collecting wood when a bear came by. He didn't want to hurt me or anything. He just pushed me around. I rolled over and sat back up again and he'd push me around some more. Just like a dog would play with you. My parents saw it and they chased it off. I don't remember it. When I was a teenager, my mom finally told me what had happened."

"Eddie," I say after a protracted pause, "why didn't you tell me this before?"

"I don't know. I guess it just didn't seem that important."

Eventually, we arrive at Sagina's place but the gate is chained with several locks. Although the house is visible in the distance, there is neither smoke coming from the chimney nor vehicles parked outside. Benally says this leaves only one other place he could be.

We travel farther into the forest, where towering ponderosa pine shade patches of snow and a faded carpet of last year's needles. We follow fresh tire tracks to a ridge, which offers a view out over the valley a hundred feet below.

Someone has been here recently, Benally says, scrutinizing the tracks in the soil. Several someones, it would seem. When I ask where we are, he points to a cleft just below the cliff where a thin trail leads down into the valley. A bear's den. This is why Sagina comes here with his patients—to stand on this ridge and perform the rituals and offerings to the bear. Judging by the freshness of the tire tracks, we must have just missed a ceremony.

Benally is unfazed by the disappearing medicine man. He remains convinced we will eventually track him down. But it seems he is avoiding me, dodging and weaving each time I draw near. On the ride back down the mountain, I find myself plotting a journey north to Red Mesa—and wondering how one goes about acquiring a gun.

SERGEANT INVESTIGATOR Edward Meyers and I are up and patrolling Utah's La Sal Mountains before the break of day. We drive past several lone tents and trailers before arriving at Camp Jimmy Dade. A pack of excited boys and dogs run between the pickup trucks, tents, and trailers, as adults polish off their morning coffee. At first glance, the place has the look of a Boy Scout Jamboree. This impression is short-lived. We get long, hard stares from most of the houndsmen; only two return our greetings. Even at this early hour, chewing tobacco is evident in protruded lower lips, sagging breast pockets, and in faded rings on the back of Wrangler jeans. Soon, Jimmy Dade starts his engine and the hunt is under way.

We drive slowly, tailing the last truck to pull out of camp with a "strike" hound chained to the top of the dog box. A Walker, it feasts its magnificent nose in the onrush of air as its fellows settle for sniffing through the crowded vent below. All are focused, quiet, and intent. For half an hour we travel bumper to bumper, but the dogs are unable to pick up the scent. At one point, a houndsman stops to check telltale signs.

We listen to the radio for any code that speaks of action. Eventually, it is announced (in plain English) that a bear has been spotted and is on the run. All trucks immediately pick up the pace and speed toward the specified mountain slope. As soon as we arrive, Meyers and I look up and see a black bear sprinting across an open field. Seconds later, we see six hounds closing the gap behind.

The other men drive off the side of the road and run to the back of their rigs. They immediately free their hounds, which tear up the thirty-degree slope. The moment they catch the scent is unmistakable; they bark and bound along the pungent trail— but in the wrong direction. The houndsmen curse, kick gravel, and then run after their dogs. When they reach the scent trail, they yell and grab the hounds by the radio collar and shove them in the right direction.

Meanwhile, the bear has disappeared around the bend. While these men sort out the wreck, Meyers and I hop back in the truck and drive around the corner. There, in a ravine below the road, we find a pack of hounds ringing the trunk of a large ponderosa pine. They are in a frenzy, barking and rearing up on hind legs, bouncing off the base of the tree. The houndsmen and their families all gather around as still more dogs join the fray—the ones either too slow, too late, or too inexperienced to know what to do. I wade in until I'm swamped with excited tails and antennas whipping my knees. I survey the faces of the over two dozen people around me. Men, women, and children all caught up in the excitement and anticipation of what's to come.

On a branch thirty feet above is a single, terrified bear. It desperately hugs the tree, its chest rising and falling in rapid succession. It still cannot catch its breath. After five months in hibernation—and a sudden, incredible run—it is now gasping so fast I wonder if it might just collapse and save them the trouble. Now and then, it allows itself a glance at its tormentors below. I meet its eyes and instantly recognize both the expression and body language of a fellow creature cornered, frightened for its life. After half an hour of letting the dogs have their day, the men round them up and pull them from the tree.

A woman in her thirties steps out of an idling truck, holding a child in one arm and a gun in the other. She sets the toddler down and walks toward the crowd with the rifle pointed up for safety. She stops in front of me, turns, and faces the tree.

———

I FIND A MESSAGE waiting back in Window Rock. Eddie Benally has arranged a meeting with the medicine man at nine in the morning. It turns out that Albert Sagina hasn't been avoiding me after all; it's just that his services are much in demand.

I am welcomed into Sagina's tidy home and offered a seat beside the woodstove. Among the family portraits and snapshots on the wall is a drawing of a tall, bearded Muslim on the run from an enraged bald eagle wielding an American flag. Although there is a comfortable-looking armchair directly across, Sagina pulls up a plastic milk carton and sits down three feet away from me. He says it's his favorite chair. The way his knees are these days, he can't sit too high or too close to the ground. This carton is just right.

Sagina is unsure, but figures he's around sixty years old. He prefers not to count his days. He has a dark, creased complexion and gray hair bound by a turquoise bandanna. After brief introductions, I catalog my bear experiences and explain that somehow, my journey seems to have led to this place. As I tell my tale, his expression oscillates between fascination and concern. Then I sit back and listen.

Albert Sagina was raised by his grandmother, a medicine woman who lived to be 108. When he was a boy, he traveled all over the reservation with her, learning the ways and means of the medicine trade. "When my grandmother sang the bear song, the bear came up to her," he says. "I was scared and ran. But my grandfather grabbed me by the hair and said, 'You idiot, you want to get killed?' He told me to hold my head up, look at the bear and pray to it. I was shaking like a leaf.

"My grandfather used to play with the bear to see how strong it was. He would go up to the mountains and the bear would come out and play. They'd chase each other around the piñon trees, wrestling and playing all kinds of games. When my grandfather would return to the hogan, my grandmother would say, 'Go shower off. You smell. Do some holy corn and dry yourself with that, then come back in.'"

Sagina has been working as a medicine man since 1958. He depends on the bear in both his personal and professional life. If one of his patients is dying, he goes to the bear's den and prays, asking the bear to intervene. He offers it white and yellow corn. The bear is especially helpful to people who find themselves in jail. Sagina prays with prisoners, asking the bear to forgive them for their crimes and promising that it won't happen again.

"Today there are a lot of things going on, violence on the highway and the city. If you are going into a big town or a dangerous neighborhood, you pray to the bear and he will take care of you. If a man or a boy is going to war, like Vietnam or Iraq, you have to take him to the bear cave and pray to the bear. 'Take care of this boy today and tomorrow. Wherever he's going, help him be on the safe side and come back safe to us.' That's what we pray."

The bear's power and protection is sought for all sorts of reasons. Kids dreaming of professional wrestling careers come wanting the medicine man to pray to the bear so that they might have its strength and ability to withstand pain. Sagina turns no one away.

"I don't pray for only Navajo," he says. "I pray for Germans and Japanese. As long as they have five fingers, we take care of them. You have to pray for them, you have to love them. I don't care what color they are. I prayed for a colored guy, Chinese, white, you name it. They come to see me. Some other medicine men won't pray for other nationalities. I just wonder what they believe . . . I know a lot. I'm not saying I'm number one. I just go by the rules of the holy people. You put the holy people in the front. I'm in the back. I'm just an interpreter for them—I do what they say."

The next time I see a bear in the mountains, Sagina counsels, I should explain what I'm doing. Bears understand all languages, not just Navajo. "I don't care what nationality you are, just talk to them. They understand you. A lot of animals do. When you go out in the woods, some of the animals like you and some of them don't. Just like people.

"If you are Navajo and you kill a bear, the spirit of the bear will come back and start following you. You will go crazy or it will mistreat you in the spirit way. You have to pray back and tell him why he was killed. Eddie [Benally] had to kill that bear because of the law. If they are stealing, they have to shoot them. I fixed a lot of medicine for him and prayed to the bear that Eddie didn't mean to do it. He just went by the law. Or else he won't have any money or work. He's all right now."

Although I've never killed a bear, I have certainly been in touch with their power. In that case, Sagina says the prescription is less obvious. In order for him to know what to do, I have to tell him everything. There must be full disclosure. It is only then that I remember to tell him my dream.

"Your dream is asking you why you are writing this book. What's your answer? Pray to the bear. That way you will learn more from it. Tell him you're only making a story for the people. That way, wherever you go, the bear will know. If you don't, later on it will take you. You'll get mad, mistreat your kids. You can say, 'I'm not going to do all that,' but when you get old, you will start doing things without thinking, just like the bear. You are going to kill somebody. Or if somebody scares you, you will just kill them. That's the way the bear is."

Sagina adjusts his seat on the milk carton, then rubs his knee.

"If I get a dream like that, the next day I walk up to the mountain and I pray . . . I don't know how many years ago this dream happened to you. But that's quite a long time. Get a medicine man and have a prayer done, or pray to the bear and tell him it's only for the book. It's really up to you."

Then Sagina offers to sing a bear song on me, but only if that is what I freely choose. He offers this prescription more as a suggestion—advice to a headstrong son. Other medicine men may have a different opinion. If I decide I need a song, he says, we can meet again tomorrow.

———

ABOVE THE GATHERING CROWD, beyond the upraised barrel, the bear still can't catch its breath. It now divides its attention between the barking hounds and maintaining its tired grip. As I gaze up at the dark, cowering form, I can't help but think of Chhattisgarh and the terrified women up the mahua tree.

The woman standing in front of me now holds her rifle aloft for what seems an inordinate length of time. She is posing for photos. Her husband and friends are crouched around, searching for the most dramatic angles of the tree, bear, and bear hunter. Then all at once, she's had enough. She stiffens her back, cradles the stock in close to her cheek, and squeezes the trigger. The clap echoes across the ravine as the bear instantly falls from the tree. It lands on its back with a dull thud—then jumps up and runs away.

Once again, the hounds are released and we all follow as they crash through the underbrush. It's a short race. The bear collapses below a bush a hundred yards away. The pack descends, barking and nipping at the body.

When the houndsmen arrive, they pull off the mature, experienced dogs to allow the younger, greener ones to get a taste for the enemy. One small hound is so voracious, that when it is picked up off the ground it refuses to unlock its jaws. It ends up tearing out a chunk of fur and skin. Through it all, the bear's eyes are open wide. Eventually, the men call off their hounds and begin the process of hauling the three-hundred-pound body out of the ravine. It requires the strength of six men, but the job is accomplished rather swiftly as this was a conveniently located harvest.

Up on the road, I get a better look at the body of the bear being dragged up the slope. In particular, I follow the left eye that reflects emerald green off the retina like it's caught in a flashlight beam. But this "reflection" stays no matter where I or the bear moves. It is almost as if this dim, persistent light shines from within.

The mood of the crowd is jubilant. This was a large, healthy male of about seven years. Once the body is sprawled on the asphalt, yet more photos are taken of children sitting astride its back. One little girl is asked if she wants to "ride" the bear. Although she vehemently declines, she is scooped up and placed on the body just the same. She jumps off and runs away at the first opportunity.

Finally, the dead bear is heaved up onto the tailgate of the truck and lashed to the back of the dog box. Bright blood drips down onto the pavement. The woman who shot the bear says she waited nine years for her bear permit and is pleased with the result. When I ask how much meat a bear like this will provide, she wrinkles her nose and shakes her head. Bear meat is no good, she declares. She doesn't eat the flesh of carnivores. Once skinned, the body will be dumped in the woods.

Because an animal was slaughtered for reasons other than procuring food, I can't help but think of sacrifice—the ritual act of offering up some innocent to appease the gods. I have no faith in the ego or divinity appeased by the slaying of this bear.

The hunter glances down at the pooling blood below the tailgate. "They should make a chalk outline of a bicyclist," she observes. "Maybe that'll scare the hippies into slowing down."

This party's over. There are lost dogs to round up and dirty work to be done. Soon the barking fades as the trucks roll away and silence rushes in.

THIS CIRCLE CLOSES back in Window Rock, over lunch at the Diné Restaurant. Eddie Benally wants a detailed account of what the medicine man had to say. He hangs on every word—until other patrons begin to arrive. This time, I have my back to the door and he has full view of the proceedings. He points out two Navajo men in camouflage caps who take a table as far from us as possible. These characters have been in trouble with Fish and Wildlife before. When it comes to the animals and the land, not all Navajo have respect, Benally says. Some have a sense of entitlement.

"So," he says, "what are you going to do?"

I tell him that I have consulted the experts. I don't know if I'm on the right path, but I've made up my mind about what to do—it only remains to choose where to do it. Luckily, Benally knows just the place.

ABOVE THE SWITCHBACK ROAD at Buffalo Pass, I find the panorama as described—clear across the wide open plateau all the way to Ship Rock, the serrated remains of an extinct volcano. It's a striking, preternatural sight, but the wind blows in impressive gusts and I prefer a more sheltered location. I wander into the woods.

Out of respect, I chose not to have a bear song sung on me by a medicine man. Such a privilege demands genuine participation. It has taken most of my life, but I have come to see that rituals possess no power of their own—only the meaning we give them. They require both faith and intent. Instead, I choose to invest in a private rite, one that blends Navajo tradition with my own tenuous grip on reality.

Five days ago, I met medicine woman Reena Maize at her usual spot in Ch' Hootso, Window Rock's outdoor Indian market. She had her blanket spread out on the pavement and her cures arranged in neat rows of ziploc bags. Her English was shaky. She wore a dusty blue dress and was adorned with silver and turquoise.

The oldest person I had seen in the Navajo Nation, she came highly recommended.

I sat down and told her about my journeys among the bears. Am I in any danger? That, she said, depends on me. She reached over the bee pollen and corn powder for a bag of gray-green herbs and seeds, then a smaller packet of yellowish flakes. This medicine, she explained, was collected within the four sacred mountains. If used properly, it will do the trick.

The first blend, Mountain smoke, will clear out any negative power that has attached itself to me—lingering effects of my dream and all other bear contact. The second packet contains Good Way smoke. This will help me see the right path, but only after I thank the grandchild (the bear) for all he has revealed. Then I can welcome him as my protector and he will bring good luck to me.

As she explained these things, a Navajo woman of middle age approached and purchased her own pouch of Mountain smoke. When she noticed that I had done the same, she declared that Reena Maize's blend has helped her countless times. It is the best that money can buy.

I never developed the skill for rolling your own, but I do the best I can. I shelter the medicine against the wind and light it on the first attempt. I draw the smoke as far as my mouth, then eventually deep into my lungs. With resolve, I am able to keep from coughing.

I clear my throat and address the grandchildren, the bears that live on this mountain. I knew I would feel self-conscious, but I was raised to believe confession is good for the soul. I explain what I'm doing here. Then I speak to all the bears I have seen, touched, or whose path I have crossed over the past five years. In full voice, I explain what I have done and why I chose to do it. I acknowledge that I am a thief, that I have taken something from each of them—as well as the people I've met along the way. I know I owe much in return.

At the foot of a large ponderosa pine, I remember the bear I saw killed yesterday and admit—out loud—that this is something I specifically came to see. I scatter the rest of the Mountain smoke in a ring around the tree and commit to faithfully describing this bear's final hour.

I drive to the base of the butte, to the sandstone bluffs where the wind seems to gather its strength. I step over a barbed-wire fence, then climb up the rich, ochre walls.

Inside a shallow cave, I light some of the Good Way smoke, which is pungent with sage. Here, I count my blessings. I recognize that I have remained safe throughout these journeys. I thank the bear for all I have experienced, and ask its help in making these stories worthy and true. When the medicine burns down to my fingertips, I step back into the sun. There, I pour the remains into the palm of my hand and offer it up to the wind.

AUTHOR'S NOTE

FOR FOUR DECADES, the IUCN, the World Conservation Union, has been assessing the global status of animals in order to draw attention to threatened species and promote their conservation. The 2004 IUCN Red List of Threatened Species includes 15,589 species facing extinction. This means one in three amphibians, one in eight birds, and one in four mammals are known to be in jeopardy. Six of the eight bear species appear on the IUCN Red List:

Sloth bear, *Melursus ursinus* (Vulnerable)
Giant panda, *Ailuropoda melanoleuca* (Endangered)
Asiatic black bear, *Ursus thibetanus* (Vulnerable)
Spectacled bear, *Tremarctos ornatus* (Vulnerable)
Sun bear, *Helarctos malayanus* (Vulnerable, Data Deficient)
Polar bear, *Ursus maritimus* (Lower Risk, Conservation Dependent).

The only bears not included in the list are the Brown bear, *Ursus arctos*, and the American black bear, *Ursus americanus*. The main threats facing bears are loss of habitat, hunting and poaching, and (in the case of polar bears) pollution and global warming.

IUCN classifications: Endangered (facing a very high risk of extinction in the wild in the near future), Vulnerable (facing a high risk of extinction in the wild in the medium-term future); Lower Risk, Conservation Dependent (focus of a continuing conservation program, the cessation of which would result in the species qualifying for one of the threatened categories above within a period of five years); and Data Deficient (inadequate information to make a direct or indirect assessment).

THE FOLLOWING nongovernmental organizations work to protect bears, their habitat, or both. To learn more, and support their work, find them on the Web. Please give generously.

Animal Asia Foundation
Arcturos
Ecological Reserve of Chaparri
Free the Bears Fund
International Association for Bear Research and Management (IBA)
Polar Bears International
Raincoast Conservation Society
TRAFFIC
WildAid
Wildlife Institute of India
WWF (World Wildlife Fund/World Wide Fund for Nature)

A portion of the author's proceeds from the sale of this book will go toward wildlife and habitat conservation.

SELECTED BIBLIOGRAPHY

Akhtar, Naim, Harendra Singh Bargali, and N. P. S. Chauhan. "Population Abundance of Sloth Bear (*Melursus ursinus*) and Management Implications in Unprotected Habitat of North Bilaspur Forest Division, Madhya Pradesh, India." Abstract presented at the Fifteenth International Conference on Bear Research and Management, sponsored by the International Association for Bear Research and Management, San Diego, 2004.

Baillie, Jonathan E. M., Craig Hilton Taylor, and Simon N. Steward, eds. "2004 IUCN Red List of Threatened Species: A Global Assessment." Cambridge, UK: IUCN Publications Services Unit, 2004.

Bargali, Harendra Singh, Naim Akhtar, and N. P. S. Chauhan. "Activity Patterns of Sloth Bear in Fragmented and Disturbed Areas of Bilaspur Forest Division, Chhattisgarh, India." Abstract presented at the Fifteenth International Conference on Bear Research and Management, sponsored by the International Association for Bear Research and Management, San Diego, 2004.

———. "Nature of Sloth Bear Attacks and Human Casualties in North Bilaspur Forest Division (NBFD), Chhattisgarh, India." Abstract presented at the Fifteenth International Conference on Bear Research and Management, sponsored by the International Association for Bear Research and Management, San Diego, 2004.

———. "Trapping and Restraint Techniques for Sloth Bear in North Bilaspur Forest Division (NBFD), Chhattisgarh, India." Abstract presented at the Fifteenth International Conference on Bear Research and Management, sponsored by the International Association for Bear Research and Management, San Diego, 2004.

Brown, Gary. *The Great Bear Almanac*. New York: Lyons & Burford, Publishers, 1993.

Bruemmer, Fred. *World of the Polar Bear*. Toronto: Key Porter, 1989.

C.I.A. (Central Intelligence Agency). *The World Factbook*. Washington, DC, 2004.

Campbell, Joseph. *The Masks of God: Primitive Mythology*. New York: The Viking Press, 1969.

Chauvet, Jean-Marie, Eliette Brunel Deschamps, and Christian Hillaire. *Dawn of Art: The Chauvet Cave*. New York: Harry N. Abrams, 1996.

Clottes, Jean, ed. *Return to Chauvet Cave, Excavating the Birthplace of Art: The First Full Report*. London: Thames & Hudson, 2003.

Clottes, Jean. "Chauvet Cave: France's Magical Ice Age Art." *National Geographic*: 200, no. 2 (August 2001): pp. 104–21.

Clottes, Jean, and David-Lewis Williams, *The Shamans of Prehistory: Trance and Magic in the Painted Caves*. Translated from the French by Sophie Hawkes. New York: Harry N. Abrams, 1998.

CNN.com. "Panda porn to cure bedtime blues," June 27, 2002.

Corell, Robert, et al. *Impacts of a Warming Arctic*. Arctic Climate Impact Assessment. New York: Cambridge University Press, 2004.

Craighead, Lance. *Bears of the World*. Stillwater, MN: Voyageur Press, 2000.

Ehrlich, Paul R. "Recent Developments in Environmental Sciences." Speech given on the presentation of the H. P. Heineken Prize for Sciences by the Royal Netherlands Academy of Arts and Sciences, Amsterdam, September 25, 1998.

Eliasson, Kelsey. "Polar Bear Attack in Wapusk National Park," *Hudson Bay Post*, November 2004, p. 3.

Fry, Stephen. *Rescuing the Spectacled Bears, a Peruvian Diary*. London: Hutchinson, 2002.

Gupta, Brij Kishor, Ashok Kumar Sinha, and Sant Prakash. "Stimulating Natural Behavior in Captive Sloth Bears." Abstract presented at the Fifteenth International Conference on Bear Research and Management, sponsored by the International Association for Bear Research and Management, San Diego, 2004.

Guravich, Dan, and Downs Matthews. *Polar Bear*. San Francisco: Chronicle Books, 1993.

Herrero, Steven. *Bear Attacks: Their Cause and Avoidance*. Toronto: McClelland & Steward Ltd., 2002.

Hsu, Hong-yen. *Oriental Materia Medica, A Concise Guide*. New Canaan, CT: Keats Publishing, 1996.

International Bear News. Quarterly Newsletter of the International

Association for Bear Research and Management (IBA), 11, no. 4 (November 2002) (and others).

Jumpkin, Susan, and John Seidensticker. *Smithsonian Book of Giant Pandas*. Washington, DC: Smithsonian Institute Press, 2002.

Kemf, Elizabeth, Alison Wilson, and Christopher Servheen. "Bears in the Wild, 1999—A WWF Species Status Report." Gland, Switzerland: WWF, 1999.

Kimball, John (Director), Black Bear Discussion Group. "Utah Black Bear Management Plan." Salt Lake City: Utah Division of Wildlife Resources, June 2000.

Kurten, B. *The Cave Bear Story: Life and Death of a Vanished Animal*. New York: Columbia University Press, 1976.

Kyle, Donald G. *Spectacles of Death in Ancient Rome*. London: Taylor & Francis, 1998.

Lopez, Barry. *Arctic Dreams, Imagination and Desire in a Northern Landscape*. New York: Charles Scribner's Sons, 1986.

Lorenzini, Rita, Mario Posillico, Sandro Lovari, and Annino Petrella. "Non-invasive Genotyping of the Endangered Apennine Brown Bears: A Case Not to Let One's Hair Down." *Animal Conservation* 7, the Zoological Society of London (2004): pp. 1–11.

Lynch, Wayne. *Bears: Monarch of the Northern Wilderness*. Vancouver: Greystone Books, 1993.

Mercatante, Anthony S. *Zoo of the Gods: Animals in Myth, Legend, & Fable*. New York: Harper & Row, 1974.

Montgomery, Sy. "Cambodia: Land of the Golden Bear." *Animals* 133, issue 6 (November/December 2000): p. 10.

Murphy, Dan. "Why Borneo's Sun Bears Now Attack." *Christian Science Monitor* 93, issue 91 (August 27, 2001): p. 8.

Naranjo, Luis German, Olga Lucia Hernandez, Daniel Rodríguez, Francisco Cuesta, and Isaac Goldstein. "Andean Bear Ecoregional Conservation Strategy." Abstract presented at the Fifteenth International Conference on Bear Research and Management, sponsored by the International Association for Bear Research and Management, San Diego, 2004.

"Polar Bear Attack in Churchill Downplayed," *Winnipeg Free Press*, November 27, 2004, p. A6.

Porter, J. R. and W. M. S. Russell, eds. *Animals in Folklore*. Totowa, NJ: Rowman & Littlefield for the Folklore Society, 1978.

Posillico, Mario, Alberto Meriggi, Elisa Pagnin, Sandro Lovari, and Luigi Russo. "A Habitat Model for Brown Bear Conservation and Land Use Planning in the Central Apennines." *Biological Conservation* (2003).

Postlethwaite, Susan. "A Poacher's Paradise in Cambodia: Black Market in Animals, Parts Threaten to Strip Jungles of Wildlife." *San Francisco Chronicle*, January 30, 2001, p. A10.

Quennell, Peter. *The Colosseum*. New York: Newsweek Books, 1971.

R. K. Narayan, trans. *The Ramayana*: A Shortened Modern Prose Version of the Indian Epic (Suggested by the Tamil Version of Kamban). New York: Penguin Books, 1977.

Rockwell, David. *Giving Voice to Bear: North American Indian Myths, Rituals, and Images of the Bear*. Niwot, CO: Roberts Reinhart, 1991.

Rodríguez, Daniel, Francisco Cuesta, Isaac Goldstein, Luis Germán Naranjo, Olga Lucía Hernández, Andrés Eloy Bracho, eds. "Ecoregional Strategy for the Conservation of the Spectacled Bear (*Tremarctos ornatus*) in the Northern Andes." WWF (World Wildlife Fund), Fundación Wii, EcoCiencia, WCS (Wildlife Conservation Society), 2003.

Romero, Simon. "Cambodia Re-emerges." *New York Times*, October 19, 2003.

Servheen, Christopher, Steven Herrero, and Bernard Peyton, "Bears: Status and Conservation Action Plan." Gland, Switzerland, and Cambridge, UK: IUCN/SSC Bear Specialist Group and Polar Bear Specialist Group, 1998.

Stirling, Ian. *Polar Bears*. Ann Arbor: University of Michigan Press, 1998.

Stucchi, Marcelo, and Judith Figueroa. "The Andean Culture's Importance in the Conservation of Andean Bear in Peru." Abstract presented at the Fifteenth International Conference on Bear Research and Management, sponsored by the International Association for Bear Research and Management, San Diego, 2004.

Swenson, Jon E., Norbert Gerstl, Bjørn Dahle, and Andreas Zedrosser. "Action Plan for the Conservation of the Brown Bear (*Ursus arctos*) in Europe." Convention on the Conservation of European Wildlife and Natural Habitats (Bern, Convention). Bern, Germany: Council of Europe Publishing, 2000.

Tertullian, Quintus Septimius Florens, and Minucius Felix. *Apology & De Spectaculis (Minucius Felix's Octavius)*, Loeb Classical Library,

T. R. Glover and G. H. Rendall, translators. Cambridge, MA: Harvard University Press, 1992.

Ward, Paul, and Suzanne Kynaston. *Bears of the World*. London: Blandford, 1999.

Warner, Marina. *From the Beast to the Blonde, on Fairytales and Their Tellers*. London: Chatto & Windus, 1994.

WildAid. "The Bokor Conservation Project: Surviving Together— Cambodia, Second Half Report 2002." Phnom Penh: WildAid, 2002.

Williamson, Douglas F. "In the Black: Status, Management, and Trade of the American Black Bear (*Ursus americanus*) in North America.": TRAFFIC North America, WWF (World Wildlife Fund), April 2002.

Wong, Siew Te, Christopher Servheen, Laruentius Ambu, and Ahmad Norhayati. "Food Habits of Malayan Sun Bears in Lowland Tropical Forests of Borneo." *Ursus* 13 (2002): pp. 127–136.

———. "Home Range, Movement and Activity Patterns, and Bedding Sites of Malayan Sun Bears *Helarctos malayanus* in the Rainforest of Borneo." *Biological Conservation* 119 (2004): pp. 169–181.

———. "Impacts of Fruit Production on Malayan Sun Bears and Bearded Pigs in Lowland Tropical Forest of Sabah, Malaysian Borneo." *Journal of Tropical Ecology* 21 (2005): pp. 1–13.

Yoganand, K. "Is the Sloth Bear in India Secure? An Analysis of Distributions, Threats, and Conservation Requirements." Abstract presented at the Fifteenth International Conference on Bear Research and Management, sponsored by the International Association for Bear Research and Management, San Diego, 2004.

ACKNOWLEDGMENTS

I AM GRATEFUL to family and friends for their indulgence and patience during extended absences, and to Nicole de Montbrun for making the call that led me down the path to this book. Heartfelt thanks to my talented editors, Kathy Belden at Bloomsbury and Susan Folkins at Penguin Canada, for their insight and finesse, and to my agent, Georges Borchardt, for his faith—and for making this project possible.

This book exists because many people gave generously of their time, knowledge, research, and experience. Over the course of these journeys, I was the grateful recipient of kindness, encouragement, protection, aid, food, drinks, shelter, transportation, and friendship. I would particularly like to acknowledge and thank: (British Columbia) Bob Herger, Tom Ellison, Ian McAllister, and Ernie Cooper; (India) Avneesh Pandey, Harendra Singh Bargali, and Phool Singh; (China) Jill Robinson, Luo Lan, Jerry, and Frank; (Peru) Javier Vallejos-Guerrero, Heinz Plenge, and Rob Williams; (Cambodia) Hem Puthea, Delphine Van Roe, Oran Shapira, Sim Chean, Nev Brodis, Matt Hunt, and Nick Marx; (Manitoba) Angele Watrin Prodaehl, Catherine Senecal, and Frontiers North Adventures; (Italy) Mario Posillico, Giorgio Boscagli, and Maurizio Carforgnini; (France) Jean Clottes, Julien Monney, Philippe Fosse, and Jean-Michel Geneste; and (USA) Eddie Benally, Edward Meyers, Steven Begay, Larry Joe, Albert Sagina, and Reena Maize. I owe a great debt to you all.

Thanks to Bernard Peyton for his advice, to Chris Servheen for his attention to detail, and to both men for their groundbreaking work among some of the world's least-known bears. Thanks to Peter Karsten, who generously contributed the handsome sketches contained herein. Thanks are also due to the Vancouver FCC (Deborah Campbell, J. B. MacKinnon, Charles Montgomery, Alisa Smith, and Chris Tenove) for the challenge and inspiration.

I am especially grateful to Lily Harned, my supportive wife, closest friend, and first reader. No one paid a higher price for this book.